Killing the Indian Maiden

Killing
the
Indian
Maiden

Images of
Native American Women
in Film

M. Elise Marubbio

THE UNIVERSITY PRESS OF KENTUCKY

Publication of this volume was made possible in part by a grant
from the National Endowment for the Humanities.

Scholarly publisher for the Commonwealth,
serving Bellarmine University, Berea College, Centre College of Kentucky,
Eastern Kentucky University, The Filson Historical Society, Georgetown
College, Kentucky Historical Society, Kentucky State University,
Morehead State University, Murray State University, Northern Kentucky
University, Transylvania University, University of Kentucky, University of
Louisville, and Western Kentucky University.
All rights reserved.

Editorial and Sales Offices: The University Press of Kentucky
663 South Limestone Street, Lexington, Kentucky 40508-4008
www.kentuckypress.com

The Library of Congress has catalogued the hardcover edition as follows:

Marubbio, M. Elise, 1963-
  Killing the Indian maiden : images of Native American women in film / M.
Elise Marubbio.
    p. cm.
  Filmography: p.
  Includes bibliographical references and index.
  ISBN-13: 978-0-8131-2414-8 (hardcover : alk. paper)
  ISBN-10: 0-8131-2414-X (hardcover : alk. paper) 1. Indian women in
motion pictures. I. Title.
  PN1995.9.I48M37 2006
  791.43'652208997--dc22   2006020629
  ISBN-13: 978-0-8131-9238-3 (pbk. : alk. paper)

This book is printed on acid-free recycled paper meeting the requirements of the
American National Standard for Permanence in Paper for Printed Library Materials.

∞ ✪

Manufactured in the United States of America.

 Member of the Association of
American University Presses

To my parents, A. Thomas and M. Lavonne Marubbio:
your own passion for learning, art, social justice,
and critical thinking have formed me
and inform this work—
thank you.

Contents

Illustrations

Preface

Killing the Indian Maiden: Images of Native American Women in Film analyzes a particular figure in Hollywood cinema, which I term the Celluloid Maiden, that depicts a young Native American woman who enables, helps, loves, or aligns herself with a white European American colonizer and dies as a result of that choice. This work brings together my research into the Hollywood film industry's continual use of this figure from the silent period to the present in thirty-four A-list films. The longevity and complexity of the Celluloid Maiden figure came into focus as I combed through films from the silent period through the 1990s, Production Code files from the Academy of Motion Picture Arts and Sciences collection, film reviews, scholarly analyses, and theoretical studies on film, particularly the western.

The overall implications of a century of confining Native American women in film to such a sacrificial role can be understood only through the application of a combination of methods. Thus *Killing the Indian Maiden* addresses the films as social narratives and politically inspired works of art that inform us about our society's fears, desires, politics, conflicts, and structures of power. Most important, I consider the artistry and visual machinations of film in relation to the political message presented to the viewer. How one reads, remembers, and reacts to a film depends on how it is constructed as a visual product and how it is promoted. These elements inform how we receive and perceive it as a visual text. The cinematic beauty of a film can either overshadow or emphasize the very real racist and sexist agendas of the film narrative or iconography. To facilitate the process of reading these films as cultural texts, I utilize a multidisciplinary framework that include theories of nationalism, colonialism, and power and film studies approaches to gender, race, and Native Americans in the media. This work combines these theories and approaches with a historical analysis of the social atmosphere and political attitude toward Native Americans and women at moments relevant to the individual films under analysis.

To help elucidate the trends in depicting the Celluloid Maiden and the social attitudes of the various eras of the figure's history, *Killing the Indian Maiden* is divided into three sections: The Celluloid Princess, The Sexualized Maiden, and The Hybrid Celluloid Maiden. Each section is further divided into two chapters that focus on particular eras of film representations—the Princess of the silent period and the 1950s, the Sexualized Maiden of the 1940s and the 1950s–1960s, and the hybrid figure of the 1970s and the 1990s. This framework highlights the breadth of the overall trends that emerge while also providing depth.

Interest in the role and image of Native Americans in film history has escalated over the last thirty years. However, very little scholarship exists on the Native American woman in film, in large part because of the cultural assumptions that primary characters in westerns and action films in general must be male, and because "Indian" often seems to be interpreted as a masculine term. The most comprehensive works on film have dealt with Pocahontas, but not with the Celluloid Maiden extension of that historical image. Likewise, few analyses concentrate on the particular forms of racism constituted by Native American–white relations in U.S. history. Much of the work in critical race theory on Hollywood films focuses on the specific dynamics of black-white racial formations. Importantly, no in-depth work exists on the Celluloid Maiden theme and its social ramifications. Thus I see a great need to explore the social and political implications surrounding Hollywood's Celluloid Maiden, especially in light of the continuing reproduction in film of nationalist and racist agendas through themes of manifest destiny and antimiscegenation.

Killing the Indian Maiden's significance lies in its dedication to understanding the ways in which our culture utilizes racialized, gendered, and sexualized bodies, especially female bodies, as sites for inscribing difference. I am interested in the complex web of power relations that exists in the cultural arena informing film images. Cinema, as a white male–dominated industry, and film, as a voyeuristic medium, offer a lens through which to analyze the psychological and sociological structures created through representations of subservient, simplistic, self-destructive Others. I am concerned with how the historical and filmic relationship between whites and Native Americans in general, which informs this image of Native American women specifically, creates intercultural boundaries that continually reinforce social, racial, and gendered difference.

This book began as my love affair with film representation and blossomed during my graduate training at the University of Arizona in American Indian studies and cultural studies. I pursued my own visual approach to discussing film representations of Native Americans, nurtured by mentors, teachers, and friends who believed that I could apply my training as a visual artist to the ways in which I read film. In particular, I extend my deepest gratitude to Tom Holm, Susan White, Mary Beth Haralovich, and Daniel Bernardi for their dedication to this project and their invaluable feedback. Their combined efforts serve as my model for teaching, mentoring, and scholarship. I owe a special thanks to Tom Holm for his years of friendship, advising, insight, and prodding. Tom's guidance and belief in my abilities prompted this research, and his spirit emerges on every page of this book. Without him, this research would have awaited another scholar; this book would still be a manuscript on my desk. Similarly, Susan White has proven a dear friend and an invaluable teacher. The cultivation of my visual approach to reading film and her attention to my writing craft attest to her skill as a teacher. She has helped me navigate the difficulties of harnessing artistic vision and honing it with academic methodology. Mary Beth Haralovich, who donned her cape and swept into this project when I desperately needed a film historian's perspective, has my undying gratitude. Daniel Bernardi's work on race and Whiteness informs this book and emerges as the grounding that helps me understand the trends I see across the span of film history. His advice to me at key moments in the writing process kept me going and owning my own work. In addition, Annette Kolodny's work on the feminization of the landscape helped me connect the pre-American images of Native women and the landscape to the film industry's use of the Celluloid Maiden trope.

The research for *Killing the Indian Maiden* was completed with the generous financial support of the American Association of University Women's Educational Foundation in the form of a 2002–2003 American Dissertation Fellowship and the Charles Redd Center for Western Studies at Brigham Young University in the form of the Annaley Naegle Redd Student Award in Women's History. Thank you. I am also indebted to the following archives, libraries, and support staff, whose acquisitions, knowledge of the materials, and willingness to help made doing research a pleasure: Russell C. Taylor, supervisor of reference services, and James D'Arc and staff at the L. Tom Perry Special Collections Library, Brigham Young University; Madeline F. Matz and Christel Schmidt at the Motion Picture, Broadcasting, and Recorded Sound Division, Library of Congress; Barbara Hall and staff at the Margaret Herrick Library, Academy of Motion Picture Arts and Sciences; Charles Silver at the Celeste Bartos International Film Study Center, Museum of Modern Art, New York; Millie Seubert at the Film and Video Center, George Gustav Heye Center, National Museum of the American Indian; and the staff at the Film and Television Archive, University of California, Los Angeles.

I am especially grateful to Leila Salisbury and the editors, staff, and reviewers at the University Press of Kentucky for their votes of confidence and for helping me through the difficulties of first-time book publishing. I am also particularly grateful to Anna Laura Bennett for her keen editing eye and attention to this manuscript.

No book is written in an academic vacuum; thus, in addition to the people and institutions mentioned above, I extend my appreciation to those who provided moral support, walked me through the writing process, were there in times of stress and panic, and made their friendship felt daily. In particular, I wish to thank Jodi Kelber Kaye, Natanya Sell, and Lavonne Marubbio, whose long conversations, feedback, and editing have helped me become a better person and writer; Dan Bode, who took me on vacations while I did research in order to help me laugh and relax, and who read the manuscript with his eye for art and detail; and Abby Clouse, Gary Gibson, and Betsy Kelly, who, in addition to nurturing my soul, took care of my animals while I was away researching. A number of other friends have supported me through this process over the last few years and deserve a special note of thanks: Richard Allen, Eric Buffalohead, Robert Cowgill, Cass Dalglish, Joe Horse Capture, John Mitchell, Ron Steele, and Missy Whiteman. I am also deeply grateful to Chris Pegg, my IT guru at Augsburg College, for his help in formatting and imaging. My greatest appreciation goes to my family; their constant support and love sustain me.

A number of trends discussed in *Killing the Indian Maiden* have been presented as papers at conferences: "Native Representations in Popular Culture Media: Where Have All the Hollywood Indian Women Gone?" Twenty-fifth Annual Southwest/Texas Popular Culture Association/American Culture Association Conference, San Antonio, Texas, April 2004, and "Cultural Trauma/American Ambivalence: The Native American Woman's Violent Erasure from the National Body," Society for Cinema and Media Studies Conference, Minneapolis, Minnesota, March 2003. A portion of the Cecil B. DeMille *The Squaw Man* material was initially published in different form in "Death of the Squaw Man's Wife: The Politics of Cecil B. DeMille's Adaptations of Edwin Milton Royle's *The Squaw Man*," in *2003 Film & History CD-ROM Annual*, edited by Peter C. Rollins, John E. O'Conner, and Deborah Carmichael (*Film and History*, 2004). Significant portions of chapter 1 were published as "Death, Gratitude, and the Squaw Man's Wife: The Celluloid Princess from 1908–1931" in *Polemics: Essays in American Literary and Cultural Criticism*, volume 1, edited by David Holloway, 85–117 (Sheffield: Black Rock Press, 2004).

Introduction

Emergence of the Celluloid Maiden

A NUMBER OF YEARS AGO, while I was wandering through a collection of prints at the University of Arizona's Museum of Art, an engraving by William Blake caught and held my attention. The image, entitled *Europe Supported by Africa and America* (1792), presents three young women, scantily clad, dwarfing the landscape on which they stand. The simplicity of Blake's composition enhances the social commentary woven into the figures, offering a complicated critique of Europe's colonial relationship with Africa and America. The two darker-skinned women flank Europe, keeping her upright and suggesting their stability in contrast to her weakness; however, the thin rope Europe holds around them and her firm grip on Africa's hand inform us of her unquestionable control over them. Reinforcing this impression, the metal bands around the other women's arms recall the ankle and wrist shackles used to confine African and American slaves. The fragile and pale Europe appears modest, with downcast eyes and long, flowing hair covering her pubis, while Africa and America stare boldly out of the frame toward the viewer, with their private parts visibly displayed. Their direct gaze acknowledges the viewer, inviting a response. In conjunction with their darker skin tones, which contrast sharply with Europe's fairness, their representation suggests a variety of colonial and racist discourses about Africans, Native Americans, and other women of color as sexually promiscuous, licentious, and exotic in their sexual boldness and freedom. The power of Blake's work resides in part in its applicability to the ongoing process of representation. Although created in 1792 to critique the three hundred years of colonialism prior to that date, the image offers a complicated

William Blake, *Europe Supported by Africa and America*, 1792. (Collection of the
University of Arizona Museum of Art; museum purchased with funds provided by
the Edward J. Gallagher Jr. Memorial Fund)

commentary on the visual rhetoric of colonialism and race that remains relevant three hundred years later.

With *Europe Supported by Africa and America* in mind, I began to explore the ongoing representation of Native American women in Hollywood films, my interest piqued by the lack of in-depth analysis of the subject. I found that, all too often, discussions about the images of Native women were relegated to an occasional line, paragraph, or page within an article discussing Indian stereotypes in film, suggesting that most film scholarship assumes the Indian to be male.[1] Intrigued, I started moving backward in time and rereading old favorites—Robert Berkhofer's *The White Man's Indian: Images of the American Indian from Columbus to the Present*, Leslie Fiedler's *The Return of the Vanishing American*, and Rayna Green's "The Pocahontas Perplex: The Image of Indian Women in American Culture." I found that, despite what the omissions in scholarship might suggest, the woman was front and center in the formation of colonial European and American consciousness about Indians. She and her male partner formed the concept of the Indian as either the noble savage or the ignoble savage that merged into the stereotypic reality now deeply embedded in the consciousness of American culture.

The creation of the term "Indian" as an idea and an image originated with the colonization of the Americas as the conquerable Other, someone whose differences of race, culture, and beliefs justify their extermination, oppression, or exploitation.[2] Noble/ignoble stereotypes surfaced in art, literature, and politics as definitions of Native peoples and, thus, as justification for their conquest, assimilation, or genocide. In its simplest form, the noble savage—both male and female—tends to represent innocence, purity, and an ideal man unfettered by civilization and corruption. A child of nature, the noble savage befriends the white man and, in its filmic rendition, comes to represent the possibility of assimilation into white culture. We recognize them today as the white hero's sidekick or the Princess figure, Tonto or Uncas and Pocahontas being our primary examples. The ignoble savage, often described as bloodthirsty or cannibalistic, provides the antithesis of the noble savage. In both male and female forms, the ignoble savage is often violent, morally questionable, and a very real physical and psychological threat to the colonizer. American political and social iconography depicts his or her resistance to assimilation as a sign of weak moral fiber or the inability to change. We know them today in various and unflattering forms: the reactionary warrior, like Magua, who fights for his land and threatens white womanhood; the drunken Indian whose weakness and inability to assimilate surface in his or her alcoholism; the squaw figure who in her youth is sexually active and in her old age is a worn-out hag. The noble and ignoble savage figures are inextricably bound to America's image of itself as a nation built on manifest destiny and the conquering of the savage and the wilderness. They are America's racial Other and alter ego: rejected in order to justify the violent treatment of them as part of progress and civilization, yet also desired for the freedom, land, and innocent state they represent.[3]

The perpetuation of the Indian in American iconography and cinematic representations results in an ambiguous relationship that is deeply connected with issues of race and colonialism. Daniel Bernardi suggests that in "U.S. cinema . . . people of color are generally represented as either deviant threats to white rule, thereby requiring civilizing or brutal punishment, or fetishized objects of exotic beauty, icons for a racist scopophilia."[4] This is certainly true for Native Americans, who are continually slaughtered, beaten, and wiped out in westerns and pulp fiction. The Indian woman's position, however, while based on the same binary noble/ignoble savage image, is further complicated through her gender and sexuality. Her gender makes her a target for rape, while her death ensures the end of a generation. Deeply influenced by traditions of patriarchy and violence toward women, the representation of Native American women in Hollywood cinema provides the colonizer, the white hero, and the viewer with a fetishized body of exotic and raced beauty—a body all too often victimized through violence and death because of its colonized position. Her status as a raced and gendered object of colonialist and patriarchal power also may be symptomatic of her decreasing presence in film history.

As I researched Hollywood's depiction of Native women, I found myself continually drawn to the Celluloid Maiden, the young Native woman who dies as a result of her choice to align herself with a white colonizer. There are a variety of representations of Native American women in Hollywood film history—the squaw, the young maiden, and the hag, for example—and various scenarios in which they appear. However, I was drawn to the Celluloid Maiden because of its multidimensionality and longevity. The figure amalgamates many of the others mentioned above, taking on the complexity and power of a cultural icon and overshadowing them in its levels of symbolic meaning. With great consistency, the Celluloid Maiden surfaces in every decade from the 1910s through the 1960s in two different, but related, representations that I call the Celluloid Princess and the Sexualized Maiden, and in the 1970s and 1990s as a hybrid of the two. Each rendition addresses a different facet of American cultural ambiguity—often quite violently—toward Native American women and the interracial mixing embodied in the figure.

The structured outline for this figure promotes a racial formation, which, according to Michael Omi and Howard Winant, occurs "through a linkage between structure and representation. Racial *projects* do the ideological 'work' of making these links. *A racial project is simultaneously an interpretation, representation, or explanation of racial dynamics, and an effort to reorganize and redistribute resources along particular racial lines.* Racial projects connect what race *means* in a particular discursive practice and the ways in which both social structures and everyday experiences are racially *organized*, based upon that meaning."[5] Within the Celluloid Maiden figure, Native culture, sexuality, and race are conflated, becoming interchangeable markers of difference. The linking of these elements within the film narrative, in conjunction with social mores and ideologies of a particular moment in time, positions them within larger discourses of nationalism and what it means to be American.

As a recurring cultural stereotype, the Celluloid Maiden plays an important role in the United States' ongoing nationalist, colonialist, and imperialist history. It reiterates particular structures of power and racial hierarchies in the articulation of Americanness or national identity based on a white, heterosexual, male norm. As Benedict Anderson makes clear, nations are "imagined communities," social constructions that depend on fixed stereotypes to legitimize a particular kind of nationalism. In order to maintain the "ideological construction of otherness" that, according to Homi Bhabha, is fundamental to the stereotype and to colonial discourse in general, the United States and other cultures have relied on relatively rigid and unchanging images, what Bhabha refers to as "fixity."[6] No concrete relationship exists between the Celluloid Maiden and actual Native American women; rather, the figure works as a colonial rhetorical strategy to promote a national American identity defined against a raced and "savage" Other.

The more romantic component of the figure, the Celluloid Princess, like her male counterpart the noble savage, symbolizes the "best" of Native America and the possibility of assimilation of the racial Other into a predominantly western European cultural ideology. The key qualifiers constituting the Princess figure include her connection to nature and the American landscape, her innocence and purity, her link to nobility, her exotic culture and beauty, her attraction to the white hero, and her tragic death. In all the Celluloid Princess films, the maiden's death frees the hero to fulfill his destiny as the American Adam—the icon of American progress, exceptionalism, and the American nation.[7]

The concept of an American Adam, as identified by R. W. B. Lewis, ties the western European American hero to the American myth of the garden and to America as an Edenic land in which to begin again. The American Adam embodies the idea of a hero "emancipated from history, happily bereft of ancestry, untouched and undefiled by the usual inheritances of family and race." This figure informs the myth of the frontier and, according to historian Richard Slotkin, explains and justifies the rapid growth and emergence of the colonies into a nation-state. Within this myth, the "conquest of the wilderness and the subjugation or displacement of the Native Americans who originally inhabited it have been the means to achieve a national identity, a democratic polity, an ever-expanding economy, and a phenomenally dynamic and 'progressive' civilization." The myth also incorporates the idea that progress, which each political era interprets differently, means territorial expansion defined by conflict, violence, and "savage war" between Europeans and Anglo-Americans and "non-European, non-White natives for whom the wilderness was home."[8]

Anticipating Slotkin's conclusions, Leslie A. Fiedler similarly describes the mythic structure of the frontier West but suggests that at the heart of the western story and its alien landscape lies the encounter between a "transplanted WASP and a radically alien other, an Indian." Such confrontations result in either a metamorphosis of the white Anglo-Saxon Protestant into a hybrid white-Indian or an annihilation of the Indian. In either case, the hybrid white hero replaces the Indian either symbolically or physically, through violence.[9] Within this mythic paradigm of the frontier West, the Princess component of the Celluloid Maiden figure represents a nonviolent means, a tool, by which the American frontier hero temporarily merges symbolically with the Indian and the alien landscape.

Within the symbolic language of this American myth and the myth of the frontier in film, the Celluloid Princess stands metonymically for Native American acquiescence to the sovereignty of the United States. Because western iconography always depicts Native American culture as already vanishing and thus legitimately (if regretfully) conquered, her voluntary union with the white hero validates subsuming her disappearing culture into his dominant one. By placing her in this double bind, the film industry uses the Celluloid Princess as paradoxical sign. She initiates a cross-racial union and the integration or absorption of one group into another, but by carrying through that union, she transgresses taboos against interracial mixing and must pay the price with her life. The Celluloid Princess films portray her death as a tragedy, an unavoidable consequence of western expansion and conquest. The contradiction inherent in her racialized construction reveals the tension between two ideological structures. The romanticization of the myth of the frontier conflicts with the reality of conquest, while the idealized image of an "integrated society" whitewashes the reality of racial politics that complicates such an ideal.

In contrast to the Princess, the Sexualized Maiden figure represents the ramifications of interracial mixing on American society. Like the Princess, but to a heightened degree, she symbolizes the danger of crossing racial taboos. A more erotic figure than the Celluloid Princess, the Sexualized Maiden embodies enhanced sexual and racial difference that results in a fetishizing of the figure. A sexual fetish, according to Freud, binds erotic desire to the threat of castration.[10] Hollywood film taps into this fetishism by heightening the figure's sexuality and her potential for physically harming white male characters, using it as evidence of her immorality, innate savagery, and potential to destroy American society. As a result, she becomes the female representation of the ignoble savage.

The fundamental characteristics of the Sexualized Maiden include the following in combination or as individual traits: She may be the mixed-blood offspring of a white man and a Native woman. As such, she symbolizes a temporal moment after colonization and assimilation take place. The figure's inevitable embodiment of the wanton squaw stereotype—the degraded metaphorical Princess figure found in literary and historical retellings of frontier encounters—surfaces as a reminder of her moral and social depravity. Finally, the Sexualized Maiden's combination of racial exoticism, sexual promiscuity, and physical threat to the hero often emerges in a femme fatale depiction that carries with it certain socially based fears about the sexually aggressive woman. The films using this figure ultimately suggest that the woman's inherently bad qualities reside in her blood as by-products of her Native heritage and her savage nature. This "bad blood" causes or justifies her death. Thus the Sexualized Maiden's presence in Hollywood films never symbolizes the successful racial integration of society; rather, like the half-breed Indian man, she throws into relief the degradation of society brought about by interracial mixing, assimilation, and tolerance of immoral behavior. Her death relieves the community of a dangerous, tainting force.

The Celluloid Maiden figure continues a much longer pictorial history as a part of the legacy of nationalizing myths that contrast Native women as markers of a supposedly vanishing race with the inevitability of western European cultural supremacy in the form of manifest destiny. Like their predecessors, as illustrated in Blake's engraving, the Celluloid Maiden images reflect the social, political, and moral attitudes toward Native Americans and interracial mixing and the national identity of the cultural moment that reproduced the figure. As a group, they illustrate an ongoing ambivalence toward race and the colonial history of the United States.

THE GENEALOGY OF THE CELLULOID MAIDEN

To uncover how deeply the roots of the Celluloid Maiden reach into the cultural symbolism of American myth and media, one must reconstruct the figure in terms of its historical relationship to earlier representations of Native American women and the American continent. Three icons in the genealogy of the figure—the primordial mother earth concept, the dangerous Native American Queen, and the innocent Indian Princess—inform the cinematic representations seen in the twentieth century.

The phrase "mother earth" feminizes the space we inhabit, connects us to it as children, offers us a maternal security, and situates the land within a larger discourse of gender. The phrase carries extraordinary political and psychological weight. By anthropomorphizing the earth, we claim familial rights that may or may not become national or international claims of ownership as people battle over the right to, and use of, the land. Feminizing "mother" earth opens up the sexual relationship implied in the idea and role of a mother. The feminization of the land as mother and as a sexualized female body has long been part of Western colonial history and discourse of power. The feminization of the land is part of what Annette Kolodny explains may be "America's oldest and most cherished fantasy: a daily reality of harmony between man and nature based on the experience of the land as essentially feminine—that is, not simply the land as mother, but the land as woman, the total female principle of gratification—enclosing the individual in an environment of receptivity, repose, and painless and integral satisfaction." Within this male fantasy, America emerges as a "human, and decidedly feminine" landscape—a nurturing paradise—that opens herself to the colonial explorer and colonist. Kolodny offers additional examples from the writings of members of the early British expeditions of 1584 to what is now Virginia and North Carolina, in which they convey an Edenic view of the land as "wonderful plenty." Similarly, in 1597, Sir Walter Raleigh refers to Guiana as a virgin: "a country that hath yet her maydenhead, never sackt, turned, nor wrought." He further sexualizes the landscape by insinuating that the conqueror's right to the female body, and thus the land, comes through conquest.[11]

Fifteenth-century drawings and etchings also reinforce the image of a feminized nature by depicting the major landmasses as women "representing the characteristic face of that continent."[12] As in Raleigh's description, many such works used visual images that gendered and racialized the continents in addition to portraying the land's abundance. William Blake's etching, as discussed above, mimics these earlier works, recalling and critiquing their construction of the American wilderness as a nature/culture binary that depicts nature as a sexualized woman, a premodern state, and an uncultivated wilderness in contrast to the superiority of western European culture. Metaphorically, America functions as an uncivilized and untamed female body that simultaneously attracts and terrifies the colonial male.

Equally ambiguous and intriguing as the feminized American landscape, the Native American Queen image embodies the qualities of the feminized and premodern New World, evoking a desire for the land's bounty and hinting at its dangers. European explorers, writers, and artists often describe the Native American Queen as "tawny" hued and Amazonian in size. These adjectives code the figure racially and place it within a mythological narrative of exotic warrior women whose bare-breasted eroticism and military prowess make them potentially disruptive to the western European patriarchal order. The following composite by Rayna Green illustrates the Queen's dangerous power: "Draped in leaves, feathers, and animal skins as well as in heavy Caribbean jewelry, [the Indian Queen] appeared aggressive, militant, and armed with spears and arrows. Often, she rode on an armadillo, and stood with her foot on the slain body of an animal or human enemy. She was the familiar Mother-Goddess figure—full-bodied, powerful, nurturing but dangerous—embodying the opulence and peril of the New World."[13] The Native American Queen incorporates the warrior woman and the mother-goddess figure in a portrait of power, military prowess, raw sexuality, and lush and potent beauty.

Such metaphors recur throughout colonial texts from Amerigo Vespucci's *Mundus Novus* (circa 1504–1505) onward, generating the images of a feminized and matriarchal New World whose lush landscapes, abundant resources, and untamed natural wilderness entice and threaten the colonial male.[14] For example, Jan van der Straet's famous drawing *The Discovery of America* (circa 1575) frames America and Europe together within the New World landscape. A naked America lies in a hammock surrounded by her weapons, exotic animals and plants, and evidence of the customs (for example, cannibalism) of the indigenous population. Vespucci, fully clothed and carrying symbols of European scientific knowledge, looks down at the startled woman. The warrior-Queen's nakedness and physical repose invite the colonizer's gaze, his exploration, and his exploitation, but her sisters in the background roast and eat a human leg, suggesting his actual vulnerability. Like the feminized land, the Queen is dangerous precisely because her seductive qualities mask the physical hardships that the colonizer will encounter conquering her and the new land.[15]

The Queen figuratively represents the psychological reaction Europeans expected of the indigenous peoples to colonial action and the rape of their motherland, and her militant stance, with a "foot on the slain body of an animal or human enemy," suggests that she will fight back.[16] The Queen acts as the fantasy landscape's alter ego that does not embrace Europe's intrusion into her space. As such, she, like the male ignoble savage, symbolizes the potential disruption of the colonial process. Together, these two beings—the primordial land and the Native American Queen—embody the exoticism of America and the untamed and biologically racialized savagery that forms the Indian in the Western colonial imagination. The Queen's bold display of agency against the colonial invader will, in turn, validate military action against her and Western dominance over her. Ultimately, as the conquest and taming of the wild land continue, images of the Queen fade, to be replaced in Western literature and art by the Princess figure.

From this history, and in combination with the political agendas of European American culture, rises the "dusky woodland" goddess—the Indian Princess, a smaller, gentler, less threatening version of the Queen.[17] Strong, and with a hint of the wild, she appears a child of nature both metaphorically and literally. The Princess's heritage and connection to a tribal community tie her to the "native soils of America," to borrow S. Elizabeth Bird's phrase, and to her primordial motherland's fecundity.[18] Untainted and innocent of vice and sexual degradation, she symbolizes the purity of nature. With these qualities, which make her sexually exotic and appealing, she embodies the unspoiled essence of a "virgin" land—an uncultivated wilderness untouched by man. Unlike the Queen, the Princess poses no physical or military threat; rather, her attraction to the colonizer and to western European culture, which sometimes results in her abandonment of her culture, homeland, and people, make her a more passive figure. Her diminutive frame, coupled with her childlike desire to learn, especially from the white hero, makes her more malleable than the Queen, and certainly more inviting to the colonizer.

Early American writing wielded the Princess as a political tool and counterpoint to the Native American Queen, presenting her as the "first symbol of the United States, representing the Western wilderness reclaimed by civilization."[19] This observation pinpoints a key component of the Princess myth that remains fundamental to her film persona as well: she is an American-made symbol that refers to very particular ideologies and social processes constructed into an image of the American nation. The phrase "representing the wilderness *reclaimed* by civilization" underscores her creation as a tool within western European colonial rhetoric; thus her abandonment of traditional Native society for Anglo-American society simply recognizes the United States as her destined community. This phrase further implies that her wildness, reflected in her tribal heritage and her dark coloring, are extinguishable, and that she possesses qualities of civility that need only to be reclaimed. In other words, her innate Whiteness simply needs to be awakened and brought forward.[20]

As did the mother earth and Queen images, the Princess figure equates Whiteness with civilization, which is juxtaposed to racialized peoples and primitive society. Early American colonial society, governed by Anglo-Europeans who shared ideologies and cultural backgrounds with the early European colonizers, maintained these binary codes. Hollywood cinema also does so, through its use of the Celluloid Maiden. Thus, while the Princess's "dusky" coloring indicates her biological race and difference from the citizens of the European American Republic, her descent from the Native American Queen elevates her to American nobility, as does her social position as the chief's daughter, making her socially more acceptable to Anglo-European society than is her "squaw" counterpart. In addition, the Princess's desire for Western contact suggests an ability to assimilate into Anglo-American culture—to attain Whiteness. Her participation in colonization through assimilation presents an image of a nation formed out of the nonviolent mixing of different races and cultures. This symbol effectively and peacefully unites components of American history without acknowledging the traumatic and devastating consequences that the nation-building process actually imposes on those forced to assimilate. The indigenous reaction to colonial invasion projected onto the Queen figure vanishes with this omission, effectively silencing an entire history of genocide and military action empowered by ideologies of manifest destiny and cultural superiority. Thus the Princess figure works as a cultural bridge, a symbol that links the landscape as an idealized entity to biological nature and that negotiates between nature and the primitive on one side and culture and progress on the other. This point has not been lost on the film industry, and it is a major factor in the Princess's timeless appeal as a media figure.

The qualifiers that make the Princess a bridge also distinguish her from the Queen warrior and mother. Though the Princess's innocence and unabashed sexuality hint at her female ancestors' wild and untamed sexuality, unlike them, she never engages the more violent element of her character; thus she maintains a moral purity linked to chastity and control. This adds to her attraction. The two other stereotypes—the female Indian drudge figure, notable for her many children and haggard body, and the wanton squaw—capitalize on the Native woman's supposed promiscuity and suggest the ramifications of sexual aggression and savageness. In contrast, the Princess always remains exotic and sexually exciting without being debased. The Princess's combined qualities justify the patriarchal interference in her life and the erasure of the Native American Queen as a political force. Less capable than the Queen of fending for herself, the Princess figure indicates the need for parental guidance, which she chooses in the form of white patriarchal culture. In so doing, she acknowledges the inevitability of white domination and justifies the paternalistic action of the United States against Native American people.[21]

Our most famous incarnation of this Princess figure is Pocahontas, whose myth blends with that of the Princess. As late as 1995, we see an animated version of this stereotype portrayed as a buxom young woman who communes with Grandmother Willow and the animals of the forest, dives off hundred-foot cliffs, and watches her new English love sail off toward the horizon. Thus the animation presents her innocence, connection to an anthropomorphic nature, and desire for the white colonizer. Historically, Matoaka (Pocahontas) was born around the year 1595, rescued Smith in 1607, was abducted by Captain Argall in 1612 and sent to Jamestown, converted to Christianity in 1613, married John Rolfe in 1614, gave birth to Thomas Rolfe in 1615, sailed to England with her husband and child in 1616, and died in 1617.[22] Her real-life narrative contains many parallels to the Princess image, as Robert S. Tilton's and Rebecca Blevins Faery's works on Pocahontas illustrate, which may explain why it blossomed into such a popular legend. According to Tilton, "Her act of bravery in saving the life of Captain John Smith was recast and retold more often than any other American historical incident during the colonial and antebellum periods." Her conversion and marriage, Faery explains, became a "persistent and popular means of domesticating the female America," who "traded her Native identity and culture for an English name, an English husband, and an English God."[23]

As Tilton's and Faery's works outline, two distinct phases emerge from the story of Pocahontas: the first dealing with her rescue of John Smith and the second focusing on her marriage to John Rolfe and the birth of their son. Both manipulate Pocahontas's image to represent a particular American national identity, and each provides a very different outcome. According to Tilton, the story of her marriage to Rolfe and of their son's birth is "specific to the beginnings of the Jamestown colony" and links "the formation of the bloodlines of many of the great families of Virginia" to her aristocratic heritage. In other words, her lineage, based on a European notion of power and influence that transformed her father's (Powhatan) tribal status to that of a "king" and hers to that of a "princess," procures an "aristocratic" line for their colonial descendents. Her marriage narrative remained popular in the pre- and early Republican period while colonists attempted to distance themselves from England and establish their own identity as an American nation. By the early eighteenth century, however, Pocahontas's relationship to Smith surfaced as a more popular national narrative. The young Republic no longer needed to prove its difference and independence from the parent country, and Pocahontas's image became more useful for legitimizing continued colonial action against Native Americans. This resulted in a romantic narrative in which "Pocahontas . . . rescued Smith, and by implication all Anglo-Americans, so that they might carry on the destined work of becoming a great nation."[24] Both the Pocahontas-Smith love narrative and the Pocahontas-Rolfe marriage narrative carry over into cinema, literally in films about Pocahontas and metaphorically through the image of the Celluloid Princess figure.

THE CELLULOID MAIDEN FIGURE

The various historical figures traced above inform the Celluloid Maiden figure. The Celluloid Princess most closely resembles the Princess type, while the Sexualized Maiden draws on the Native American Queen, the sexually promiscuous Native woman who counters the Princess figure in literature, and the femme fatale. These two figures merge at various times in the late twentieth century to create a hybrid.

The Celluloid Princess emerges during the silent period in romantic tragedies that set the stage for subsequent figures. "Indian films"—films that highlight the Indian character—present the image of the Celluloid Princess as a primary character torn between two cultures. In the earliest works, she appears as a helper figure—a young girl—who saves the white hero from attack by savage Indians but who dies in the cross fire of battle. The narrative structure of these short, one- to three-reel films relies on a conflict between savagery and civilization that erupts in warfare and results in the domination of white settlers over the Indians. These include *Red Wing's Gratitude* (1909), *The Broken Doll* (1910), and *Iola's Promise* (1912). The helper returns as a secondary character in two feature-length films in 1920—*Out of the Snows* (1920) and *The Vanishing American* (1925). In contrast, the films about the lover figure focus on a marriage between the woman and a white hero who has come west to escape or to find adventure. In a liminal space between her culture and western frontier settlements, the two live a short but idyllic life that disintegrates when the maiden realizes her husband really loves another, or that he must return east and wants to take their child with him. The lover generally commits suicide, allowing her hero to return to his destined life in the East. *The Kentuckian* (1908), *The Indian Squaw's Sacrifice* (1910), *White Fawn's Devotion* (1910), and *The Squaw Man* (1914, 1918, 1931) explore this plot. By the 1920s, the Celluloid Princess figure fades to a secondary position, where she adds an exotic accent to the hero and heroine's story. Two examples of this diminished importance of the Princess figure from the twenties include *Out of the Snows* (1920) and *Scarlet and Gold* (1925).

The Princess figure disappears during the mid-1930s and 1940s but reappears in the 1950s in pro-Indian westerns such as *Broken Arrow* (1950), *Across the Wide Missouri* (1951), *Broken Lance* (1954), and *Last Train from Gun Hill* (1959). Pro-Indian films challenge the western norm by offering sympathetic portrayals of Native Americans, condemning the marginalization of Native Americans by the federal government and contemporary federal Indian policy, and tackling racism head-on. In contrast to those of the silent period, the 1950s films raise the level of idealization in the Princess figure and, as a result, enhance the symbolic components of the figure. In addition, the character again recedes into a secondary position in the plot, which, by the end of the decade, results in its minimal presence on screen.

In both eras, the presence of the figure signals a national identity crisis regarding the composition of the American national body. During the silent period, such fears revolved around the recent "closing" of the frontier and the shift from a rural to an urban lifestyle. Important during this period, as well, were the integration of Native Americans into the social fold, the massive immigration of eastern and southern Europeans and of Asians that threatened to alter the nation's racial topography, and the ramifications of World War I on the American psyche. The Celluloid Princess reemerges in the 1950s as a cultural mediator during an era confronted with the growing influx of Native Americans into the urban centers, increasingly violent reaction to the civil rights movement, and escalating anti-Communist crusading. The changes the character undergoes during the decade mirror this controversial political climate and register the attempt by some in Hollywood to voice dissent about growing censorship and conservatism.

The Sexualized Maiden figure grows out of the silent-period Celluloid Maiden's maturation into a highly effective representation of America's psychological reaction to race, unbridled sexuality, and powerful women. Films such as *Scarlet and Gold* (1925), *Frozen Justice* (1929), *The Squaw Man* (1931), and *Laughing Boy* (1934) illustrate the rise of the more sexual Celluloid Maiden type in the silent period and early 1930s. More overtly racist depictions appear in a particularly sadistic run of films during the 1940s, 1950s, and 1960s.

The 1940s films *The Northwest Mounted Police* (1940), *My Darling Clementine* (1946), *Duel in the Sun* (1946), and *Colorado Territory* (1949) offer a cohesive set of the figure's characteristics—beauty, mixed-blood heritage, overt sexuality, marginalization from white society, and deadliness to men—that exhibits the rapidly changing sexual mores, racial dynamics, and power structures of the era brought on by the ending Depression and World War II. The provocative quality of the films signals the changing standards in film censorship; the resulting erotically charged image presents a physically and psychologically dangerous body barely contained. The character's scanty clothing accentuates her pinup girl figure, which in turn strains to control a volatile psyche. The underlying theme in these films equates the woman's sexual taint with a disease carried through her Indian bloodline. She represents a great danger from within civilized society because her taint resides, hidden, in blood, surfacing only through her uncontrolled, passionate nature. This underlying theme resonates with the rising popularity of Freudian psychology during the late 1940s and the growing concerns about interracial mixing that surfaced after World War II.

The 1950s and 1960s films—*Arrowhead* (1953), *The Searchers* (1956), *In Cold Blood* (1967), and *Mackenna's Gold* (1969)—appear somewhat disjointed in their depictions of the Sexualized Maiden, but the ideological and social remnants of the two eras unify the group and highlight the sexual racism so ingrained in the figure. Less concerned with the figure's sexuality and more attentive to expressing or exploring racism, the 1950s films rely on language and actions that reflect the physical results of extreme bigotry. The overt depictions of racism in these films capture the tenor of the country's heightened state of paranoia brought on by the threat of communism and the escalating racial conflict emerging out of the period's desegregation policies. In contrast, the 1960s films characterize the shifting dynamics of the civil rights movement by inverting the aggressor and submerging the issue of race in the film's structure. These later films highlight the psychological instability of the Sexualized Maiden figure as the cause of violence against a bewildered white hero. Consistent with the then-popular idea that overlooking racial difference eases integration, the narratives of the 1960s films outwardly appear to accept integration and miscegenation while reinforcing easily identifiable stereotypes and racial assumptions through their depictions of the Sexualized Maiden. This later group of films also includes the first distinct crossing of the figure into a more contemporary setting and a different genre—that of the urban crime thriller. Additionally, *The Searchers* and the urban crime drama *In Cold Blood* set a precedent for the hybrid Celluloid Maiden by incorporating characteristics of a fallen Princess into their Native woman.

With the merging of the Celluloid Princess and the Sexualized Maiden in the revisionist westerns of the 1970s and the 1990s, a certain level of promiscuity and negativity seeps into the figure. Like the pro-Indian westerns of the 1950s, the 1970s films—*Little Big Man* (1970), *A Man Called Horse* (1970), *Jeremiah Johnson* (1972), and *The Man Who Loved Cat Dancing* (1973)—rework the classic western portrayal of the "whites as representatives of civilization and the Indians as barbarians" by reconsidering the "impact of westward expansion on Native Americans."[25] The tumultuous civil rights era and the countercultural movements of the 1960s greatly influenced these films, as reflected in their tone of disillusionment with corporate and political America, racial inequality, and military violence. In keeping with the radical and countercultural tone characteristic of the Vietnam War era, the 1970s films construct an antiestablishment plot that utilizes the open and appealing sexuality of the hybrid Princess figure as a mechanism to woo the hero away from civilization. Unlike their predecessors, these films celebrate the Native American lifestyle as a viable alternative to American culture. Incorporating both the positive and negative aspects of previous Celluloid Maidens, the hybrid Celluloid Maiden is the pivotal character for deconstructing the myth of the frontier, while the white hero, whose defining metamorphosis into Indianness happens because of his reaction to her, emerges as a tangential participant. She symbolizes the white hero's moment of rebirth and self-awakening and his emergence as an

counter culture

amalgamation of two worlds whose roots are formed in Native America. Her sexuality is key to the character's ability to sway the hero and to mediate his psychic conflicts, since, in the process of "going native," he comes dangerously close to abandoning all tenets of the civilized mind. This trait of her persona refers to the dangerous power of the Sexualized Maiden as a sign of antiassimilation. Likewise, it works as a double-edged sword that highlights her Otherness. This twist on the role of the Celluloid Princess indicates an attempt to manipulate the figure to fit an era at odds with the traditional myths of American exceptionalism and the frontier hero.

After a hiatus in the 1980s, the hybrid figure surfaces in a mix of cross-genre films in the 1990s—*Thunderheart* (1992), *Silent Tongue* (1993), *Legends of the Fall* (1994), and *Legends of the North* (1995). These films illustrate a waning interest in sustaining an antiracializing multiculturalism even while they utilize a revisionist approach that critiques the nation-building process and racial power relations celebrated by the western. The diversity found within the group indicates the film industry's attempts to combine its two components into a figure able to mediate temporal and generic changes. As did the 1970s films, these base their character on the Celluloid Princess type, but they accentuate traits common to the Sexualized Maiden, such as mixed-blood heritage, sexual aggression, and violence. The films adapt only one or two of these elements and eliminate the older combination of eroticism and sadism, creating a more well-rounded and contemporary character that tests the boundaries of the figure. The tensions within each film between its revisionist intent and its reliance on standard generic methods of presenting the Celluloid Maiden, however, reflect a long-standing ambiguity in cinema toward embracing the iconic status of the figure and criticizing the culture that produces it. While the era offers great latitude in the development of the Celluloid Maiden, it also illustrates the film industry's continued reliance on the figure's colonialist and racialist construction. From 1992 to the mid-1990s, the use of an increasingly traditional Celluloid Maiden figure parallels the decade's movement from the height of the debates over the quincentenary of Columbus's arrival in the Americas, with their anticolonialist rhetoric, toward a neoliberal avoidance of tackling racial issues head-on.

Although the figure crosses genres, the myth of the frontier, the assumption of American exceptionalism, and the ideology of white patriarchal superiority that dominate the western genre always inform it in some fashion. The western embodies the primary elements of the myth of the frontier, as discussed above, and, as historian Jane Tompkins points out in *West of Everything: The Inner Life of Westerns*, depicts the West as a symbolic space for freedom and "the opportunity for conquest." This space offers a culturally sanctioned arena in which the white western hero temporarily transgresses the line between civilization and savagery as he sets into motion the former and conquers the latter. This transgression molds his character, making him the quintessential icon of progress and colonial prowess. Formed from the landscape that physically dwarfs him, he wants to dominate and "sometimes . . . merge with it completely."[26] Both the Celluloid Princess, as the metaphorical or metonymical embodiment of nature and the western landscape, and the Sexualized Maiden, as a representation of the dangers of Native America, offer the hero a way to subjugate the land, either through marriage or through physical and sexual violence. In keeping with these manifestations of the West, the Celluloid Maiden always dies. The colonial paradigm of the western demands the death of the Celluloid Maiden, and this residual element more than any other crosses into other genres. On a symbolic level, the death of the maiden signals the continuing action of colonialism by erasing the symbol of Native America and the American wilderness. The appearance of this aspect in such Native-centered and Native-produced films of the 1990s as *Dance Me Outside* (1994) and *Grand Avenue* (1996) indicates the extent to which American colonial rhetoric and symbolism affect even those living with the negative consequences of those stereotypes.

The continual replaying of the Celluloid Maiden's tragic narrative suggests that mainstream America remains uncertain about its relationship to the Native American people it continues to colonize and displace. Conflict exists between the United States' embracing of a feminized Native American figure and its rejection of this figure through racializing practices. On one hand, there appears to be a need to return to a mythic moment in American history when the white male frontiersman represented manhood, modernity, and progress, while the Native woman symbolized the vanishing purity and adolescent state of a past American territory. Although this moment idealizes the Native American woman and nature as quintessential to the formation of the white male's American identity, it also reifies her as an expendable commodity to be consumed by the nation-state. As Richard Slotkin points out, the United States has achieved its national identity as a progressive civilization through "the conquest of the wilderness and the subjugation or displacement of the Native Americans."[27] Along the same lines, the young woman's assimilation into the colonizer's culture eradicates the sovereignty of Native American peoples.

On the other hand, the representations of the noble Native American maiden yearning for the love of her white colonizer suggest that mainstream white America produces a racialized Other as a contrast to and measure for what it is to be American. The films often position the Native American maiden as culturally and socially inferior to a refined and pure white woman whose ultimate union with the hero signifies the moral and social acceptability of this choice. This results in a racialized and sexualized hierarchy in which the Native American woman appears racially and culturally inferior to, and sexually more aggressive than, the white woman. The Native woman's love for the white man and her need to be accepted into the colonizer's culture are seen as a desire for civilization and an ideal Whiteness attainable only through a rejection of her Indian culture and through physical and emotional submission. Within this hierarchy, her sexual freedom, in comparison to the white woman's relative restraint, reinforces her exoticism and eroticism, as well as her inferiority. When coupled with her yearning for Whiteness and a white man, her body symbolizes a sexual, transgressable space in which the white male can undergo socially taboo experiences or activities, such as interracial love or, in some cases, rape. In either case, her abandoned body ensures the safety of racial purity for mainstream white America; the Native American woman symbolically vanishes, allowing for the culturally sanctioned union of the white heterosexual couple. Both these scenarios reframe nationalist and racist agendas around the Native woman's body and end violently with her death. They also suggest that the civilizing process requires assimilation into the white mainstream while underscoring the ideology that white racial superiority is, and must remain, the national identity. The legitimization of such racial and cultural hegemonies promotes emotional, psychological, and physical violence against women of color and validates and perpetuates cultural genocide as a by-product of progress and assimilation.

The cultural narratives suggested above are not new — the films that utilize the doomed indigenous woman evoke past American and European political ideologies that romanticize imperialism and nationalism by means of "artistic" renditions of the Native American woman. Hollywood has used the figure for over ninety years in high-end productions by well-known directors and producers. These "prestige" pictures exhibit the privilege of time, money, and individuality in comparison to the industry's B films and assembly-line products.[28] The quality of these films and their dedication to the figure underscore the figure's relationship to mainstream America and Hollywood film. Overall, the thirty-four Celluloid Maiden films I analyze utilize the Native female body as a vehicle through which colonialism is continually presented visually and metaphorically, as a narrative space in which to articulate fears about interracial mixing and assimilation—often directed toward raced Others in the United States—and as a metaphorical and symbolic arena in which nationalist rhetoric about America as a white nation-state and global superpower plays out.[29] A number of primary themes enhance these trends. All the films reinforce American myths of the frontier, manifest destiny, and the ideal of Anglo-European America's premodernization innocence through this iconic image. The reliance of mainstream culture on these myths and various depictions of the Celluloid Maiden during different eras maintains the racial Other as an exotic or erotic danger to a homogenous national identity. The film industry remains committed to replicating mainstream cultural and social concerns regarding interracial love. In sum, the Celluloid Maiden figure works as a racial formation that reinforces cultural narratives of nation building and national identity. These narratives exclude the racial Other from the overall image of the nation and, often inadvertently, condone acts of violence against women of color.

The Celluloid Princess

One

Death, Gratitude, and the Squaw Man's Wife

The Celluloid Princess from 1908 to 1931

Historians of American culture have long and effectively argued
that the identity of the Native American and Native American's
encounters with European invaders constitute a palimpsest upon
which our current preoccupations and understandings and world-
views are constantly reinscribed.

— David Mayer

THE NATIVE AMERICAN AS PALIMPSEST — a textual body effaced,
erased, and written over — evokes images of violent silencing. Tellingly,
the metaphor also reveals a certain amount of repression, uncertainty,
and ambivalence related to the action of reinscribing and covering alternative narratives. The metaphor is particularly relevant to early cinema,
which, as Roberta Pearson explains, "reflected and refracted the complex and contradictory position and representation of Native Americans
within contemporary U.S. society and culture," and to early cinema's
representation of the Celluloid Indian Princess.[1] In the early twentieth
century, the recent "closing" of the western frontier by the 1890 cen-
sus, assimilationist policies for integrating Native Americans into mainstream white society, and tensions created by the largest immigration of
eastern and southern Europeans in the country's history fueled growing

anxiety about the racial and cultural boundaries of Americanness. Early cinema inscribed many of these complex issues on the figure of the Celluloid Princess and, through her interaction with white society and her violent death, reflected the anxiety and social turmoil that marked the early twentieth century.

The complexity of images and cultural attitudes woven into the early Celluloid Princess makes her an important figure among the thousands of Indian images found in early westerns and in Indian films, whose primary narratives focused on Native Americans.[2] Presented in romantic tragedies as a young Native woman whose attraction to western European culture or the white hero situates her between her own culture and American frontier culture, she symbolizes the possible merging of the two and the differences between them. The Princess's qualities of innocence, virtue, and vulnerability make her attractive to the white characters and also contrast her to the other Indians in the films, who are often depicted as degenerate, violent, and untrustworthy. Her presentation as a pagan deeply tied to her culture and heritage, however, marks her as distinctly different from the white American characters. She is the essence of the noble and vanishing savage who bridges two very different cultures and worldviews but is unable to fully divorce herself from one culture to integrate into the other.

The Celluloid Princess's placement between two worlds in these films encapsulates the cultural ambiguity of the Progressive Era (approximately 1900–1925) and early Depression period toward Native American–white relations and the anxiety underlying the social and political debates about assimilating Native Americans into the mainstream. The inevitable setting of the Princess films on the western frontier and in the past reflects a colonialist romantic nostalgia for, and connection to, the myth of the frontier, and the belief that Native Americans represent a disappearing way of life. The frontier landscape comes to represent the untamed wilderness and a place of conflict and conquest of those who would hinder the progress of western European civilization—Native Americans and Mexicans especially. The presentation of the Princess as futilely straddling two cultures within this space points toward concerns about the ability of Native Americans to assimilate, about the pace at which assimilation should happen, and about what integration and possible miscegenation would mean to American culture. Inextricably wound into these concerns were the political debates about the fate of Native Americans. Some citizens argued for the continued use of reservations and the separation of cultures; others argued for assimilation through education, changing cultural formations, missionary intervention, and the continued allotment of lands to individuals rather than tribal groups.[3] The ideology of white racial and cultural superiority underlies the political formation of these views and suggests that American civilization and progress are superior to what was deemed savagery, social regression, and at best cultural stasis.

When read within the milieu of the Progressive Era and the early Depression era, the Celluloid Princess and her interaction with other characters work through the tensions created by the changing face of America and offer insight into the political and social attitudes toward Americanness, Native Americans, and raced immigrants at that time. The nation grappled with rapid change and social anxiety as it adjusted to the shifts from rural to urban and from a majority western European Protestant population to one mixed with growing numbers of eastern and southern Europeans, Asians, Catholics, and Jews. Though it was an era marked by its commitment to antitrust legislation, overseas imperial expansion, land preservation, social and political reform, and education, it was also a period when foreigners and those of profoundly different social and cultural orientations from the dominant ideal were looked upon with suspicion and fear. Especially in the first decade of the twentieth century, older questions about what it meant to be American and what made up the American character were revived.

Simultaneously, there emerged a growing nostalgia for the America of the past, including the rapidly disappearing landscape with its awe-inspiring wilderness and "picturesque" peoples—especially Native American peoples. One Progressive watchword was conservation. For many contemporary Americans, preservation of the remaining wilderness, including its distinct races of peoples and its artifacts, was inextricably bound to the preservation of an American national identity. The elements forming this identity were synonymous with manifest destiny and a western European Protestant America and included open spaces, the conquest of the "savage" country and its people, free land for farming and ranching, and abundant natural resources. The popularity of Wild West shows, Theodore Roosevelt's Rough Rider image, and the growth of the Boy Scouts reinforced such notions and solidified the American West and the western hero as national iconic structures. In addition, fueled by imperial nostalgia for this rapidly disappearing America, museums and private citizens competed to increase their collections of "primitive" or vanishing peoples' material culture.[4] This paradoxical need to recreate and continually reinforce the romanticized image of nineteenth-century western frontier America while also promoting the economic and cultural forces that caused its disappearance manifested itself in Indian and western films.

The emerging film industry (also marked by rapid growth and change), which included foreign companies operating within the United States, manufactured Indian and western films as "the international form of American motion pictures." American companies marketed their products as real American films and those of foreign manufacturers as inauthentic in an attempt to ensure the ability of "the United States' industry to compete against foreign manufacturers at home." In other words, western and Indian films became the hallmark of American film, and the American industry used them to distinguish "authentic" American westerns from those made by foreign companies, even those working within the United States, such as Pathé.[5] This clearly nationalistic endeavor culminated in the production and consumption of the greatest number of these types of films in American cinema history—as many as "5,400 features, documentaries, shorts, and serials" between 1890 and 1930. It also established the western as the nation's "richest and most enduring genre" and as a "vehicle for disseminating the Western formula to the culture at large."[6]

In this period of social and cultural unrest, the genre bolstered the popular belief in American progressivism by presenting civilization and progress as superior to savagery, social regression, and cultural stasis. The primary representations of Native Americans were divided between images of hostile "savages" and those of the "noble red man." According to Michael Hilger's representational sampling of silent films from 1908 to 1929, the savage image broke down into two primary categories that, essentially, were used either as a means for promoting the superiority of the white hero or as cultural commentary on political, social, and moral themes of the day. Films utilizing the savage image included themes of vengeance, drunkenness, kidnapping and torture, and attacks on whites. In contrast, those depicting the noble red man emphasized themes of friendship and loyalty, generosity and courage, white-Native interracial romance, Native-Native romance, victimization, and precontact narratives. These film topics offered formulas with which to address the racial, moral, and cultural problems confronting the American nation while indoctrinating the viewing public into a particular ideology regarding American history, the colonizing process, and national character. As Jowett summarizes, "The ever-popular Western became a morality play particularly attuned to the American scene, with the frontier serving to remind the mass of city dwellers of the simple and clear cut differentiation between good and evil found in the country."[7]

During the early decades of the twentieth century, the film industry was an agent of acculturation as well as differentiation. The structure of the Celluloid Princess films offered a particularly engaging way to indoctrinate immigrants into American culture, through images based in a clear racial hierarchy and with messages about separate and unequal cultural integration. Although they represent only a fraction of the Indian films made from 1908 to 1931, these films establish the Celluloid Princess figure as an American icon and create the framework for the future representation of Native American women in American cinema.[8] During these years, the American film industry presented the Celluloid Princess in two types of cinematic representations that differ in plot formation and social subtext but inform each other. Easily categorized as "helper" or "lover" figures, they work within the noble red man categories of generosity and gratitude to whites and interracial relationships. A number of basic similarities, rendered differently within the films, exist between the helper and lover figures that serve to link the two characters. The essential qualities that signify the Celluloid Princess exist in some form in both figures: she is innocent, attached to an exotic culture, and linked to ritual and the American landscape; she yearns for the white hero or western European culture; and she sacrifices herself to preserve Whiteness from racial contamination. Within this context, Whiteness symbolizes an ideal image of purity, ultimate civilization, and culture that is held as a utopian model of excellence and desire. While the helper films center the maiden as the focus of the action, the lover films shift the focus to the white hero. Of great importance to the subtext of the films, the mode of death differs—the helper is killed while the lover commits suicide.

The helper figure appears almost exclusively in the early short films (one to three reels long), such as *Red Wing's Gratitude* (1909), *The Broken Doll* (1910), and *Iola's Promise* (1912), but also surfaces as a minor figure in two feature-length films of the 1920s—*Out of the Snows* (1920) and *The Vanishing American* (1925). A primary character in the early shorts but a secondary figure by the 1920s, the helper often appears as an innocent child figure whose involvement with the hero never manifests itself as a love relationship. Her attempt to warn her white friends of an impending Indian attack always results in her accidental death. The action-packed narratives, which emphasize gratitude and generosity, highlight the female lead's athleticism and her desire to repay a kindness done to her by a leading white character. On the surface, these films appear to support an assimilationist agenda and a romantic nostalgia for Native Americans; however, their structure and heavy reliance on the savage image undermine such a reading and result in a validation of westward expansion, conquest, and separation of groups.

The lover films are also commentaries on assimilation and, like the helper films, present an innocent and noble Native woman who dies because of her interaction with white society. Unlike the helper films, which center on a desexualized child maiden, these focus on a sexually mature figure who participates in interracial love. Often called "squaw man" films because the white hero marries an Indian "squaw," their themes of interracial marriage reflect concerns about cultural difference, miscegenation, and interracial families. The blueprint for later manifestations of the Celluloid Princess, this early Princess figure differs from those of other eras in the combination of plot elements that define her character.[9] Four key themes surface in these films: her character holds a primary role in these stories; she is a full-blooded Native woman and usually a chief's daughter; she often has children who are being taken from her to be educated in the East; and she commits suicide. At no other time during our film history do these four themes emerge so often and with such interconnected purpose. The result is an exotic romantic tragedy that transfers easily from the shorts—*The Kentuckian* (1908), *The Indian Squaw's Sacrifice* (1910), and *White Fawn's Devotion* (1910)—to the longer feature length films: *The Squaw Man* (1914, 1918, 1931), *Scarlet and Gold* (1925), and *Oklahoma Jim* (1931).

[margin note: major characteristics]

THE HELPER FIGURE

Americans during the first decades of the twentieth century were involved in what historian Robert H. Wiebe describes as a search for order.[10] The helper films of 1908–1913 emerge within this quest as a particular metatext about white America's anxiety in regard to the rapidly changing racial dynamics of society. They exhibit vestiges of the social evolutionary race theories popular at the time, such as social Darwinism, that organized groups along biological and cultural lines as a way to explain difference. An ordering of chaos in their own right, the films promote a visual replica of a mythic frontier that normalizes particular social formations and ideologies about race and white cultural superiority. Their formulaic design captures as a vignette a volatile moment between hostile Indians and white settlers on a frontier, either in the West or the Northwest Territories, that erupts in violence. Embedded in the structure are two ever-present racializing binaries: the savage/civilized dichotomy that situates Indian culture as inferior and regressive against western European culture as superior and progressive, and the ignoble/noble dichotomy that categorizes the "savage" into a further binary opposition. The plots revolve around the helper—noble savage—character and her negotiations between the ignoble savages and the settler community.

Social Darwinism and similar social evolutionary doctrines inform the overall racializing narrative of the helper films. Evolutionism, made popular in the social sciences during the mid-nineteenth to early twentieth centuries through the work of Herbert Spencer, incorporates notions of survival of the fittest with racial categorization, economics, and social growth. In its most vulgar form and usage, social Darwinist thought perceives race, class, and "breeding" as connected signs of evolutionary progress. Ethnologist Lewis Henry Morgan, using Native American cultures as his template, elaborated on social evolution by suggesting that the history of the human race was based on an "upward path from savagery through barbarism to civilization—three 'distinct conditions . . . connected with each other in a natural as well as necessary sequence of progress.'"[11] In this schema, Native Americans possess the ability to attain the level of civilization accorded western European culture, but only through a series of social and evolutionary transitions.

The helper films' three-tiered composition creates a narrative hierarchy, based on cultural and racial difference, that is encapsulated in Morgan's theory and in the myth of the frontier and that results in social friction and, ultimately, violence. The western frontier of the mid- to late nineteenth century—a transitional period before the frontier was officially declared closed and a time of ongoing Indian wars, changing dynamics in western communities, and the taming of the land and its people—forms the overarching narrative space and invokes the ideological construct formulated in the myth of the frontier. According to historian Richard Slotkin, the myth of the frontier is "our oldest and most characteristic myth." Produced over a period of three centuries, it explains and justifies the rapid growth and emergence of the colonies as a nation-state. Within this myth, the "conquest of the wilderness and the subjugation or displacement of the Native Americans who originally inhabited it have been the means to our achievement of a national identity, a democratic polity, an ever-expanding economy, and a phenomenally dynamic and 'progressive' civilization." The myth also incorporates the idea that progress, which is understood differently in each era, means territorial expansion, defined by conflict, violence, and "savage war" carried out by Europeans and western European Americans against "non-European, non-White natives for whom the wilderness was home." The figure of savage war, "an operative category of military doctrine," bases its logic in the notion that Western culture cannot coexist with "primitive natives" in any other way than through a subjugation of the latter group. "Ineluctable political and social differences," inherent in "blood and culture" that prevent cohabitation without violence, underscore this racial philosophy and justify colonial action.[12]

Framed by the logic of this mythic space and the savage/civilized dichotomy constructed into the character types, the frontier of the helper films emerges as a place of oppositions in which abusive, aggressively violent, and savage Indians confront kind, nonviolent, and civilized whites. Indian camps replete with war dances and other signs of a vanishing culture visually counter the white towns or approaching wagon trains, metaphors of progress and American community. Racial and cultural markers of the exotic and primitive—tepees, beaded buckskin, and foreign rituals of worship and warfare—are juxtaposed to familiar figures of civilization from dime novels and Wild West shows: westward migration, white women and children on the frontier, and towns. In addition, these early films often frame the savage Indians in long or medium long shots that physically distance them from the audience, while they frame the hero in medium shots and close-ups that offer a more intimate connection with the audience.[13] The visual coding of cultural difference within the larger racial ideology formed by the myth of the frontier works to conflate race and culture, associating Indian heritage with racial stereo-types of savagery and ideologically supporting a social Darwinian racial hierarchy with western European culture at its pinnacle.

The helper films extend the savage/civilized dichotomy described above by incorporating characters that cross over the division. Occasion-ally, as in *Iola's Promise*, these films incorporate atypical white characters whose actions are so vastly different from the majority of white charac-ters that they appear as anomalies connected metonymically (through type) with the ignoble savage stereotype.[14] Most often, however, they complicate the dichotomy by including a noble savage who racially and culturally falls into the savage category, but whose noble spirit elevates her from the other, ignoble savages. The majority of Indian characters in the film fall into the ignoble category as savage reactionaries to white expansion who are abusive to their women and sadistic to white captives. The Princess helper stands alone as a romantic noble savage figure—the Indian willing to give her life for the western European culture that at-tracts her—and as the pivotal character propelling the action forward. The following excerpt of a review of *Red Wing's Gratitude*, released in 1909 by Vitagraph, illustrates the helper figure's positioning within the standard helper film plot, highlights a bit of the romantic tragedy of her character, and underscores her position within the racial structure outlined above: "Red Wing is an Indian girl who is brutally treated by her father. He is driven away by some emigrants when abusing her, and in retaliation carries away one of the little emigrant girls to be tortured. Red Wing takes her in her canoe down river. Then comes an exciting pursuit, in which Red Wing is mortally wounded, but lives long enough to see the white child in the hands of her friends and the Indians beaten off."[15] Typically in the films, a white man saves the helper from an abu-sive situation, or a group of settlers extends kindness to her, as occurs in *The Broken Doll*. The Indian maiden illustrates her gratitude through an act of heroism that results in her own death. Variations such as age of the helper or cause of the intercommunity conflict exist within this format but do not affect the overall narrative purpose.

The rhetoric used in the various film companies' advertising, which often surfaces in the intertitles as well, emphasizes the tragic abuse and isolation of the helper and the reactionary violence of her people. The contrast between the helper figure's psychological depth and the other Indian characters' stereotypical portrayals also reinforces a racial structuring based on cultural traits and implies the racial and cultural inferiority of her people and their evolutionary distance from whites. Biograph's advertising rhetoric for *The Broken Doll: A Tragedy of the Indian Reservation* (1910) exemplifies this clearly. According to the *Biograph Bulletin*, the film focuses on a preadolescent girl from the reservation who "has never known a kind word or attention" from her own people. Categorized by the *Bulletin* as "semi-civilized" and "unfavored," the girl finds kindness and a regenerated spirit through her contact with white settlers. She is befriended by a miner's daughter, who, after seeing the child beaten, pities her and gives her a doll. The doll is the Indian girl's only cherished possession, and when it is broken by an Indian who considers it an "effigy of a white baby," the child "buries it in true Indian fashion" on a pyre in the mountains. Grateful for their kindness, the Indian girl warns the miner's family of an upcoming Indian attack, precipitated by the killing of a drunken Indian by a white man. A battle ensues and the "little one, wounded during the conflict, has just strength enough to reach the little grave where she falls, making it a double one, and her pure soul parts with the little body sacrificed upon the altar of gratitude."[16] The rhetoric of the film summary underscores her youth, innocence, and gratefulness. In addition, it implies the unfavorable character of the other Indians and her own "semi-civilized" state, which is reemphasized by her burying the doll in "true Indian fashion." These cultural markers exist within texts that establish Whiteness and western European culture as the norms and thus also function to code Indians as racially separate from whites.

The films themselves heighten the expected aura of tragedy by visually highlighting the helper's dangerous situation, her incredible, childlike sincerity, and the long, painful struggle to her place of death. D. W. Griffith's Biograph films did this particularly well, and, like *Red Wing's Gratitude*, his films *The Broken Doll* (1910) and *Iola's Promise* (1912) position the abuse of the heroine and her death as bookends for actions that establish her as a noble and tragic figure.[17] Griffith would go on to use such framing of the innocent, tortured child figure effectively in later films, such as *Broken Blossoms* (1919) and *Birth of a Nation* (1915). While plot variations do exist in the action, age of the heroine, and place of her death, this type of tragic experience, her innocence and childlike purity, and her attraction to western European culture never stray from the formula.

The Broken Doll, which accentuates the level of tragedy by making the heroine a preadolescent, clearly illustrates the effectiveness of this approach. The opening and closing shots of the young girl are ones of suffering; they frame a sequence of abuses that follows brief moments of happiness brought on by her interaction with whites. Indeed, the audience is introduced to the helper in a scene that underscores issues of child abuse.[18] As the tribe walks down a mountain from the reservation to town, the girl slips and falls. In a medium long shot that frames just the girl and her mother and accentuates the threatening posture of the older woman, we see the girl crouched on the ground while her mother yells at her and throws her back down to the ground. The mother turns and continues walking. Subsequent scenes show the child shoved by her mother for gawking at the townspeople, slapped for talking to the miner's daughter who gives her the doll, and grabbed and shoved by an Indian man when she shows him her doll—the "effigy of a white baby." Peppered among these examples of abuse and Indian family dysfunction are scenes that emphasize the child's sweet temper and enthusiasm for learning white ways and making new friends. This type of attention to emotions and situations throughout the film enables the audience to empathize with the girl and mourn her suffering, whether or not they can read the sparse intertitles. In these ways, the narrative solidly establishes an aura of romantic tragedy surrounding the noble figure positioned against violent savages by the time she is shot. In the final scenes, the viewer sees the fatally wounded girl emerge from the battle, torturously climb the mountain, and die next to her doll. A particular section in the sequence, which foreshadows a similar scene in *Birth of a Nation*, captures from above the girl's struggle up the mountain, the height of the mountain, and its dangerously steep and craggy terrain, illustrating further her heroics, strength of character, and isolation.

The helper films are often erroneously categorized as romantic Indian films, a popular type of film that emerged in large numbers at this time and that concentrated on the "noble red man" motif.[19] Other examples of the genre include Griffith's Biograph titles *The Redman and the Child* (1908), *The Indian Runner's Romance* (1909), and *The Mended Lute* (1909) and Native American director James Young Deer's films *The Cheyenne Brave* (1910), *The Yaqui Girl* (1911), *Lieutenant Scott's Narrow Escape* (1911), and *Red Deer's Devotion* (1911).[20] These films portray Indian life and customs in a romantic light and vilify whites as the cause of their vanishing or their inability to integrate into western European culture. They emphasize the noble qualities of Native Americans and their spiritual relationship to the vanishing wilderness. Ignoble savages—violent reactionary figures—if they appear at all in the plot, recede into the narrative background. In contrast, "savage" Indian films present the Native American as a bloodthirsty enemy of white America. Griffith's Biograph titles *Fighting Blood* (1911), *The Massacre* (1912), and *The Battle at Elderbush Gulch* (1914); Thanhouser's *The Forest Rose* (1912); Selig's *A Daughter of the Sioux* (1909); and American's *Geronimo's Last Raid* (1912) exemplify this type of film.[21] In these films, no noble figure rises above the reactionary Indians as a contrast; rather, the "savages" represent a lurking threat on the frontier that lives to attack, maim, and slaughter settlers. The helper films do not establish an overall romantic nostalgia for a vanishing way of life or the vanishing American. Instead, they utilize the romance of the symbolic noble figure as a foil for the ignoble savage, who is also a prominent figure in the plot. Thus helper films combine the noble red man and the savage Indian motifs so prominent during the era.

The helper's aura of romantic tragedy is fundamental to maintaining the noble/ignoble savage and savage/civilized binaries coded into the structure. The sympathy created for the Indian girl accentuates the abusive and violent behavior of the other Indians, ensuring antipathy to them and reinforcing their distinct difference from her. In effect, she reinforces how very dangerous Indians are to each other and, by extension, to whites. The juxtaposition also emphasizes the benevolence, virtue, and generosity of western European culture. Additionally, the nuances of her personality, compared with other Indians' one-dimensionality, move her out of the narrow stereotype they define and position her as a liminal character. She is neither completely savage, as are her tribesmen, nor civilized. Rather, she exists between the two worlds as an anomaly, symbolizing the possibility of assimilation and a move away from the primitive past, associated with tribal culture, and into a more progressive and civilized future, associated with westward expansion and western European culture. By means of the helper's positioning as a focal point between the two extremes that stresses the savage/civilized binary and her romantic representation, the films repeatedly put into visual form the myth of the frontier.

These silent films, in effect, initiated a viewing public—a vastly

Who decides what's authentic

diverse public—into the visual language of the myth. Film reviews of the time outline the type of Indian images that were demanded and considered authentic. For example, the following review of *Red Wing's Gratitude* concentrates on authenticity and "correctness in every detail" in the portrayal of Native Americans: "An Indian picture of unusual interest because the leading roles are assumed by real Indians, who direct all the movements, Indian fashion. They wear their clothes Indian fashion, and they are made by Indians, ensuring correctness in every detail." According to Eileen Bowser's study of early cinema, "authenticity was an important advertising point" for the Indian films, even more so than for the westerns of the period. Vitagraph, considered one of the best studios for film quality after Biograph, promised *Red Wing's Gratitude* to be "an unusually real and interesting picture of actual Indian life" and hired two "real" Indians to help direct the film and provide the appropriate Indian atmosphere. According to editorials in the trade papers—the *Moving Picture World* and the *Motion Picture News*—from 1909 to 1915, "authenticity" seemed to range in meaning from proper western scenery and historicism to acting style and appropriate costumes for Indians. A 1909 review underscored stoic posture, minimal emotion, savage actions, and belted dresses on the Indian maidens as marks of reality. Similarly, W. Stephen Bush's 1911 article "Moving Picture Absurdities" demanded "real Indians" with "keen sight," "stoic" behavior, and absolutely good or evil personalities. Other critics craved films that offered "illustrative and historic recorders of this noble race of people, with their splendid physique and physical prowess."[22] The "accuracy" called for in these reviews simply reinforced cultural assumptions about Native Americans as either noble or ignoble savages. Neither the industry's incorporation of Native Americans as actors, directors, and advisers in the filmmaking process nor the protests by Native American groups to their Indian agents and the U.S. government about their representation in film did much to alter these stereotypes.

More damaging, perhaps, were films, like D. W. Griffith's *The Broken Doll*, that manufactured realism through an ad hoc mixture of Indian "tribal and masquerade styles . . . mourning and burial rites and battle-preparations, mixtures of imagined gestures, choreographed steps, and half-baked anthropological scraps." According to Eileen Bowser, "Most people assumed that movies aspire to reality, for reasons having to do with the new emphasis on the story film," such as the helper films provide. The new focus relied partly on the change in acting style from the histrionic—a style based on very set theatrical poses—to verisimilitude, based on "natural" actions and responses.[23] The focus was also the result of the appearance of Indian cultural artifacts or facsimiles in films, which suggested reality and visually linked audience memory to tribal artifacts on display in museums, reenactments of Indian battles and rituals performed in Wild West shows, and exhibitions at the 1904 world's fair. The result is a dangerous play of reality and fantasy within which the Native American's relationship to white America is always that of the primitive and racialized Other.

Films made in the early 1910s refract the reality of contemporary debates over Native Americans' place in the American national body. These debates attempted to answer the question of whether Native Americans should remain separate from western European culture on reservations or should be fully integrated into the dominant culture. Technical problems such as method and rate of acculturation complicated the assimilationist side of the argument, while diminishing lands and growing poverty on the Indian reservations complicated the other. The multiple ways in which these issues may be read within the context of the films' narrative structures reflect the power of their use of binaries and mythic space. For example, David Mayer argues that Griffith's *The Broken Doll* is an "intervention in the separation-assimilation controversy" that takes the middle view on the controversial topic by having the Indian characters "get into difficulties when . . . they leave their reservation . . . [and] when they attempt to assimilate."[24] Although this is a valuable reading, one might also argue that the white characters' attention to the helper figure suggests an acceptance of assimilation only when the subject of assimilation presents the qualities of the helper figure. Neither of these readings takes the filmic structure into full consideration or considers the actions of both groups. The helper's transitional placement between cultures and her metonymic connection to a primitive and threatening people suggest the impossibility of assimilation even in light of the white characters' seeming openness to the idea. Read within the context of the three-tiered composition of mythic space and binary oppositions, the films promote more forcefully a "conquest of the wilderness and the subjugation or displacement of the Native Americans."[25]

D. W. Griffith's *Iola's Promise* (1912) offers a particularly interesting addition to the antiassimilationist reading. Iola, the young Indian girl, is

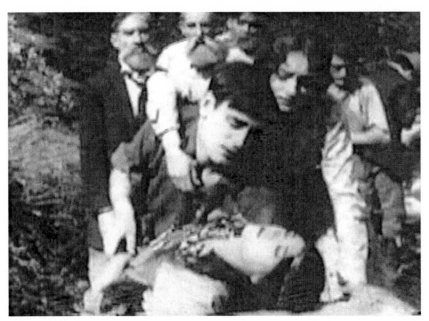

Iola's Promise. D. W. Griffith, Biograph, 1912.

"held captive by a gang of cutthroats, from whose clutches and abuse she is rescued by Jack Harper, a prospector." Out of gratitude, Iola promises to help Jack find the gold he seeks. "He is amused at this and says 'Will you?' 'Yes.' 'Cross your heart?'" Although Iola does not understand the "cross-your-heart action," she sides with Jack and the other whites against her own people. She heroically saves Jack's fiancée, Dora.[26] During the attack on the wagon train, Dora and her father are taken captive by Iola's people and tied to a stake. Iola, played by Mary Pickford, disguises herself in Dora's cloak and hat in order to draw the Indians away from the two hostages. A crosscut sequence shows the turmoil of the moment: Dora and her father's escape, Iola shot by her own people, Jack and the miners' arrival, the ensuing battle, and Iola's collapse in the gulch. Just as the surviving whites arrive, Iola points out the gold in the gulch and dies in Jack's arms.

The framing of this final scene is key because it hints at the possibility of assimilation while simultaneously denying the option. The shot frames Iola forefront and center. Jack cradles her in his lap while Dora leans over him with her arm around his shoulder. This trio configuration appears again in the lover films, but not in the other helper films, suggesting that the possibility of an interracial relationship exists between Jack and Iola. Indeed, Iola's ability to "pass" for white while wearing Dora's cloak and bonnet implies that she can be assimilated. Jack's tender embrace suggests an attraction that is not unwarranted, considering the sexual undertone created in the first scene by the attempts of the "cutthroat" to rape Iola, but her death ensures that Dora and Jack remain the dominant couple. The shot's composition and the character costuming and placement visually and culturally contrast Iola, who is again in full Indian dress, with the whites. Furthermore, the arrival of miners, suggesting the defeat of the Indians, and Iola's pointing out the gold as she dies imply the right and inevitability of white control over Indian land and resources. Thus, although the final sequences and ending illustrate an uncertainty about assimilation, the narrative structure ensures the more dominant philosophy of the myth of the frontier and the whites' right to the land.

Production of helper films waned after 1912, in part because they did not make the transition to the longer narrative formats that became more common thereafter. Elements of the character, however, do re-emerge in altered form in the 1920s and are worth noting. *Out of the Snows* (1920) and *The Vanishing American* (1925) utilize the helper as a minor character whose difference from the early helper points toward alternative trends in representing Native American women. In *Out of the Snows*, Anita is a mixed-blood woman, of Indian and white parentage, who falls in love with a Canadian Mountie and helps him to solve a mystery that reunites him with his fiancée. Two things stand out in Anita's representation as incongruous with the early helper image but typical of the Sexualized Maiden figure, which rises in popularity during the 1920s–1940s: Anita is of mixed heritage, implying a sexual union never achieved in the helper films, and she is sexualized through her love for the Mountie, again opening the possibility of a mixed-race relationship. *The Vanishing American*, adapted from Zane Grey's nostalgic novel, buries the helper figure in a very minor character who is forced to work for an unscrupulous white Indian agent while her lover is off fighting in World War I.[27] The facts that she does not willingly help the white agent and that she dies from abuse suggest she fits more readily within the racial injustice stories than in helper narratives. Thus, although both films continue the noble and tragic helper motif, they change fundamental aspects of the formula; such alterations modify the reading and purpose of the character.

The examples of helper films available from 1909 to 1912 illustrate a consistent prejudice against Native Americans reflective of the larger societal insecurity about assimilation and the changing racial dynamics of America during the period. Lynching of African Americans occurred weekly in 1910. Rising immigration numbers (8,795,386 between 1901 and 1910) included large groups from eastern Europe and southern Europe—groups often considered racially inferior by the Anglo-Saxon majority. The racialization of non–western European Americans did not remain internalized within U.S. social politics but also surfaced globally in American coding of foreign nations like Russia, China, and Japan as barbaric and their citizens as evolutionarily unequal to white Americans and Europeans.[28] The structure of the helper films, so overtly grounded in a white racial superiority, evokes a need to maintain a clear distinction between groups. It also underscores a continual social uncertainty about the merging of raced groups into the dominant ideal of a white America. The films do not offer a viable solution for a country unable to halt or even slow the immigration and integration process. Thus the helper's placement between two battling cultures and her ultimate death can only suggest an inability or a hesitancy on the part of white society to subscribe to the melting pot ideal of the American nation.

THE LOVER FIGURE

Emerging in conjunction with the helper films, the lover films indicate the same evolutionist racial theories and similar cultural anxieties. They cast a different light on these issues, however, by presenting the frontier as a place where cultural interaction moves past the volatile moment of helper films to a time when mixed-race families face the reality of their future. This is not to suggest that friction and violence do not exist between groups or that this is an assimilationist panacea. Rather, this frontier is a transitional space where the cultural taboo of interracial love unfolds as both romantic and problematic, primarily because of the cultural distinctions between groups. Difference, embedded in the ideological framework as primitivism and evolutionary stasis, perpetuates racial and cultural binaries within which Native Americans are presented as fundamentally deviant from a white norm. A subplot that runs through these films warns that both culture and race define a person's character. The Native woman—the lover figure who aids and marries the white hero—simultaneously heightens the exoticism of the place and of cross-cultural unions and underscores the problems of miscegenation through her unwillingness or inability to acculturate into white society. The lover figure exists in a system as clearly bounded as that of the helper films. The lover narrative provides a solid mythic configuration in which the threat to America's white hierarchical social system and racial purity, brought on by assimilation and interracial marriage, is temporarily contained through the Native woman's suicide. The structure, plot, and central theme proved a more popular format than the helper films for addressing these concerns. As Andrew Smith observes, "It would be hard to over emphasize the importance of the 'squaw-man' story to early American cinema. Filmmakers retold the story hundreds of times, and it was the dominant plot of the Indian western genre."[29] Lover films easily made the transition from shorts to feature-length format.

The films utilize the western frontier and the savagery/civilization metaphors as templates to shape the concerns mentioned above quite differently than did the helper films. Rather than the frontier's being a site of constant friction between races and of savage war, in these films the East and West both contain elements of danger linked with excess, but those of the West are presented as more damaging to society. The dangers of the East, or civilization, are associated with decadence—a downfall of progress—such as drinking, gambling, embezzlement, or an idle lifestyle, which can be reversed. Those of the West are more complicated, physically violent, and linked to breeding and environment. On one hand, danger, equated with social regression and criminal behavior, materializes in both whites and Indians, as the following examples illustrate: in *The Indian Squaw's Sacrifice* (1910), "a Mexican and white desperado . . . roll" the hero for his money; "low-down Redskins" do the same in *The Kentuckian* (1908); and white cowboys in the *Squaw Man* films physically threaten the hero and Indian woman. Such examples warn against social deviance as the nefarious effect of certain environments. Miscegenation, on the other hand, emerges as the primary source of danger to white society and is metonymically connected, through the frontier, to these other examples of social deviance. Although the spatial context of the frontier justifies interracial mixing and miscegenation, the films ultimately depict them as morally regressive acts (on the part of the hero), which the Native woman initiates and which endanger the racial and moral structure of western European culture. As such, the relationships must either be contained within the space or destroyed. The resulting child, a sign of the father's transgression but also a well-loved offspring, must be removed from the West in order to be purged of his "savage and exotic" heritage. Thus this West is savage not because of reactionary Natives but because of its existence on the edge of the laws and mores of the American nation.

All of the lover films follow a general plot outline that distinctly resembles that of the famous contemporary play by Edwin Milton Royle, *The Squaw Man*.[30] Royle's story, originally published as a one-act play in 1904, was expanded into a four-act play in 1905 and into a novel in 1906. According to Andrew Smith, "The drama was a huge domestic and international success and had a remarkably long run. It opened at New York's Wallack's Theater on October 23, 1905, became a national road show the following season, and [came] back to Broadway in 1907 and 1908." The early shorts *The Kentuckian* (1908), *The Indian Squaw's Sacrifice* (1910), and *White Fawn's Devotion* (1910) borrow from Royle's general plot, while Cecil B. DeMille's three feature-length films with the same name adapt it quite literally. Such remakes of famous theatrical productions and literature were quite popular in the early history of film and helped cinema achieve legitimacy in the eyes of the upper- and middle-class theater patrons.[31] This may be one reason for the lover films' popularity and their ease in transitioning from shorts to feature-length format.

Similar to that of Royle's play and novel, the films' basic plot revolves around a white hero who is wealthy, educated, and in trouble with the law. He escapes to the West, where a young Indian woman saves his life and nurses him back to health. The woman's exotic qualities and her nobility—symbolized by her willingness to sacrifice herself for the hero—as well as her attractiveness and resourcefulness, indicate to the viewer that she represents a Princess figure and legitimate their union to a certain extent. "The inevitable happens" and the woman becomes pregnant, forcing the couple to marry. A few years into the marriage, the hero receives word from the East that it is safe for him to return or that he has inherited money. Because his wife cannot or will not acculturate into white society as it exists in the East, he must make a decision between staying with his Indian wife and returning east with his child.

The option of leaving his child behind is never seriously considered. The Indian wife's suicide resolves this dilemma. She kills herself so that her husband can move back east to inherit money (*The Kentuckian*) or marry his true love (*The Indian Squaw's Sacrifice* and *Scarlet and Gold*), out of shame (*Oklahoma Jim*), or because she cannot live without her husband and child (*White Fawn's Devotion* and the three film versions of *The Squaw Man*).

The framework conveys the predominant message that interracial relationships between Indians and whites cause emotional, social, and cultural problems that are rooted in the moral and evolutionary inequality between these two races. The family exists in a liminal space between the two cultures, suggesting that, as a unit, they do not fit into either. The helper's self-sacrifice, along with her love for the white hero, underscores her position within the structure as a noble savage and implies that she recognizes her status as a hindrance to both her husband and their child. While the mixed-heritage child—usually a son—ties the two cultures together and foreshadows a mixed-race American nation, his heritage and "savage" environment remain latent threats that must be erased through proper education, separation from his mother, and removal to a superior and more civilized space—the East. The woman's sacrifice ensures her son's future as a civilized American. Western European breeding and whiteness are suggested as culturally and racially superior to Native American culture, which is depicted as vanishing, backward, and inferior. The woman's plight warrants the viewer's sympathy, yet she never emerges as a heroine. Rather, issues of race strangely mingle here with nostalgia for the American frontier as a place of refuge and exile, imperialist nostalgia for the noble yet backward and vanishing Native American, and simultaneous intrigue with and repulsion for interracial mixing.

The *Biograph Bulletin*'s summary of Biograph's 1908 film *The Kentuckian: Story of a Squaw's Devotion and Sacrifice* offers an example of the cultural work done by both the narrative template and the advertising campaign. The text tells us that "Ward Fatherly is the son of a wealthy and indulgent Kentuckian" who finds himself in trouble for killing a man in a duel. He escapes to the "Western frontier, whither he has gone incog, working as a miner." Here he meets a young Indian girl, who rescues him when "a couple of low-down Redskins" knife him. "She drags the wounded Kentuckian to her tipi and nurses him back to health. The inevitable happens—they are married. A lapse of several years occurs, and we find the little family—the Kentuckian, his Squaw, and a little son—living in blissful peace." A friend arrives to give Ward the news that he has inherited his father's estate and must return immediately to the East. "He feels, on the one hand, that he cannot take his Squaw back and introduce her into the society of his set, and on the other, he knows it would break her heart to leave her. No, no. He must give up all and stay where he is." According to the plot summation, the "Squaw at once realizes the situation. She must, for her love for him, make the sacrifice, which she does by sending a bullet through her brain, thus leaving the way clear for him—a woman's devotion for the man she loves."[32]

Three disturbing social attitudes that appear in all the lover films are clear in *The Kentuckian*'s statement; they reveal the ideological constructs underlying the filmic structure of these narratives. First, the woman's race, which is coded into the term "squaw," makes her unacceptable to cultured society. In addition, the term erases her individuality and reduces her to an object, in contrast to Ward. Second, as an honorable white man, the hero makes the undesirable choice and stays with her. The rhetoric of honor dramatically reinforces the "necessity" of this sacrifice for the viewer through the statement "No, no. He must give up all." And third, her responsibility as a devoted wife means the ultimate sacrifice—a "bullet through her brain." These points incorporate two philosophical stances attributable to the patriarchal ideology of the era that reduce the woman's agency and position within the social order of the narrative. As a subordinate character and a member of the colonized group, she poses a hindrance to his status in white society; she is, therefore, expendable. In sum, the quote illustrates a hierarchical formation that positions white society, white men in particular, at the zenith, and Native Americans as dependents somewhere on the periphery, of culture and refinement. As the controlling and patriarchal entity, white society sacrifices its own happiness and cultural progress for the colonized, feminized, and needy Native American subject.

Read within the politics of the time, the patriarchal ordering of society seen in these films, while not surprising, refracts a particular power relationship between Native Americans and the federal government. At the time, federal Indian policy maintained a distinctly paternalistic attitude toward Native Americans, who were considered as lagging in the evolutionary march from savagery toward a more civilized state. Indian policy between 1880 and 1920 enforced American cultural ideals about farming, family organization, and religion through boarding school programs, land allotment, and missionary intervention in order to accelerate their progress. Attempts were made to eradicate Indian lifestyles by curtailing Native religious beliefs and customs; eliminating communal living, sovereign cultural institutions, and Native languages; and enforcing Western educational ideals. Beginning in 1881, Indian agents were allowed to forbid "rites [and] customs . . . contrary to civilization." In accordance with the General Allotment Act, or Dawes Act, of 1887, reservation lands were taken out of tribal holding and divided into family plots, while the excess was sold to white farmers. The Board of Indian Commissioners, the group responsible for evaluating federal Indian policy, officially began in 1888 to encourage an education system that in "effect calls for the destruction of Indian tribal identity and the fostering of individualism among Indian students."[33] The ideology that validated these actions surfaces in the rhetoric of *The Kentuckian* advertisement discussed above and in the way these films define the Native American woman in relation to the white hero and other white characters.

The films also resonate with evidence of a backlash to women's freedoms that mirrors conservative reaction in the early twentieth century to women's suffrage and the growing number of women entering the workforce outside the home. Victorian ideals about women's status within the home, the family, and society were being challenged by "young women [who] were becoming too independent and free of restraints in the post-Victorian society" of the mid-1910s.[34] The film industry marketed its products to both independent women and more conservative Victorian viewers. Serials like Pathé's *The Perils of Pauline* and more serious dramas promoted the "new woman" and featured strong, independent heroines whose freedom from Victorian strictness resulted in their higher education, less restrictive clothing, work outside the home, and politically active presence. In contrast, many melodramas focused on the dangers that awaited the young, unprotected woman outside the home, such as white slavery, prostitution, and dangerous men. The lover films promote a certain strength of character in the Indian woman but also contain her within a familial power order, suggesting that these films participated in the social dialogue about women's place in society but leaned toward a more conservative perspective on the topic. In sum, the Indian woman emerges as a primordial, original woman whose

strong but subordinate

docile and subordinate personality contrasts to the new woman—the contemporary white woman.

The lover films' ideological framework, described above, does not change significantly over the twenty-three years of their production, but minor plot variations do occur that illustrate the latitude for expression available within the format. In some cases, instances of "slippage" within the dominant ideology of the film offer glimpses of alternative attitudes. A number of films display particularities that distinguish them from others found in this group. *The Kentuckian* and *White Fawn's Devotion*, for example, insert scenes that indicate cultural latitude for accepting miscegenation and mixed-race families. Others, especially Cecil B. DeMille's *Squaw Man* films, utilize scripting, casting, and scene composition to underscore the more racializing aspects of the lover film plot.

The Kentuckian offers a narrative example of romantic slippage during the couple's wedding ceremony that softens the overall tone presented by the film's advertising. A "fully robed Episcopalian" minister performs the rites while Ward places a ring on his bride's finger.[35] The simply composed shot tightly frames the three characters so that both the clergyman and the ring are clearly visible. The *Squaw Man* films also use a minister to provide Christian legitimacy to the marriage ceremony, but none of them focus so purposefully on a wedding ring or on the reciprocal love of the couple. *White Fawn's Devotion* (1910) exhibits an interesting case of narrative slippage by reversing the plot sequence after fulfilling it. In this film, White Fawn and her husband are happily married and living in "Dakota" with their daughter when he receives notice of his inheritance. Suspecting that her husband "will probably forget his half-educated Indian wife waiting longingly for his return" and believing that "she now stands in his way and in the way of their child's advancement," the woman stabs herself.[36] To this point, the film has followed the traditional plot sequencing, but now it uses it as the springboard for an alternative ending. The daughter finds her father hovering over her mother and thinks he has murdered her. She tells her mother's people, who chase the man, capture him, and are about to kill him when White Fawn appears, only wounded. Her husband decides to stay with his family and forgo his inheritance in the East. The three twists added to the ending are key to representing a discomfort with the narrative outcome of the other films: the inclusion of a daughter rather than a son, the wife's recovery, and the husband's decision to remain. The substitution of a daughter for a son raises two possible readings. On the one hand, the issues of heredity and inheritance are easier to flout if the heir is a girl. On the other, the use of a female child works against the patriarchal ideology that values male over female children, and this seems more reflective of the high regard Native cultures traditionally have for women. The woman's remarkable recovery gives a certain amount of agency to the lover character that disappears when the attempted suicide succeeds.[37] In addition, romantic love triumphs over cultural barriers when the husband decides to remain in the West with his family. Both these films illustrate the degree of latitude available within the film plot while emphasizing its boundaries.

Cecil B. DeMille's three *Squaw Man* films, in contrast to *The Kentuckian* and *White Fawn's Devotion*, build upon racializing ideologies to underscore a decidedly more antiassimilationist narrative. As do Royle's texts, the *Squaw Man* films begin in England, depicted as a lush, green land of education and refinement, and move to the American West, constructed as a place of exile and savagery. Similarly, the beautiful, educated, and refined Diana symbolizes England and is positioned against Nat-U-ritch, who is coded as culturally and intellectually inferior to Diana.[38] Jim Wynnegate, Diana's childhood friend and true love, whose self-exile to avoid embezzlement charges protects Diana's name and her husband's reputation, is the connecting element between these two locations and two women. While in exile, Jim rescues Nat-U-ritch, the daughter of Tabywana the Ute chief, from the white cowboy Cash Hawkins; she returns the favor twice, by killing Hawkins before he can shoot Jim and by rescuing Jim from a nearly fatal accident. Her love for him is unquestioned. Jim's social isolation and her adoration result in an interracial union that marks him derogatorily as a "squaw man" and gives them a mixed-race son, Hal. The text's most disturbing conflict arises after Diana's husband—Jim's cousin—dies, clearing Jim's name and leaving him the family estate. Diana and a solicitor arrive in America to find Jim and bring him home. Rather than return to Europe with Diana, Jim makes the difficult decision to stay with Nat-U-ritch, who could not survive his departure, but to send Hal to England to be educated as a white man. These choices, made without Nat-U-ritch's consent, result in her heartbreak and suicide.

Over a seventeen-year period, 1914–1931, the *Squaw Man* films promoted classist and nationalist themes of supremacy and antimiscegenation mingled with an imperialist nostalgia for the Native American and the frontier American West. All three of these DeMille films (1914, 1918, and 1931) closely adhere to Royle's story and the lover film template but, like the other lover films, carry their own distinct generic markers. Each also underscores the racializing theme of social regression, in which violence is endemic to the Native characters, the displacement of Native Americans by whites is inevitable, and the superiority of western European culture is unquestioned. Through casting, scripting, and cinematographic choices, DeMille emphasizes this theme differently in each film, in ways that reflect the shifting climate of American society's attitudes, fears, and assumptions about Native Americans and racial minorities.[39]

The Squaw Man (1914), cowritten and coproduced by DeMille and Oscar C. Apfel, dramatizes the trauma involved in the breakup of the mixed-race family while emphasizing the supposedly inevitable and justified displacement of Native Americans by whites because of their "primitive" culture and unwillingness to acculturate fully into white society. The final scene encapsulates these trends most economically of the three versions. Jim kneels in the foreground holding Nat-U-ritch's body; a pair of Hal's moccasins dangles from her hand. Diana, shielding Hal from the sight, stands slightly behind Jim and to the left. Next to her and to the right of Jim and Nat-U-ritch, Tabywana poses in stereotypic Indian stoicism, complete with his arms crossed and a full eagle headdress. The ranch hands and the sheriff's men cluster in a semicircle around this inner group while Tabywana's men encircle them. As the screen fades to black, Jim looks toward Diana. Jim's embrace of his dead wife's body illustrates the tragedy of the situation. The placement of Diana slightly behind Jim and with Hal suggests a new future for Jim. Hal's positioning within Diana's motherly embrace foreshadows a new family unit of Jim, Diana, and Hal. Nat-U-ritch's death eliminates her as a threat to Hal's destiny as an Englishman, and it also releases Jim and allows him to start a new life with Diana. This reconfiguration and Nat-U-ritch's suicide imply a consensus that the interracial relationship was ill fated. Such rationale on the part of whites both without and within the film locks Nat-U-ritch's fate with that of a vanishing people, a position from which even her marriage cannot extricate her. Unlike the book and the plays, the film never presents the possibility of Nat-U-ritch's going to England with Jim. Her connection to the landscape and her world, continuously

The death of Nat-U-ritch: Scene from *The Squaw Man*. Cecil B. DeMille, Jesse L. Lasky Feature Play Company, 1914. (*Motion Picture World*, February 28, 1914)

illustrated through her Native costume and the presence of her people, overshadows any "civilizing" or "westernizing" that her marriage to Jim might suppose.

Nat-U-ritch's suicide also implies the powerlessness of Native American women to act against interventions by the dominant culture. The film captures this lack of agency by recreating a familiar scenario in Native history. Hal's removal parallels that of many Native children who were forcibly taken away from their parents to be educated in religious and military schools as part of the civilizing mission of the period. His inclusion in the final scene and in Diana's embrace, and his forced witnessing of his dead mother's body, promotes the paternalistic and hard-edged view that Native Americans need to face the reality of their dying culture and embrace assimilation. Lillian St. Cyr's (Nat-U-ritch) performance and emotional response to the reenactment educated the cast about the trauma of such experiences. As Dustin Farnum (Jim) reported to the press, "When we were rehearsing the scene where the baby is taken from Nat-U-ritch to be sent back to England this pure-blooded

Indian girl broke down and went into hysterics. It was pitiful. It was twenty-five minutes before we could proceed with the picture. In all my years on the stage I never saw anything like it. It was absolutely the reverse of what we have been taught about Indians."[40] The power and reality that St. Cyr brought to the film as a Native actress is unparalleled by the performances of actresses later cast in the part. Her performance and the large Native cast of this version separate it from the subsequent versions.

Further readings of the final scene's racial hierarchy reinforce the bigotry and Anglocentrism of the story. The accumulation of cast members in the last scene works to underscore Nat-U-ritch's position in the hierarchy of the community and to accentuate that her central position in this last scene comes only because of her death. Diana's arrival forces Nat-U-ritch to the periphery of the set and the action, where she lingers around the edges of the drama, as do Tabywana's warriors in the final standoff. The other Native characters work as props that accentuate her connection to Native America and to a savage element that always threatens white civilization. Nat-U-ritch's use of ritual and costume throughout the film and her inability to assimilate into Jim's world continuously link her to the savageness they represent. They are all racially, culturally, and socially coded as inferior and exotic, and they, especially Nat-U-ritch, are presented as residing on the periphery of civilization, never fully in it. The warriors' placement and the dynamics of the arrested battle between them, Jim's men, and the sheriff's posse suggest that her death severs their link to civilization. The visual composition of the final shot, which places them in the rear of the image, also reinforces the idea of their vanishing power and their inevitable vanishing into the historical background. According to Andrew Smith, during the first few decades of the twentieth century, "a general rise in racism sparked by increased immigration, the ascendancy of westerners to national political prominence, nostalgia about Indians brought on by the closing frontier, and new ideas about the fixity of racial and cultural differences led white intellectuals, social reformers, and policy makers seriously to question whether Indians could ever rise to the so-called 'civilized' state. Increasingly, European-Americans believed that Indians saw the world in fundamentally different ways from themselves and that the natives had neither the will nor capability to change."[41] DeMille's film certainly reinforces such a belief. The progress of history and culture out of the violent West (depicted by the posse and Tabywana's warriors) and toward civilization (represented by the British group) is propelled by Nat-U-ritch's death.

One must conclude that DeMille designed the scene to reinforce such a metatext. The film suggests that interracial relationships threaten the "natural" racial hierarchy of civilized society—a fear that resonates with Progressive Era concerns about immigrants whose ethnic heritage and non-English languages set them apart from the English-speaking, predominantly western European Protestant American populace. Like the Native American characters in the film, many immigrants also seemed to refuse to integrate fully into American culture, choosing instead to retain their ethnic communities, languages, and ties to their homelands. Such nonconformity, especially during the period of rising unrest in Europe prior to World War I, subjected them to similar manifestations of fear and racist rhetoric. Immigrants were pushed to assimilate, but with a caveat that, though one must integrate culturally, one should not attempt to do so through miscegenation with members of the dominant white American culture. The film's very limited use of intertitles and clearly designed visual narratives make it easily accessible to a nonliterate and non-English-speaking viewing public, thus making its cautionary message unmistakably clear to the immigrant members of the viewing audience.

An analysis of the casting choices for the Nat-U-ritch character over the seventeen-year period spanned by the *Squaw Man* films allows a unique glimpse at the public's changing ideas of how this figure, and perhaps Native women in general, should act. Each actress's portrayal affected the film's overall tone significantly. Lillian St. Cyr, also known as Lillian Red Wing, brought an authenticity to her 1914 character that neither Ann Little's nor Lupe Vélez's subsequent performances could, through her insertion of cultural knowledge, the latitude and realism she brought to a narrow role, and her obvious emotional reaction to Hal's removal. Casting St. Cyr seems progressive in retrospect because of the tendency to cast white actors and actresses in most Indian lead roles—Mary Pickford in Griffith's Indian films, for example. According to the press reaction, Ann Little's portrayal in 1918 was more indicative of a popular conceptualization of Native Americans, as illustrated in a review of her acting as a "wonderful characterization of the female Redskin, with her expressionless features, changing little in suffering or in joy."[42] Her reduction of the character to an emotionless woman signals the inability of 1918 America to accept Native Americans outside a rigidly confining racial stereotype—one that would survive in Hollywood well through the 1950s. Lupe Vélez's portrayal follows the trend set by Little, conveying an insignificant range of intellect and emotion, and the layering of her sexuality onto the one-dimensional characterization simply adds one stereotype to another. The choice to hire Vélez for the 1931 film, based in part on her sexuality and screen persona, foreshadows a trend in Hollywood to depict mixed-race Native and Hispanic women as overtly sexual and promiscuous. The ethnicity of each actress also highlights the changing attitudes of the industry, illuminating both the tendency of the film industry to assume that certain ethnic groups could portray Native Americans and minorities more accurately than could actors from the group itself, and the racial ideology informing such assumptions.[43]

The 1931 version of *The Squaw Man* illustrates DeMille's renowned skill in reading the times and desires of his audience. He adapted Royle's story and his previous film versions for a 1930s audience by combining elements of his previous two characterizations of Naturich and by making her screen image reflective of other popular culture representations of Native "princess" figures. According to Marilyn Burgess and Gail Guthrie Valaskakis's study of frontier stereotypes, from about 1915 through the 1940s, advertising images on cigar boxes, food products like Land O'Lakes butter, calendars, and paintings depicted a highly romanticized and sexy young woman surrounded by pristine nature. The sexualizing of the Naturich character and the casting of Lupe Vélez illustrate a desire to make the Naturich character more erotic to the viewing audience. The choices also suggest an awareness of popular culture uses of the Indian Princess figure. Known later in her career as the "Mexican Spitfire," Vélez, like many Latin American women in Hollywood at the time, was associated with verbal epithets evoking passion, violence, spice, or heat.[44]

Aside from Naturich's sexualization, the plot remains virtually the same until the final scene. Jim and Diana have reunited, but Hal's presence and Jim's decision to stay with his wife make their physical union impossible. Their love for each other, which is clearly established in the early part of the film, resurfaces when Jim tells Diana his life will be over when they leave, and she responds that she will love Hal as she "has never ceased to love [Jim]." Shortly after this exchange, Diana departs with Hal. A grief-stricken Naturich sneaks into Hal's bedroom and shoots herself while holding a crude wooden horse she has just made for him. The final sequence is a tightly composed shot within the child's room, with Naturich dying against his bed. Jim rushes in, calling her name, and cradles her in his arms. Behind them, the sheriff's and Jim's men crowd into the frame to watch as Naturich opens her eyes, looks at Jim, says "un-ner-stan," and dies. The camera pans down from her face, past the bedstead, to the horse that has fallen to the floor. Her death in the small square room, surrounded by white men who, with the exception of Jim, are enemies intent on punishing her, takes on the symbolic meaning of her life in Jim's world. This tilt down to the handmade horse (a prop from the 1918 film) reinforces her primitive status, and her verbal acknowledgment that she "un-ner-stans" suggests she is aware that there is no place for her in Jim's world.

This scene recalls the opening credits, which superimpose the title of the film onto a silhouetted Indian hunched over on a fatigued horse—the archetypal figure of the vanishing American. Naturich's suicide and dying words are a most poignant reminder that she must accept her place in the world as part of a vanishing people and not deprive Hal of his place at "Eton and Oxford." Such overt social Darwinism is not balanced by the bilingual moments in the film, the very beautiful cinematography, or the picturesque framing throughout. In fact, when combined with the moral guidelines of the time, Royle's ending and DeMille's changes add another layer to be analyzed.

During the 1920s and early 1930s, Hollywood evolved as an industry into a "viable commercial enterprise" with a keen sense of its audience. According to film historian Arthur Knight, DeMille, "better than any other director of the era . . . seems to have apprehended a basic duality in his audience—on the one hand their tremendous eagerness to see what they considered sinful and taboo, and on the other, the fact that they could enjoy sin only if they were able to preserve their own sense of righteous respectability in the process."[45] Royle's play and novel and the DeMille films' renditions of *The Squaw Man* offered precisely this duality for the audience. Popular culture's commitment to the continual remaking of the text suggests that Naturich's death preserved a common sense of morality and acted as retribution for the immorality of both the interracial premarital sexual relationship between her and Jim and her killing of Cash Hawkins. Naturich shoots herself with the gun she used to kill Cash Hawkins, bringing the film's violence full circle. Her punishment is already neatly coded into Royle's texts and the earlier films, but by 1931, the Motion Picture Production Code's very strict guidelines and the religious fervor of the time demanded more. The twist in the 1931 version ensures that she admits her transgression.[46]

The 1931 version of *The Squaw Man*, with its new ending, also registers the racial and sexual ambiguity toward minorities, especially Native Americans, in the 1930s. By 1931, politicians had recognized the failure of the allotment system and forced assimilation policies. The 1928 Meriam report shocked the nation with its catalogue of serious problems caused by the federal government's forty-four-year policy. Simultaneously, but still in keeping with the ambivalence seen earlier in the decade, a romantic and imperialist nostalgia for the idea of Native American culture as a utopian alternative to modernity overshadowed the reality of the 1924 Indian Citizenship Act and the actuality of those Native Americans surviving in white America. The result was a federal policy shift toward recognizing cultural pluralism that would come to fruition in John Collier's 1934 Indian Reorganization Act (also known as the Wheeler-Howard Act) and in the celebration of ethnicity apparent in Southwest artists' colonies.[47] The addition of fervent racism, fueled by economic woes, continuing Americanization drives (the anti-immigration policies of the 1920s were still in effect), and the religious and social moral backlash to the cultural promiscuity of the 1920s, resulted in a complex and ambiguous melding of imperialist nostalgia, sympathy, and condemnation.

Within the milieu of Hollywood's racial hierarchy, this complex and ambiguous mix developed into the cinematic entrenchment of stereotypes of Native Americans that continue today—the noble versus ignoble savage and the Princess versus the squaw—and white or Hispanic actresses' portraying Native American leading characters. The 1931 version depicts Naturich as a Princess figure—beautiful, exotic, and willing to give her life for the white hero—but reinforces this status through her social standing as the Ute chief's daughter. Her beauty shifts into sexuality with the overlay of another Hollywood stereotype, that of the voluptuous and seductive Latina whose morals are contaminated by her innate sexual nature. At this point in Hollywood history, as Richard Dyer's work has illustrated, white actresses and white female characters

came to epitomize the values and purity of western European culture.[48] White actresses played Native American women who were symbolically pure and innocent, while Hispanic or Latina actresses played those who were not—and rarely at this time did Native American women play Indian women in title roles. In addition, white actresses, like Eleanor Boardman (Diana), were positioned against women of color, whose sexuality and immorality accentuated the white character's sterling qualities. The 1931 film's casting choices suggest some of these politics, as does the decision to sexualize Naturich and alter the ending. Naturich's "un-ner-stan" encompasses this racial and hierarchical structure and condones it. She accepts her transgression, her social status, and her inability to be white like Diana or to provide Hal with what Whiteness can—education, money, title, class, and a secure future within the social system. The lover film template inscribes the woman's punishment into the narrative. DeMille's third version more blatantly punishes the racially coded woman for transgressing the sexual color line—he forces her to verbalize her guilt. DeMille's decision to portray Naturich as he did reflects the discrimination and hostility to minorities that existed on all levels of American culture in the 1930s. The combination of Naturich's sexuality and immoral behavior—her premarital sex and killing of Cash Hawkins—also foreshadows the Sexualized Maiden figure that surfaces in 1930s and 1940s westerns.

Lover films peaked in popularity in the mid-1910s, virtually disappeared during the 1920s post–World War I period, and reappeared in 1931 with DeMille's last version of *The Squaw Man* and as a minor narrative in *Oklahoma Jim*. The lapse in production of these films during the Jazz Age of the 1920s may have resulted from their moral theme and plot. The films speak against the transgression of cultural taboos such as miscegenation and premarital relations and in favor of paternalistic family structures and rigid social order. Such themes seem incongruous with the 1920s' search for freedom, violation of social order, and women's liberation. Nonetheless, the stock market crash of 1929 resulted in the closing of more than five thousand banks and businesses nationwide and the country's sinking into financial depression. The Jazz Age was over; by 1931, millions of people were out of work, and food and work riots emphasized the overall desperation in the country.[49] Like the 1910s, this was a time of cultural chaos marked by intense xenophobia and an increasing demand for "aliens" to conform to white American ideals, as well as a return to religious and moral roots for many Americans. Once again, the lover films offered a lens through which to project the trauma of the moment.   ✦

DEATH OF THE CELLULOID PRINCESS

Cinema, specifically the highly representational systems of Indian and western films, offers through the lover and helper films a palimpsest on which to rewrite Native American–white history and to articulate national struggles based on racial and cultural difference. Mary Douglas notes that "the body is a model which can stand for any bounded system. Its boundaries can represent any boundaries which are threatened or precarious."[50] Within these films' narratives and within the construction of American society, the Princess figure (helper or lover) stands for the bounded system of a contained colonized subject within the larger national structure. Even as the representative of the best of Native American society, the Princess is potentially disruptive because she politically destabilizes the framework, so clearly promoted in these films, of a racially white nation. The films maintain and order the national racial paradigm through the young woman's suicide or manslaughter.

Not only the fact but the manner of the Princess's death is of crucial importance. The lover films place the responsibility of the Native woman's death in her own hands and code it as an act of acquiescence to a dominant social order. Western Judeo-Christian cultures generally view suicide as an extreme act of violence against one's own body, the result of losing emotional, psychological, or physical control. With this in mind, one may read the Princess's suicide as either an act of agency against, or an act of submission to, the bounded system. The Princess, always positioned as the colonized subject, never quite fits the national ideal. Thus her suicide violates or threatens the system's parameters by transgressing the cultural and religious taboos against taking one's life that are inscribed into that system. From this perspective, she refuses her position. It is more likely, however, that her suicide verifies how deeply ingrained she is in the system. The lover films follow a trend, quite popular in the silent period, that portrays her suicide as an act of grief or self-sacrifice brought on by her inability to understand, navigate, or conform to white society.[51] In light of this, her death serves as punishment for transgressing cultural taboos against miscegenation and reaffirms the national system rather than sabotaging it. The suicide also executes a metaphor, common during the late nineteenth and early twentieth centuries, that suggests that killing the savage within is the best way to assimilate Native Americans into mainstream culture. Such a "death," achieved through educational and religious training designed to eradicate Native languages and cultures, transforms Native Americans (usually children) into Christian Americans. The Celluloid Princess literally performs what assimilation demands; her act reinforces a particular national space that excludes ethnic identity and sovereignty. Her violence displaces Western cultural guilt about the ramifications of colonialism as it is depicted through her character.

The Native woman's suicide also offers an easy solution to the problem of civilizing Native Americans, stopping resistance to the colonial process, and accelerating assimilation into white society. Andrew Smith draws a similar conclusion in his discussion of Nat-u-ritch in Edwin Milton Royle's play *The Squaw Man*: "If the fictional Nat-u-ritch is fated to a circumscribed social position because of her cultural and racial differences, so by analogy are all Indians. As a member of an inassimilable people, her suicide is the final and inevitable solution to the problem of Indian/white relations. Her death represents the death of all tribal peoples in the United States. When she is gone, when they are gone, so are the intractable problems surrounding assimilation."[52] Though Smith refers to Royle's texts, his words speak to the period's concern with the ramifications of interracial relationships. Although the Princess figure is designed to promote assimilation, as Smith points out and the films corroborate, she is unassimilable, and thus her relationship threatens society's "natural" racial hierarchy and class order. As powerful a metaphor as suicide may be, it does not survive as a trend beyond the silent era, suggesting that the appeal of suicide as a moralistic ending was tied to the melodramatic style of the era.

The helper films, on the other hand, rely on a battle sequence in which the helper dies as "collateral damage" in a "savage war." Generally, she is shot while escaping her own people (*Red Wing's Gratitude* and *Iola's Promise*) or in cross fire. In other words, no one person bears the guilt for her death, but the films place the burden of responsibility on her own people. To a greater extent than the lover's suicide, this emphasis on ambiguity or Indian fault relieves white viewers of any associative guilt in the resultant vanishing or extermination of Native Americans (or any colonized group) through frontier expansion and American nation building.

The elements that make the helper and the lover such successful palimpsests for reinscribing early-twentieth-century Native American–white relations and other social issues transfer into later manifestations of the Princess figure. Thus the importance of these early Princess films lies not only in their illumination of contemporary American racial and social concerns but also in the foundational blueprint they provide for Hollywood's future representations of Native American women.

Subsequent Princess figures resemble the lover figure most obviously, but the narrative structures of the films tend to reference the influences of the helper narrative's mythic space. The Princess figure will continue to save the hero—either physically, as does this early prototype, or spiritually; she will usually be a full-blooded Native woman of high tribal social standing; and her exotic qualities will be accentuated and become a primary reason for the white hero's initial interest in her. The secondary positioning of the lover will grow more pronounced over the century, as will the emphasis on the western format that registers the influence of the helper films. Although the *Squaw Man* films begin to incorporate these changes, *Oklahoma Jim* (1931) exhibits these tendencies most clearly of all the early films. Natoma, the chief's daughter, occupies a minor moment in the film that initiates the white hero's adventure and his love relationship with Betty, a white woman from the East. Natoma's suicide, committed out of the shame she feels in having been tricked into a false marriage with a white man, initiates the eventual battle between her people and the white settlers. The format of the film, as the *Film Daily* states, is a "Good Old Fashioned Western with Indian Reservation atmosphere . . . [and] enough action and fighting to please all the fans."[53] Thus we see the friction between Indians and whites from the helper films and the interracial relationship, high social status, and suicide of the lover films. Future Princess films will do away with the suicide motif and replace it with the collateral damage trend of the helper films.

Such adaptations of the early Princess figure underscore how well it answers the needs of American culture for an exotic escape into racializing and romantically nostalgic relationships with groups that do not fit the national ideal of a white hegemonic nation. They also reflect a continuing need, on the part of mainstream American culture and the film industry, to act out interracial frustrations through the body of the Native American woman, who represents the colonial relationship between Native America and the American nation. The early Princess films, in part because of their temporal closeness to the historical closing of the western frontier and the ending of the Indian wars, present this need most overtly. During chaotic moments of intense national identity crises, however, the Princess film resurfaces, manipulated to fit the social needs of the day, suggesting that the figure's use as a palimpsest is deeply ingrained in the American national psyche.

Two

White-Painted Lady

The 1950s Celluloid Princess

The girl inside the wickiup is in the holiest time of her life. For these four days she becomes White-Painted Lady, Mother of Life . . . for this night only this girl is even more holy than most, maybe, because she has been away from us for a very long time. She is very old for this ceremony; it is very special.
                                    —Cochise to Jeffords in *Broken Arrow*

THIS WELL-KNOWN INTRODUCTION of Sonseeahray from Delmer Daves's 1950 film *Broken Arrow* precedes the white hero Jeffords's and the audience's first encounter with the exceptional Indian woman who will marry him and help bridge the tensions between his culture and hers.[1] As a beautiful young maiden who embraces the white hero, she symbolizes the best of Indian culture and the possibility of assimilation into western European culture. The quote also presents the 1950s paradigm of the Celluloid Indian Princess who aligns herself with a European American colonizer and dies for that choice. Though the 1950s figure is reminiscent of the Princess of the silent film era, her idealization surpasses that of her cinematic ancestor, with filmic and narrative attention focused on her social status, beauty, and exotic heritage. The Celluloid Princess who emerges works within the pro-Indian westerns of the time as an index of liberalism, cultural pluralism, and racial integration during a moment in history characterized by racial and political paranoia linked to cold war policy, rising anti-Communist activity, and national desegregation policies. Her symbolic possibility, however, coded as her innate Whiteness and willingness to assimilate into western European culture, clashes with deeply ingrained racism and results in violence enacted on her body that underscores the racial and ideological tensions of 1950s America. Her resulting containment within the Princess role as the exotic Other reflects the aura of the cold war as well as the colonial rhetoric of dominance.

Homi Bhabha explains that colonial discourse depends on the notion of "fixity," the rigid and unchanging, to maintain the "ideological construction of otherness" that is fundamental to the stereotype.[2] The particular elements that create the Celluloid Princess as an acceptable icon for racial integration also confine her as a racial Other and fix her within a cultural, historical, and racial framework. These elements may include her noble or high social standing, either as a chief's sister, daughter, or granddaughter or, like Sonseeahray, connected metonymically to deities, holiness, and goodness; her youth, innocence, and purity; her connection to nature and the American landscape's primordial essence; her desire for the American hero (symbolic of Whiteness) and her resulting death; and her racial exoticism. Within the western's colonial discourse of American nation building, the combination of these elements equates the Celluloid Princess with the notion of a virgin continent and an untamed wilderness that desires the white male colonizer and the progressive march of civilization. Thus the Celluloid Princess stereotype underscores an interpretation of the American national space as legitimized by conquest and regulated by a color line — a demarcation between the white colonizers and the darker-skinned colonized that the white male crosses with ease.

When seen as cultural texts of an era, the pro-Indian films utilize the Celluloid Princess figure as a mitigating element between a liberal, utopian, mixed-race national image and the reality of cultural violence against those who are racially and culturally different from a national white norm. The tensions created by such juxtapositions of ideologies register the controversial political climate of 1950s America. Cold war policy and the resulting fear of communism, right-wing politics, the beginning of the volatile civil rights era, and the height of the federal government's termination and relocation program for Native Americans are hallmarks of the early 1950s. World War II shook the United States out of its isolationist tendency and placed the postwar nation in a position of political and economic dominance. The Truman administration promoted such a position by supporting overseas programs like the Truman Doctrine and Marshall Plan and by "creat[ing] an atmosphere of crises and cold war" in which the Soviet Union was "not just a rival but an immediate threat." Indeed, the Soviet Union appeared a very real danger after exploding its first atomic bomb (1947), and with other independence movements—Mao's overthrow of Chiang Kai-shek's U.S.-supported government (1949), the Korean War (1950), and Indochina's and the Philippines' local uprisings—the risk of communism increased in scope. According to Howard Zinn, the Truman administration reacted in "a series of moves abroad and at home [that established] a climate of fear—a hysteria about Communism—which would steeply escalate the military budget and stimulate the economy with war-related orders. This combination of policies would permit more aggressive actions abroad, more repressive actions at home."[3]

Over the next decade, repressive actions at home would include a disloyalty search program initiated by executive order in 1947, a series of anti-Communist bills in 1954, the return of the House Un-American Activities Committee, and the investigation of 6.6 million persons between March 1947 and December 1952. No one was immune. Universities fired those unwilling to sign loyalty oaths; schoolbooks were banned if considered subversive; and once again, the Hollywood film industry found itself under scrutiny for Communist tendencies.[4] The result for Hollywood was an industry-wide purging of those considered Communist threats—a blacklisting of stars, writers, and technicians. According to Robert Sklar, a large component of Hollywood "adopted an attitude of compliance," retreated from fighting the accusations, and in some cases participated in the process.[5]

Simultaneously, but with less vigor than the anti-Communist crusade, Truman's 1947 civil rights program attempted to deal with the country's racial problems. During the war, the United States had openly denounced racism while continuing to segregate its troops, to base pay scales on race, and to ignore the racial tensions and frustrations among its diverse population. Postwar, however, the country's civil rights record became "an issue in world politics." In the aftermath of a war on Hitler's fascist doctrines, U.S. racist policies and attitudes toward its citizens of color jarred terribly with its rhetoric of world leadership and democracy. Although desegregation was ordered for the military in 1948, it would take more than a decade to be completely enforced. On the civil level, it was not until after the 1954 Supreme Court decision in *Brown v. Board of Education of Topeka*, which outlawed segregation, that mainstream Americans began to see a shift in the deeply entrenched racial structures of the nation. Even this monumental decision did not significantly change the balance of power, integrate American society, or alter the racism felt by African Americans and other racial minorities.[6]

The era's politics affected Native Americans differently than it did African Americans. While segregation remained the norm in black-white relations, integration was the catchphrase in Indian policy. Postwar federal Indian policy shifted once again, from that of the cultural pluralist approach of John Collier's 1934 Indian Reorganization Act to one of termination and relocation. The relocation portion of the policy was influenced in part by the "performance of Native American men abroad and native women in the war industries at home" and by the growing number of Native Americans already seeking work in cities after the war. Supporters of the program pushed to relocate Native American families to large cities (many quite a distance from the homeland) and integrate them into the urban populace. Federal programs were established to help with the transition but were inadequate to deal with the magnitude of problems that such moves entailed. The termination portion of the policy, encapsulated in House Concurrent Resolution 108, encouraged the federal government to eliminate the reservation system and governmental responsibility to tribes considered well established and monetarily self-sufficient. By 1954, Congress had passed termination bills for the Menominees of Wisconsin, Klamath of Oregon, Coushattas of Alabama, mixed-blood Utes, Southern Paiutes of Utah, and a group of small western Oregon tribes. The policy was disastrous for the tribes involved because it neglected the myriad economic components necessary for a community to survive. Thus, although they had been self-sufficient to an extent, their economic base was often inadequate to allow successful separation from the federal system.[7]

On the whole, the 1950s is a period remembered for its national paranoia and repressed anxiety about anyone who did not fit the national ideal—the white, democratic, Christian, nuclear family norm—and about one's own place in relation to that norm. The western reached its peak during these years in part because of its ability to capture these fears and ideals.[8] During the 1950s, four pro-Indian westerns emerged that countered Hollywood's trend of supporting repressive actions. These films challenged the national ideal mentioned above through their promotion of racial integration and assimilation while clearly registering the national unease and tension of the period. As a group, *Broken Arrow* (1950), *Across the Wide Missouri* (1951), *Broken Lance* (1954), and *Last Train from Gun Hill* (1959) exhibit sensitivity to the complexities and various manifestations of racism. They speak directly to the Native American–white integration issues that arose in the wake of the termination policy while also depicting an overt reaction to integration and racial desegregation that alludes to national race relations as a whole. Each offers a sympathetic portrayal of Native Americans and, through its narrative, condemns "White America's marginalization of the Indian."[9] All present happily married interracial couples who plan for, or have, children. With the exception of the town in *Broken Lance*, the communities in which they live accept their union, but they represent liberal enclaves surrounded by nonsupportive elements.

The films build from the blueprint created in the silent-period Princess films but relegate the Princess character to a role secondary to the hero's. The early 1950s films *Broken Arrow* and *Across the Wide Missouri* utilize the western mythic structure seen in the silent-period helper films, in which the Princess figure bridges the savage and civilized forces at war on the frontier. An attempt at intercultural political union is added, and "savagery" is extended to include whites as well as Indian reactionaries. The conflict between the groups, however, remains a fundamental component in the narrative structure and results in a battle and the Princess's death. *Broken Lance* (1954) and *Last Train from Gun Hill* (1959) draw from the silent-period lover films in that the Native woman's tribe never appears as a fundamental cultural entity in the films; her cultural heritage manifests itself only in memories, clothing, and peripheral figures who link her to an unseen community.

The release of these few films coincided with the similarly romantic, antiracist, and pro-Indian westerns *The Big Sky* (1952) and *White Feather* (1955), which allow the interracial couple a happy future. Both types of film ideologically competed against films like *The Searchers* (1956), whose ambiguity toward racism complicates its anti-Indian stance, and virulently anti-Indian or "vehemently racist" westerns, such as *Arrowhead* (1953), that would eclipse the assimilationist pro-Indian westerns and maintain prominence until the early 1970s. But, as a group, the

1950s Princess films exist somewhere between the utopian extreme and the everyday reality. Indeed, as Michael Coyne points out, the pro-Indian westerns "condemned white perfidy against the Indian, but did so from their secure positions within the existing power structure."[10]

INNOCENCE, PURITY, AND WHITENESS

After an extensive lapse, from 1931 through the 1940s, the Celluloid Indian Princess emerges in the 1950s as a secondary, but highly icono-graphic, figure in the form of Broken Arrow's Sonseeahray (Debra Paget). Noted "at the time as a breakthrough in the sympathetic treatment of the Native American," the film, with its interracial marriage that "shattered the barriers of color and hate," promoted a "theme of tolerance and inte-gration [that] served as an indication of America's evolving policy toward Native Americans."[11] As the first of the pro-Indian films released that decade, Broken Arrow—and Sonseeahray—set the standards for subse-quent films' depictions of the Princess figure.[12] Accentuating the quali-ties of goodness and innocence found in the silent-period figures but erasing the hint of taint attached to the earlier figure's sexual freedom, the film heightens the figure's exotic status while drawing connections between her spiritual status and Christianity. In addition, her high social standing and "innate Whiteness"—her desire to assimilate into western European culture—make her an acceptable candidate for incorporation into the American nation. These decisions may have been vital to audi-ence acceptance of the themes of miscegenation and cultural similarity, especially given the period's anti-Communist tenor, which deemed any ideological difference from the conservative mainstream Christian per-spective anti-American and a threat to national unity.

Sonseeahray's incarnation as "White-Painted Lady, Mother of Life" and her powers of healing and prophecy situate her solidly within the symbolic and primordial world. When Tom Jeffords (James Stewart) and the audience first encounter Sonseeahray through the rounded door-frame of the wickiup, she is "in the holiest time of her life," and her beauty and healing powers enchant him. Sonseeahray is not the first Na-tive American woman presented in the film; however, the women shown in the preceding scene of the sunrise ceremony appear as a homogenous group of dancers—props within the composition. In contrast, Sonseeah-ray stands alone, metaphorically and physically. This technique of isolat-

Broken Arrow. Delmer Daves, Twentieth Century-Fox, 1950.

ing her or having her accompanied only by a matronly figure, in contrast with other women who appear as background figures and in groups, works throughout the film to elevate her within the narrative and within the visual composition of the film.

Jeffords's first glimpse of Sonseeahray shows her seated on the floor of the wickiup, wearing a white buckskin dress and a ceremonial head-dress.[13] A warm orange backlight contrasts to the darkness outside, giving her headdress a halo effect and illuminating the interior space. The light does not recreate a realistic interior firelight; rather, it seems to emanate from within her, suggesting that she is radiant with holiness and the ritual power of the moment. Her motionless pose, the lighting, and the rounded doorframe recall iconic images of Mary and other Christian saints. Her symbolic and primordial status in Apache culture is reinforced through her incarnation as White-Painted Lady, Mother of Life (Changing Woman in Apache tradition). As the two men enter and Cochise (Jeff Chandler) kneels before her, the viewer becomes aware of her petite frame, her ornate dress, and the solemnity of the occasion.

Holding his hands out to her, Cochise explains, "White-Painted Lady, I have wounds." The camera centers on her while she responds, "Yes, but each scar is a mark of love for your people. The path of your people is stretched long behind you. And you are the head, and you are the heart, and you are the blood. The killer of enemies is your father and you are his son. You will be well." Next Jeffords kneels before her, and she hesitates. Startled, she continues, "Give me your arm. Does it hurt you? . . . It will never hurt again. Your life will be long. The good things will be yours. The sun will shine for you." Her prophecy foreshadows his fame as a peace broker between the Chiricahua Apache and the white citizens of Tucson, which is the basic story of the film, but ironically overlooks her own death, caused by their transgressive love and inter-racial marriage.

Through her various names, Sonseeahray resembles a pancultural goddess figure. For four days, she is White-Painted Lady, Mother of Life, a name that confirms her connection to the earth, reproduction, and sustenance. Another of her names, Morning Star, links her to the heavens, specifically the planet Venus, also called the morning star. Her names entwine classical Western mythology, Apache cosmology, and the other-worldly: Morning Star unites her to the Roman goddess Venus, protector of gardens and fields, who is also identified with Aphrodite, the Greek goddess of love, and all coalesce in White-Painted Lady. Sonseeahray's purity, more so than that of any other Celluloid Princess, encompasses the earth and the spirits so thoroughly that she attains goddess status. And, through her connection to Tom Jeffords, the white American hero—the American Adam—she becomes the American Eve.

The American Adam, according to R. W. B. Lewis's groundbreaking work of the same name, is an authentic American hero formed from the American soil who possesses "heroic innocence and vast potentialities." The figure emerges between 1820 and 1860 in the work of such writers as Thoreau, Cooper, and Whitman as an archetype within an American mythology focused on American individualism and rooted in the American experience on the continent. As Lewis explains, he stands for "the hero of a new adventure: an individual emancipated from history, happily bereft of ancestry, untouched and undefiled by the usual inheritances of family and race; an individual standing alone, self-reliant and self-propelling, ready to confront whatever awaited him with the aid of his own unique and inherent resources." The American Adam is an archetypal man ready to fulfill the American myth—the new beginning for the human race, divinely granted after "the first chance had been so disastrously fumbled in the darkening Old World." In such a myth, the American Adam, working within the New World Eden (an unmarked space waiting to be populated by this new breed of man), symbolizes American exceptionalism; his uniqueness sets the stage for American nationalism and expansionism. As Americans push westward across the continent, the American Adam emerges more and more clearly in the western heroes modeled after Cooper's Natty Bumppo, men such as Daniel Boone and Davy Crockett, and later in figures such as Buffalo Bill Cody. Like them, he undergoes ritualistic trials as he advances into new worlds that affect him and that he "radically affects." Often he is "beaten, shot, betrayed, abandoned—but leaving his mark upon the world, and a sign in which conquest may later become possible for the survivors."[14] With as powerful a legacy as the Princess, the western Adam hero is very much entwined with the Princess's history, and both are enmeshed in the myth of the frontier's fundamental tenets of conquest and manifest destiny.

Throughout the film, Sonseeahray and Jeffords meet near water and among the trees, promoting the idea that she lives in a garden, a place of refuge that Jeffords visits and misses when he returns to the desert and Tucson. The Princess and, according to Robert Baird, the American Adam were easily transposed from literature into the film industry's "American Westerns . . . including . . . *Broken Arrow*," in which the "American Adam undercurrent is manifested . . . during a pastoral 'honeymoon' scene."[15] This scene efficiently ties together Jeffords's and Sonseeahray's coding as Adam and Eve and places them in an American Eden. Their honeymoon retreat is also a green, lush, water-filled spot—an oasis devoid of intruders and signs of civilization—where they discuss their future children. By this point in the film, Sonseeahray's innocence has been established through her naive belief that Jeffords skins himself while shaving, her introduction to a mirror, her shock at kissing and the "new feelings [it puts] in [her] heart," and her obvious youth in comparison to Jeffords. These moments reinforce Sonseeahray's sexual purity and make her connection to the prelapsarian Eve more concrete. The honeymoon scene opens with a shot of Sonseeahray walking along a lake toward Jeffords's reclining figure. She bends over him.

SONSEEAHRAY: "You are asleep?"

TOM: "No . . . I'm quiet because I'm so happy. I'm afraid if I open
my mouth my happiness will rush out in a funny noise, like Ya
Hoo!"

SONSEEAHRAY: "What does that mean? It is an American word?"

TOM: "Uh huh. I think it was a word made by Adam when he
opened his eyes and saw Eve."

SONSEEAHRAY: "Who are they?"

TOM: "Don't you know?"

SONSEEAHRAY: "The world is so big, and I know so little."

This short interchange reinforces her pagan innocence about his world.
It also establishes America as an Eden, Tom Jeffords as an Adam figure—something already suggested through his frontier hero status and
his desire to forge a new and peaceful West—and a deified Sonseeahray
as his Eve.

Her innocence is shattered in the following scene, when she, Jeffords, Cochise, and a few other Apache men are ambushed by anti-
Apache ranchers. When Jeffords falls, injured, during the fight, she
grabs a knife to stab the man who shot him, and she is shot. As she dies,
Jeffords crawls to her and, in a gesture frequently associated with the
Celluloid Princess, cradles her in his arms. Within the scenario that
emphasizes her goddess status, her death reads as a divine intervention
that ensures Jeffords's peace initiative, brings the two warring cultures
together—a metaphor for the resolution of the cold war, perhaps—and
speeds the assimilation of Native Americans into the American nation-
state. Her death also symbolically silences the dream of an American
Eden populated by the American Adam and a truly American Eve's offspring. Sonseeahray's high social status, purity, and desire to assimilate
into Jeffords's culture make her an ideal candidate for incorporation.
Nonetheless, her death highlights the undercurrent of racial tension in
the narrative and the inability of Jeffords's people to accept her. Daves
handles this material with a level of care that suggests a certain hesitancy
in presenting their story. The secondary positioning of the interracial
love story within the larger narrative, the extreme representation of Sonseeahray as a deity, the Adam and Eve theme, and her death act as insur-
ance against offending the audience, but they result in a film that was
considered too "insistent in its magnanimity."[16]

While *Broken Arrow* is atypical in its character's goddess status, the critiques of American national identity and of the racism of a structure that excludes people based on their racial heritage appear in all the Princess films. Because of a number of influences, including the anti-Communist crusades in Hollywood, filmmakers used the western's vocabulary to "allegorize a wide range of difficult or taboo subjects like race relations" and cold war politics. The genre was, according to Slotkin, a

> safe haven for liberals, because its identification with the heroic fable of American progress covered its practitioners with a presumption of patriotism that was essential in Hollywood during the years of the "Red Scare." Because it was safely "in the past," the tale of White-Indian conflict and peace-making allowed filmmakers to raise questions of war and peace and to entertain the possibility of coexistence without the kind of scrutiny to which a film set in or near the present would have drawn. Moreover, the same setting would allow them to address the race question without offending southern sensibilities.[17]

The pro-Indian film narratives allowed filmmakers to reinitiate each generation of viewers into the cultural meanings of America's foundational myths of the Indian Princess figure, the white American hero, and the American frontier West at the same time that they critiqued these myths from within the generic structure. Westerns encapsulate a mythic moment in American history when manhood, modernity, and progress, as represented by the white male frontiersman, unite with the vanishing purity and savagery of America's past, as represented by the Native woman. The Celluloid Princess films use the woman's death as a safety net that allows the moment to celebrate the Native American woman as quintessential to the formation of the white male's American identity. But her death also reinforces her status as a political tool used by the nation-state. In light of the liberal tendencies of the films, the underscoring of American imperial and colonial methods seems a subtle critique of U.S. cold war policies and suggests an inability to break out of a structure based on similar ideologies.

Across the Wide Missouri (1951), released only a year after *Broken Arrow*, tones down the idealism of its predecessor by accentuating the Princess figure's position as a political commodity. The trapper Flint

Mitchell (Clark Gable), to ensure his safe passage into the beaver-rich Blackfoot country, "buys and marries a young Indian squaw, Kamiah, when he learns that she is the granddaughter of Bear Ghost, the Blackfoot chief. Love plays no part in his original calculations; he merely figures that she is his guarantee of peace with the Indians."[18] Through a fellow trapper, Flint learns that Kamiah is Blackfoot but has been raised by the Nez Percés, who stole her as a child. His friend Brecan, who lives with the Blackfoot tribe, comes to buy Kamiah and return her to her family. Selfishly, Flint outbids Brecan. His marriage to Kamiah (María Elena Marqués) legitimizes his trail blazing and, in essence, the American nation's inevitable expansion of the frontier. Such political marriages were frequent from the early 1600s to the late 1800s among the French, English, and Spanish fur traders. The unions often increased the trappers' chances of survival and success in Indian country; Native women acted as domestic helpmates, translators, sexual partners, and indigenous medical experts.[19]

The film softens the effect of Flint's callous act of buying Kamiah by highlighting her initial interest in him, her strong will, and her option to refuse his bid. The film accentuates their attraction to each other but relies on the stereotype of the beautiful and innocently erotic Princess figure to legitimize their love. Kamiah's status as a Princess figure is emphasized through a contrast of her with other young women in the early scenes of the film. Stereotypical vignettes of Sexualized Maidens and squaw figures work to emphasize Kamiah's innate beauty, sexuality, and high social status.

The opening scenes of the film take place in a meeting camp where trappers and tribes mingle and trade. Young Snake women are seen standing around the whiskey counter choosing men to go "into the willows" with them—a narrative reference to the wanton Indian maiden stereotype. Kamiah first appears straddling a horse, also a suggestive image, but accompanied by a matronly figure whose presence erases any hint of unseemly sexuality. The scene underscores her beauty and innocent sexuality by focusing on her long bare legs and high-split dress that allows her to easily sit astride the horse. As she watches Flint buy horses, a Scottish captain (Alan Napier) attempts to buy sexual favors from her. Flint points out to her would-be suitor that the Nez Percé women are very proper; indeed, her noble stature and chastity are proven when she whips the captain for his indecent proposal. Her beauty and spunk win

Across the Wide Missouri. William A. Wellman, MGM, 1951.

Flint over and "little by little he falls in love with his adoring squaw."[20] Under her influence, Flint eventually metamorphoses into a loving family man who respects his wife's Indian heritage and welcomes her family as his own; the film, however, does not downplay his continuing use of her knowledge of the Blackfoot country and her connections as means to an end.

Across the Wide Missouri's metanarrative complicates a straightforward championing of its prointegration narrative by highlighting the hero's underlying agenda and the opposing Indian group's reactionary stance. On one hand, the film presents a pro-American national supremacy in the form of the American frontier hero and his son (Howard Keel), who narrates the story. His opening remarks are telling in terms of the story's agenda. "This is my country. This is where I was born. The first nine years of my life were spent in this Indian village with many of my mother's people. This man is my father. . . . He was a breed of men, mountain men, who lived and died in America . . . men who walked the Indian trails and blazed trails where no man had ever been before." This overarching narrative celebrates American exceptionalism, American imperialism, and territorial occupation. The son closes the narration and the film by stating that, after Kamiah's death, his father "belonged to the Indian country now heart and soul. Now he opened the West to . . . civilization." The imperialist tone differs from that of *Broken Arrow*, which is more overtly concerned with integration and cultural equality, by underscoring Flint's actions and groundbreaking nation-building efforts as a frontiersman. Notes on the original screenplay by Talbot Jennings highlight this intention: "The idea of this picture, beyond solid and exciting entertainment, is to show . . . the kind of men who developed in the greatest degree the traits that have always been—and still are—most characteristic of the American people—skill and self-reliance."[21] The movie emphasizes Flint's individualism and skill as a frontier trapper but also critiques these characteristics of American exceptionalism by accentuating his self-serving agenda, his disregard for how his actions affect others, and his initial racism toward the Blackfeet, whom he sees as impediments to his beaver trapping prospects.

On the other hand, the Blackfoot resistance to American intrusion and occupation in the film offers an alternative narrative that speaks against American imperial activity and, in contrast to the nation-building rhetoric, references the tensions of cold war nationalism. The theme was appropriate at the time, when the United States saw itself as taking over "the job of world leadership" and as a political and financial influence to help shape nations threatened by communism. During the late 1940s and early 1950s, the United States collaborated with France's imperial actions in Vietnam and entered into an "undeclared war in Korea." In addition, from the late 1940s through the 1960s, indigenous upheavals occurred in many of the Western nations' colonies: in "Indochina against the French; in Indonesia against the Dutch; in the Philippines, armed rebellion against the United States." Native groups in West and South Africa and Kenya also rebelled against the colonial governing forces and implemented strikes protesting starvation wages and injustice.[22] Internally, the United States' poor civil rights record and forced termination policy for Native Americans paralleled much of this global discord and caused problems for the United States' foreign policy.

Across the Wide Missouri, like *Broken Arrow*, touches on the tenor of the time by including two types of Native Americans—those who support assimilation and integration into western European culture (Sonseeahray and Cochise, and Kamiah and her grandfather Bear Ghost) and those who militarily oppose it (Geronimo in *Broken Arrow* and Iron Shirt in *Across the Wide Missouri*). Playing off both types, *Across the Wide Missouri* promotes cultural pluralism, to an extent, by presenting scenes within the Indian community that depict ceremony, daily life, and family interaction. The scenes open the eyes of the hero (and the viewer) to the humanness of the Native characters. For example, Flint's son describes his father's first visit to Kamiah's village, where he meets Bear Ghost: "My father told me that suddenly he saw these Indians as he had never seen them before, as people with homes and traditions and ways of their own. Suddenly they were no longer savages but people who laughed and loved and dreamed." Such humanizing moments help to break down the savage/civilized dichotomy so frequently applied to Indian-white encounters in the western. The scenes also offer a way for the viewer to understand what the renegade groups are fighting to preserve. Iron Shirt (Ricardo Montalban) and his supporters refuse to accept Flint's union with Bear Ghost, continuing to see him as a trespasser in their country. In retaliation, they assassinate Kamiah with an arrow through her heart—a metaphor for punishing her traitorous heart and her selling out to the white man. Though their resistance fails to retard the invasion of the trappers and future settlers who are led through the country by her husband, the act symbolizes historic Native American resistance to American expansion and federal Indian policies of assimilation. *Time* magazine's comment that a "Blackfoot arrow, guided by the Production Code's antimiscegenation line, cuts down Gable's bride" is valid, considering that the Production Code office continued to enforce the antimiscegenation rule. Kamiah's assassination, however, may also be read in light of contemporary Native American resistance to forced termination of tribal lands. Native Americans and Native activist groups mounted substantial resistance to termination, criticizing its underlying land acquisition agenda, the speed with which it was implemented, and the resulting loss of tribal sovereignty rights.[23] The decision to have Kamiah's own people kill her reinforces the idea that the rebels were battling against the assimilation and integration she represented through her marriage to Flint.

The liberal "family of man" narrative, together with the various and often conflicting agendas in the film, complicates the film's nation-building, individualist narrative. The love story softens the hard edges of the self-serving American exceptionalist rhetoric of the cold war and McCarthy eras; however, it does so without jeopardizing the mythic status of America's western heroes. Nevertheless, by 1954, even *Across the Wide Missouri*, a film much less utopian than *Broken Arrow*, must have seemed too simplistic for the realities of the era's race relations. As the nation moved through the 1950s' civil rights battles over segregation, the Princess films — *Broken Lance* (1954) and *Last Train from Gun Hill* (1959) — presented the effects of racism on the mixed-race couple increasingly graphically. The films focus on the first few years of marriage and of living in a white community. The romantic nostalgia for traditional tribal culture, as promoted in the few scenes in *Broken Arrow* and *Across the Wide Missouri* within the Apache and Blackfoot communities, all but disappears. These later films reference Native culture through memories, the Princess figures' clothing, and her ties to other Native characters, a technique that suggests the traditional cultures have disappeared. In addition, the figure's role in the films decreases until, as in *Last Train from Gun Hill* and *Broken Lance*, the Princess's racial heritage is more important than the character.

Broken Lance places the story of racial prejudice against an Indian woman (Katy Jurado) and her "half-breed" son Joe (Robert Wagner) within larger narrative conflicts between the West of the cattle barons and the encroaching eastern industrial capitalism, and between vigilante justice and structured law. The familiar generic plot of the old-guard westerner fighting against the inevitable tide of civilization and progress sets the backdrop for a family saga. The controlling patriarchal cattle baron Matt Devereaux (Spencer Tracy) favors his Comanche wife and their son, to the detriment of his relationship with his three sons from his first marriage. In retaliation, his other sons eventually destroy him and take over the ranch. In a flashback from Joe's point of view, the film relates the disintegration of the family and unfolds the history of Devereaux and his second wife of twenty-five years. The sensitively written narrative depicts the marriage as an intimate and loving one but underscores their neighbors' racist sentiments, which impede on the Devereauxs' lives and cause them to isolate themselves.

Three different manifestations of racism and reactions to racism stand out in the film's exploration of the social issue of miscegenation. Internally, the family deals with the townsfolk's disapproval of her Indian heritage by calling Mrs. Devereaux "Señora," because, as Joe relates to his girlfriend Barbara (Jean Peters), "people in town like to pretend she's Spanish, figure it looks better." His explanation reveals recognition of the levels of racism involved in the belief that certain ethnic backgrounds are more acceptable than others. The ideology Joe references implies a racial pyramid of sorts, in which dark-skinned Spaniards are elevated above Native Americans but still below white Americans. The theoretical premise of such conclusions stems from Western colonial ideologies about racial difference. Merging with this are social Darwinian notions of the stages of man's evolution, in which tribal peoples are considered to be lower on the evolutionary scale than light-skinned western European Americans. Such racializing categorizations do not appear so dramatically within the other 1950s Princess films' narratives, but they do form the basis for racist themes in the 1950s anti-Indian films and in some of the 1940s Sexualized Maiden films. The switching of ethnic markers does not erase the strong reaction to the Devereauxs' marriage; rather, the change accentuates shame about Señora Devereaux's Indianness. According to Joe, "Out here a white man don't marry an Indian, even the daughter of a chief. They call him a squaw man and his kids breeds. I'm a half-breed." Joe's statement to his girlfriend Barbara reflects the bitterness of being a half-breed as well as the inequality he witnesses growing up. Literally, the Princess character exists as a racial extension of these two men—as a reminder of Joe's Indian heritage and of her husband's "going native" during a moment in western history.[24]

While Barbara accepts Joe's mixed heritage with diplomacy and humor, her father, the governor and an old friend of Devereaux's, deals with it less gracefully. His prejudice against Indians motivates him to ask Devereaux to keep Joe away from Barbara. When confronted with his racism, he answers, "This is something that's born and bred in me and I'm fifty-six years old . . . and I'm governor of the state." His self-reflexive moment of shame and Barbara's rather insipid comment that she has "almost forgotten" Señora's Indian heritage represent two moments in which characters outside the Devereaux family tackle the issues of racism head-on. In each case, the character's self-conscious attempts to articulate his or her thoughts on race and to move past it contrast to the family's continual reminders of living within a racist system. As a result, these scenes highlight two ways that people address race. Barbara's memory lapse reproduces a tendency to ignore racial markers in an attempt to move past racism. The governor's statement acknowledges what his daughter cannot by raising the liberal notion that racism is socially constructed and fueled by power politics. Both maneuvers attempt to articulate, but fail to deconstruct, the deeply ingrained racializing structures based on those markers. Throughout the film, issues of racism linger beneath the surfaces of conversations and in characters' actions, but only in these two instances do characters tackle the issues head-on. Within the context of the 1950s' heightened awareness of race relations, these remarks demonstrate not only different approaches to dealing with racism but also the difficulty involved in confronting issues of race in, and finding room for those defined by race within, a society molded by racism.

According to Manchester's study of the era, the term "mixed marriage" meant a marriage between Christian sects, and "unions between whites and Negroes, as blacks were then called, were unknown to the great middle class." Thus the film's focus on two mixed-race marriages (the Devereauxs' and Joe and Barbara's) underscores how progressive and sensitive the director, Edward Dmytryk, and others working on the film were in presenting the material and the nuances of racism. These filmic moments, in conjunction with other characters' unabashed racism, and in contrast to the Devereauxs' liberalism, highlight the complexity and insidiousness of racism within communities and, allegorically, within American society during the 1950s civil rights era. The film won a Golden Globe for Best Film Promoting International Understanding, suggesting that these moments rang true to the critics as well as the film's creators.[25]

The film compromises its liberal probe of racism, however, through its depiction of the Devereauxs' love story as a fairy-tale union and Jurado's character as a tribal Princess. The reliance on this image illustrates the difficulty filmmakers had escaping the stereotype, but *Broken Lance* alters the typical Princess ending, suggesting an attempt to do just that. Early in the film, Devereaux reminisces with his wife—whom he calls Princess—in a filmic moment that informs the audience of her Native heritage: "You know the first time I saw you, riding across the plains on that little paint-pony with the antelope skin shirt and beads and feather in your hair, I thought there was nothing in the world so beautiful. I didn't know the half of it." Joe adds to the history of this touching moment when he tells his parents' story to Barbara. He relates how his father, "a wild Irishman with a mangy head of cattle and three wild boys

. . . wrestled some braves [and was taken] into the tribe and . . . married the princess." The Devereauxs' idyllic love weathers the difficulties of family trauma and social ostracism, but without Mr. Devereaux, Señora Devereaux has no place in his world. She makes two statements that reinforce this. She tells her husband, "If you die, I die," and she tells Joe, "There is no longer a need for me, my son." In the last scene of the film, set at her husband's grave, she appears dressed in her people's clothes rather than the western dress she wore at the ranch, signaling her return to them. As her son arrives with Barbara, whom he has just married, she withdraws into the foliage. While not completely concealed, she nonetheless symbolically vanishes from their view. The metaphoric implication is that her disappearance removes any physical reminder of his Native heritage, allowing him to pass into white society with his bride. She fulfills her statements above by "erasing herself" from her son's life, by vanishing into the landscape and returning to her people.

In the context of the film's promiscegenation narrative, the scene comments on the American tendencies to equate integration with assimilation and to rely on the melting pot theory of the American nation, which ignores the power of prejudice to exclude even those attempting to assimilate. During this era, the issue of miscegenation in westerns focused on "racial intolerance at the most intimate level as the truest test of tolerance. Just as full humanity is equated with full Americanism, full social integration finally depended, according to 1950s Westerns, on white willingness to welcome racial members into the family unit. It is not so much a question of accommodation as one of assimilation: either they *belong*, or they don't."[26] Joe and Barbara may enter white culture with less friction than did the Devereauxs, because Joe carries no outward signs of his Indian heritage. Although his mother assimilated into white culture through her marriage, her dark skin continued to signal her difference and inability to pass for white. Dmytryk's film, released the same year as the decision in the groundbreaking civil rights case *Brown v. Board of Education of Topeka* and the end of Senator McCarthy's reign, offers no simple solutions to problems of racial harmony and miscegenation. It often gets caught within the racial paradigms it attempts to critique, but even more than the earlier 1950s Princess films, *Broken Lance* wrestles with the complexities of racism.

Following *Broken Lance*'s successful release, Rosa Parks's heroic stance and the ensuing Montgomery bus strikes, and the shattering of

"U.S. complacency" by race riots in Little Rock, Arkansas, *Last Train from Gun Hill* (1959) pushed the display of racism to the extreme. The film points a finger at interracial problems in the United States by tackling the issue of racism against Native Americans through a sadistic act of violence. The result is a western overtly "sceptical of American society's intrinsic merits."[27]

The film's long opening scene, which introduces Catherine Morgan (Ziva Rodann), presents the impetus for *Last Train from Gun Hill's* psychological drama. A long shot focuses on the young woman, with her nine-year-old son Petey (Lars Henderson), driving a buckboard along the riverbank. They are traveling to visit her people on the reservation; her dark skin, long braids, and moccasins signal her Native heritage. The camera tracks her as she passes two young men who are sitting among the trees drinking. The overgrown area suggests an isolation that is accentuated by the dramatic music and the men's bold actions. A sequence of cross-cut scenes documents "the young brutes'" pursuit of the terrified woman and her boy.[28] The chase continues until Catherine's wagon turns over, at which point the men corner her and rip her clothes. She attempts to cover herself and backs away along the ground. The camera cuts to Petey riding off on one of the men's horses just as she screams. The sequence ends with this violent and deadly sexual assault. The rest of the film takes up the psychological quest of her husband, the marshal (Kirk Douglas), for revenge against her killer, Rick Belden (Earl Holliman), who turns out to be his best friend's son. Catherine's visual story lasts a total of four disturbing minutes.

The film presents the myth of the Princess momentarily through the image of Catherine with her son but then reverses it rapidly through Rick's actions. The film also eclipses the romantic union of the white hero and the Princess, inverting the mythic promise by presenting western European culture as more savage than the stereotypical savage Indian. Although savagery is depicted most clearly in Catherine's rape, it also surfaces in the depiction of Rick and through his references to her. In this tactic, *Last Train from Gun Hill* exhibits the overt "Indian hating" hallmarks — sexual violence and racial tagging — seen in more traditional 1950s anti-Indian westerns. Throughout the film, Rick justifies her rape and death by repeating the racist pejoratives learned from his father. Rick sees her as "just an Indian squaw," and because his father (Anthony Quinn) has told him there is "nothing prettier than a Cherokee squaw" when a man wants sexual gratification, Rick sees his behavior as acceptable. He kills her out of pure malice and hatred, spurred on by the racist belief that her cultural background and skin color make her open game for sexual sport. His racial tagging continually reminds the viewer that she is not white. In contrast to its "Indian hating" counterparts, however, *Last Train from Gun Hill* presents racism, not the inclusion of different races, as destroying families, old friendships (between the marshal and Rick's father, Craig Belden), and white society.

Catherine's brief depiction and later physical exclusion from the narrative illustrate a trend to deemphasize the symbolism of the Princess as the figure becomes a more established part of American society. According to Daniel Bernardi, during this period in Hollywood history, the "studios systematized the popularization of American whiteness."[29] In the context of the United States' formation as a nation, Whiteness represents the color of civilization. The Princess stereotype equates Whiteness with civilization, which is positioned against racialized peoples and primitive society. In addition, the Princess's desire for white contact suggests a promise of assimilation into western European culture—the ability to attain Whiteness. And her participation in colonization through assimilation presents an image of a nation formed out of the nonviolent mixing of different races and cultures. This peaceful symbol effectively unites components of American history without highlighting the very traumatic and devastating consequences that nation building actually imposes on those forced to assimilate. From 1950 through 1959, the highlighting of these characteristics decreases as the character is incorporated into white society and as the civil rights conflicts increase. In 1950, *Broken Arrow*'s Sonseeahray never enters white society, dying while on her honeymoon—a sign of white America's inability to consider a racially integrated society. Similarly, *Across the Wide Missouri* (1951) demonstrates society's discomfort with the idea by including Kamiah in a small and mobile community of whites who do not really represent established American society, but exist on its perimeter. By 1954, the films reflect a greater comfort in broaching the subject: Señora and Catherine live with white communities for extended periods of time. Catherine's character (1959) appears the most entrenched in western European culture because of her husband's status as marshal, but she is also the least-developed character and the most violently treated. Thus a trend emerges: as the Princess moves into the position of Whiteness through her assimilation, acceptance of her decreases significantly.

In addition, as the Princess assimilates into white society, her skin color darkens and the manifestations of overt racism increase. *Broken Arrow* represents the paradigm of the Princess in its depiction of Sonsee-ahray and in its casting of the blue-eyed, white actress Debra Paget in the role that epitomizes Whiteness. Over the span of the 1950s, darker-skinned and non-Anglo women were hired more frequently to play the part: the Hispanic actress María Elena Marqués, the Mexican actress Katy Jurado, and the Israeli actress Ziva Rodann. The viewer, who is originally presented with the icon of purity in a character played by a well-known white actress, cannot escape the reality of race in the later films' actresses and characters. This trend also corresponds to the federal mandates for desegregation and the rising reaction to integration. As the skin colors of the actresses grow darker, the character's role decreases until, as in the case of Catherine, her status as a Princess never really develops. This trend suggests that race had become more significant an issue than America's symbolic melting pot image suggested and that the usefulness of the romantic figure was waning by 1959. Certainly, Señora Devereaux's observation that "there is no longer a need for me" and her vanishing from the narrative foreshadow Catherine's minimal role. This is not to say that the liberal and antiracist messages of the films were no longer necessary; on the contrary, they were as important as ever. More forcefully than the earlier Princess's deaths, the film's visual and graphic erasure of Catherine implies that the symbolic possibility of the Princess fails to overcome the truth of racism and fear of miscegenation.

THE PRINCESS, THE COLD WAR, AND CONTAINMENT

As the analysis above has shown, the 1950s films promote the idea of an integrated and multiethnic nation. They do so through the presentation of the Princess as a respectable woman, the inclusion of an interracial marriage, and the possibility of her mixed-heritage children's assimilating into American society. "The process of nationalist mythmaking," however, as Andrew Higson points out, "is not simply an insidious (or celebratory) work of ideological production, but is also at the same time a means of setting one body of images and values against another, which will very often threaten to overwhelm the first."[30] Over the course of the decade, the Princess films manifest Higson's insight, and the racism, which the Princess's marriage to the white hero is supposed to dissipate, overwhelms the symbolism of their union. These films clearly articulate the tensions within American culture about racial integration and civil rights.

In their use of the Princess figure, however, the films resort to a stereotype of fixity and control. Use of the Celluloid Princess stereotype is a colonial rhetorical strategy based on a national American identity defined against a raced and "savage" Other who is both feared and desired and must be contained to maintain that national identity. Colonial discourse depends on fixity, a "paradoxical mode of representation" that "connotes rigidity and an unchanging order as well as disorder [and] degeneracy," to maintain the construction of Otherness.[31] Both within the films' narratives and within American society, the Princess's racially exotic body is potentially disruptive because she destabilizes the sociopolitical framework, so clearly promoted in the western, of a racially white nation. Continually representing the Princess image as a racialized Other with little political power and replaying her death controls disorder and fixes her within the colonial ideological discourse. *Broken Lance* appears to be an exception to this tendency, but Señora Devereaux's disappearance in the context of the romantic image of her as a young girl riding across the plains reinforces the vanishing American figure. In returning her to her people, the film aligns her with a disappearing culture—one that is literally gone from the film—and retains the fixed image of the romantic Native doomed by western expansion and nation building.

Mary Douglas gives substantial form to the structure discussed above in her statement that the "idea of society is a powerful image. It is potent in its own right to control or to stir men to action. This image has form; it has external boundaries, margins, internal structure. Its outlines contain power to reward conformity and unstructured areas."[32] The Princess's image within such a delicate framework illustrates the fragility of a system that balances the internal and external elements forming its conceptual identity. The Princess stereotype straddles the line that demarcates what is included in and excluded from the national body. Her image as a Princess and a conformist places her provisionally within the nation-state. But her transgression of social taboos through miscegenation, her potential disruption of the social order, and her pollution of the national white body through her mixed-race children justify her expulsion from the structure and her punishment. Whiteness, as we see it encoded in the ideal of American civilization, identity, and progress, depends on its polarity to the primitive as encoded into the symbolic conquered America and Americans. American identity cannot exist without this physical and metaphorical national Other. Thus the other incorporates a racialized and resistant people who have continually been viewed as threatening opposites to American civilization, progress, and white hegemony. For the Princess to achieve Whiteness—equal status in white society—through her union with the white hero, the national symbol must eliminate the concept of the Other from its construction of Whiteness. To do so represents the end of the colonial process—the end of the conquest and the "civilizing" process that define American uniqueness.

On a symbolic level within the 1950s milieu, these films reflect white America's need to control the internal disruption in the nation and to hang on to a specific notion of Americanness. The reactionaries who shun and kill the Princess figure in these pro-Indian westerns, including the Iron Band's renegades in *Across the Wide Missouri*, illustrate this need to control what they see as a disrupting force to their way of life. According to Richard Slotkin, the "central paradox of America's self-image in an era of Cold War . . . 'subversion' and the thermonuclear balance of terror" was "our sense of being at once supremely powerful and utterly vulnerable, politically dominant and yet helpless to shape the course of critical events." It was also a "problem of reconciling democratic values and practices with the imperatives of power."[33] In conjunction with this mood, the film industry attempted to negotiate between the idea of a socially integrated America and the reality of the racist system that placed political and social power in the hands of white Americans. The 1950s films' use of the Princess as an allegorical reference to domestic civil rights politics simultaneously places into relief these national conflicts and tensions through the suppression and containment of the un-American Other. The resulting complexity and the often contradictory messages that weave through these films, however, illustrate the nuances of racializing systems that link structures of racism with representations of race and national identity within their iconic images. As a group, the films call into question the ability of the nation, even at its most liberal moments, to overcome its ambivalent, often violent, relationship with Native Americans, who are both alien to and intricately woven into the fabric of American identity as a white nation-state. The shift from an idealized hope for integration (*Broken Arrow*) to denial of its peaceful possibility (*Last Train from Gun Hill*) suggests Hollywood's questioning of whether the image of the Celluloid Princess fit the rapidly changing racial structures of America.

The Sexualized Maiden

Three

What Lies Beneath the Surface

The Sexualized Maiden of the 1940s

I see a tough son of a bitch, you know, who is a half animal, and a magnificent one, crafty as hell, beautiful as hell, and unconsciously a terrible destroyer. I see a gorgeous black panther, something that is death, and yet anybody will go to it and stroke it and pet it and love it. . . . Men are afraid of her.

—Cecil B. DeMille

LOUVETTE, THE CRAFTY DESTROYER described above, is Cecil B. DeMille's envisioned Métis woman for his 1940 epic *Northwest Mounted Police*. Her original name, Lupette, parodies the word "lupine" as well as the French slang term for a "street girl," suggesting that she is both sexually promiscuous and innately animalistic.[1] DeMille's conception of Louvette as a character whose sexual and destructive nature emerges from her mixed-blood ancestry displays elements of the Sexualized Maiden figure that appears in 1940s westerns as a hybrid of the wanton mixed-blood and the femme fatale. The racially based foundation of the Sexualized Maiden is manifested in a fetishistic and phobic fascination that surfaces in visual and verbal rhetoric, such as DeMille's "beautiful as hell . . . gorgeous . . . death . . . love it . . . afraid of her." Although DeMille's conception takes this racism to an extreme, the sentiments exhibited here are evident in all the 1940s Sexualized Maiden films, whether or not the narrative sympathizes with the character. Within such a construct, the woman's background becomes the mode of representation for her Otherness, her moral and physical taint, and her disturbing sexual power. The weaving of racial and sexual stereotyping that surfaces in these 1940s films reproduces some of the social and cultural tensions of the pre– and post–World War II eras as well as a longer colonial history of American ambivalence toward miscegenation and racial difference.

Marked and marginalized by her Native heritage and mixed-blood status, the 1940s Sexualized Maiden exhibits characteristics reflective of the racialized subject in colonial discourse. According to postcolonial theory, Homi Bhabha's analysis of stereotypes in particular, the power of colonial discourse resides in its articulation and inscription of the colonial subject's difference—both racial and sexual—within an "economy of pleasure and desire and the economy of discourse, domination, and power."[2] In other words, the markers "racial" and "sexual" become modes of differentiation that identify and split the subject and also confine it within a particular social structure. As the offspring of a Native woman and a white man, the 1940s Sexualized Maiden exists as a split subject within a liminal space, never part of a Native community and often abused by or unwelcome in white society. Her father's heritage surfaces in her light skin tone, while her mother's appears in her inherent sensuality and moral darkness. Thus her racial difference is conflated with her social difference, forming the basis for her domination and sexual exploitation. The depiction of the Sexualized Maiden also incorporates identifiable traits from another socially marginalized figure—the femme fatale—whose sexuality is deadly to the men she attracts. In many instances, the Sexualized Maiden's exotic looks and sexuality elevate her to the status of a fetish, which Bhabha points out disavows difference because of its construction as a replacement or stand-in for what supposedly constitutes difference.[3] To clarify, in Freudian psychoanalysis, the fetish is tied to the recognition of sexual difference (men have penises and women do not) and the attempt to erase that difference or the psychological threat it carries of castration for the male subject. Nevertheless, the Sexualized Maiden's inevitable death, caused by her racial and sexual deviance, erases the fetish patina and reinforces her racial status. The amalgamation of these character types creates a highly effective and complicated figure whose body carries the stigma of America's psychological response to race, sex, and powerful women. The Sexualized Maiden is continually recycled in film as a degenerate type, and her stigma results in and justifies her death.

The raw and uncontainable sexuality the young woman exudes resides in her symbolic matrilineal link to the Native American Queen figure, who represents the dangerous yet intriguing Americas in European material culture from the sixteenth century through the eighteenth century. The "tawny"-hued Native American Queen, draped in "leaves, feathers, and animal skins" and "armed with spears and arrows," embodies the opulence and peril of the New World.[4] The leaves, feathers, and skins imply lush landscapes, abundant resources, and an untamed natural wilderness. But worn on her dark-skinned body, they create a racialized and fetishistic image that is both enticing in its eroticism and threatening in its metonymic relation to her physical power and militancy. She is potentially disruptive to the western European patriarchal and colonial order.

Colonialism eventually erases the Queen's militancy, but her abundant sexuality and brazenness remain in her offspring, the wanton squaw figure that Rayna Green suggests is the "Princess's darker twin"; she reflects the downfall of the Princess figure who marries or has sexual relations with a white man. Green's work focuses only briefly on this representation in literature and visual art, but equally derogatory depictions of Indian women surface throughout frontier history. David Smits's work on Anglo-American attitudes toward Indian-white racial mixing and the image of the squaw, however, uncovers various attitudes toward the Native women who participated in commerce at the military forts, offered themselves to enlisted men, or married trappers. While the services of the Native women were often valued and appreciated, the displacement onto them of western European American ideologies about sex, marriage, and gender roles in society resulted in their categorization as promiscuous and lacking in moral training. This, in turn, was often evidence of their cultural inferiority to white women.[5] Such stereotyping transferred to cinema as hints of taint in the Celluloid Maiden figures of the silent and early sound period and fully in the 1940s depictions of the Sexualized Maiden's mother, who, unlike the Princess, embodies all that is negative about Native America with none of the promise.

This amalgamation of stereotypes forms the cinematic Sexualized Maiden's legacy. In effect, her mother's promiscuity transfers through the blood, suggesting that the young girl's immoral and unlawful behavior is a sign of her inferior racial status. On a deep level, the potential for genetically passing such inferiority and immorality plays into the fear that miscegenation produces offspring that are degenerative to society as a whole—particularly to white racial purity. On a social Darwinian level, the passing on of such unfavorable traits also threatens the moral purity of society. As Charles Musser points out, "Attraction for the Other—racial, gender, and even class—is thus laid bare by the half-breed. Like the mulatto, the half-breed is the product of passion that has broken the bounds of law."[6] Her existence stands in defiance of the moral and legal laws against miscegenation still prevalent in the mid-twentieth century. Thus the 1940s Sexualized Maiden does not exude the military threat of the Indian Queen; rather, her capacity to threaten society resides in the overt sexual nature that she inherits from her mother and from the Queen, and in her ability to poison a white cultural ideal.

The Sexualized Maiden resembles the mixed-blood woman of late-nineteenth-century romantic western fiction. According to Daryl Jones, she is a volatile "temptress and a formidable rival to the Anglo-American heroine." As a "dark and alluring woman of mystery who [tempts] the hero away from the path of virtue, [she] constitutes an implicit threat" to society.[7] Hollywood borrows this fictional character, merges her with the squaw stereotype, and adds characteristics of the femme fatale. Mary Ann Doane explains that the femme fatale,

> represented as the antithesis of the maternal . . . persistently appears [in cinema] in a number of reincarnations: the vamp of the Scandinavian and American silent cinemas, the *diva* of the Italian film, the femme fatale of film noir of the 1940s. . . . Her power is . . . not subject to her conscious will . . . she is not the subject of power but its *carrier*. . . . But the femme fatale is situated as evil and is frequently punished or killed. Her textual eradication involves a desperate resistance of control on the part of the threatened male subject. Hence, it would be a mistake to see her as some kind of heroine of modernity. She is not the subject of feminism but a symptom of male fears about feminism.[8]

Similarly, the 1940s Sexualized Maiden's libidinous nature threatens the institution of the family and always results in the death of her lover.

Her status as a desirable, yet dangerous, object of male lust whose power over men threatens the patriarchal and racial order of "ideal" society elevates her to a fetish. In sum, she, like the Native American Queen figure, is a sexual and racial fetish whose ability to attract and repulse resides in her body.

Such lustfulness and potential deadliness surface temporarily as signs of moral and racial difference in early cinema's depictions of Celluloid Maidens but do not come together with this consistency until the 1940s. The five primary character traits of the Sexualized Maiden—beauty, mixed-blood heritage, overt sexuality, marginalization in white society, and deadliness to men—are most tightly woven together in the 1940s in films like *Northwest Mounted Police* (1940), *My Darling Clementine* (1946), *Duel in the Sun* (1946), and *Colorado Territory* (1949). The Sexualized Maiden of the 1940s sets the tone for the character in 1950s and 1960s westerns, films that heighten the racist reactions of white characters to the maiden and include her desire to kill or hurt the white hero. These 1940s titles are all "prestige pictures"—high-end westerns and nation-building epics—by well-known producers and directors: Cecil B. DeMille, John Ford, King Vidor, David O. Selznick, and Raoul Walsh. *Northwest Mounted Police* and *Duel in the Sun* were top box-office draws in their release years; *My Darling Clementine* received the National Board of Review's billing as one of the ten best films of 1946.[9] The latter two continue to engage scholarly attention. Such prestige suggests that the issues addressed in these films and their portrayals of the young Indian women resonated with the public as more than examples of a popular type or generic structure.

Indeed, the confluence of the Sexualized Maiden's component elements at this time in American history precludes the simple answer that the figure was just a character type in all westerns and western nation-building epics. Her inscription within the colonial discourse of racial and sexual difference ensures that she is much more than this. As a composite of particular and well-known identities, like the sexualized squaw and the femme fatale, and packaged like the popular 1940s pinup, she mixes volatile and sensitive issues into an undeniably attractive and dangerous package. And, like the Princess figure, the Sexualized Maiden's racial heritage and positioning in American culture form the basis for reinscribing colonial narratives about Native Americans. Emblematic of the colonization or assimilation process gone wrong, she threatens the

ideal moral and social order. In the context of pre– and post–World War
II America, the Sexualized Maiden represents mainstream fears about
the ramifications of miscegenation. She stands as a sign of the national
conflicts surrounding women's roles in 1940s society and the changing racial dynamics of American society. In sum, she expresses the era's
rapidly changing sexual mores, power structures, and racial dynamics
brought on by the country's emergence from the Depression, its participation in World War II, the beginning of the cold war, and the changing
film industry.

The following analyses of the Sexualized Maiden films traces the
emergent and changing elements of the character in the silent-period
and early-1930s films *Scarlet and Gold* (1925), *Frozen Justice* (1929),
The Squaw Man (1931), and *Laughing Boy* (1934) and their manifestations in the 1940s films listed above. It focuses on how racial difference and sexual difference are conflated and construed as proof of racial
degeneracy while also forming a fetishized object that promotes both
lust for and fear of the Indian woman. The cycle of dominance of and
violence toward the Native American woman that emerges in this tracing suggests that the colonialist rhetoric underscoring the Sexualized
Maiden's representation manipulates a variety of other social and cultural issues in its application. The figure, as a measure of how various
cultural movements were played out, how social anxieties were released
through the figure, and what these factors indicate about 1940s race relations, represents an externalization of American ambivalence toward
Native Americans that is an alternative to the Princess figure.

EARLY COMPONENTS OF THE SEXUALIZED MAIDEN

The sensual Indian woman, the femme fatale, and the half-breed character that combine to form the Sexualized Maiden appear in varying
combinations with the early Celluloid Maiden. The young woman's
passion emerges as the most prominent trait and ranges in degree from
premarital desire in Princess films like *Scarlet and Gold* (1925) and *The
Squaw Man* (1914, 1918, 1931) to prostitution in *Laughing Boy* (1934).
A number of the more overtly sexual characters—Talu in *Frozen Justice*
(1929) and Slim Girl in *Laughing Boy*—are also physically or symbolically mixed-blood women, which, the narratives and film advertising
imply, explains their wanton sexuality. Though a certain level of passion

factors in to all of the Celluloid Maiden stories, it motivates the Indian woman to murder in *The Squaw Man*, while Slim Girl's sexual promiscuity with white men leads her Navajo husband to kill in *Laughing Boy*. None of these films combine all the elements of the Sexualized Maiden, but they illustrate particular trends worthy of analysis.

The Princess films present a full-blood Native woman whose sensuality and relaxed mores about premarital sex seem culturally sanctioned by and indicative of her Native heritage. The narratives allude to and then restrict the display of passion, fashioning it as proof of the Princess figure's devotion to the white hero and part of the plot motivation. As seen in the advertising for lover films discussed previously, premarital relations between the Princess figure and the white hero she rescues supply a racy and erotic component to the overall narrative formula that results in their marriage. The advertisement for *The Kentuckian: Story of a Squaw's Devotion and Sacrifice* (1908) makes the connection between the sexual attractiveness of the "pretty Indian girl" and the "inevitable" happening: the woman becomes pregnant, forcing the couple to marry.[10] The films nonetheless gloss over the "moment" of consummation, focusing the attention on the marriage and child. Thus these earlier films tend to present the "inevitable" as part of the western experience for lonely white males encountering lovely young Indian girls while also making clear it is the hero's moral responsibility to marry her. Occasionally, the white lover jilts the young pregnant woman, as in *Scarlet and Gold* (1925). In this case, a "loyal Mountie marries Haida" to save her reputation, and out of respect, "she kills herself so he can be free to marry the [white] woman" he loves.[11] The 1925 film adds a level of shame to Haida's predicament that is not as pronounced in the earlier films. Partially a reference to the slipping morals of the post-Victorian and Jazz ages and a warning about the dangers of premarital relations, these plot additions emphasize the difference between Native American and white cultural norms of sexuality.

In contrast to earlier Princess films, the 1931 remake of *The Squaw Man* deliberately accentuates the sexual aspect of Naturich's character.[12] In all the versions (1914, 1918, 1931), the intensity of her feelings for Jim enables her to kill Cash Hawkins and heroically rescue Jim from a near-fatal accident. Naturich's attentions to Jim while he recuperates and his loneliness result in "the inevitable," her pregnancy, and their obligatory marriage. All the same, the 1931 remake underscores her seduction of him and plays on the popular culture stereotype of Native women's sexual freedom, in contrast to the highly contained passion and moral refinement of Jim's true love, Diana, who has sent him away to ensure her own marital fidelity.

One scene in particular highlights Naturich's beauty, passion, and seductiveness. Jim (Warner Baxter) has recovered from his accident and, at the urging of his ranch hand Bill, deems it prudent to send Naturich (Lupe Vélez) back to her father. While fetching more wood for the fire, Jim sees her huddled in the rain, her refusal to leave him made clear. Bringing her back inside, he instructs her to change out of her wet clothes in the bedroom; Naturich ignores him and walks across the dimly lit room to the fire. A long shot frames Jim in the foreground shadows near the door, watching Naturich, who is illuminated by the firelight. As Naturich undresses in front of the fire, a point-of-view shot from Jim's position frames her, and the camera dollies in for a close-up of her naked back. Uncomfortable, Jim hands her a coat to cover her nakedness, which slips to reveal her shoulder as she slowly rolls her leggings down. The camera position suggests Jim's continued gaze on her as she unbraids her long hair and brushes it out in front of the fire. Clearly attracted by her actions, Jim walks into the frame and sits down in his chair by the fire. When Naturich comes and sits on the floor next to him, he rests his arm next to her still-naked shoulder. Placing her cheek on his hand, she looks up at him while the scene fades to black, a visual innuendo of their inevitable union.

Although the sequence exists in some form in the earlier films, this version accentuates Naturich's innocent sexuality, her disrobing, and Jim's voyeurism. The January 16, 1931, scenario directing this scene instructs Warner Baxter, "She looks half child and half woman, and quite adorable. . . . We feel that he is seeing Naturich for the first time as a woman." Jim's attraction to Naturich must have led to an explicit embrace in some production discussions; Lenore Coffee wrote to DeMille on January 27, 1930, "I think it is terribly dangerous for him to *ever* take her in his arms or touch her deliberately. Any physical contact must be legitimately for a purpose—like helping her off with some wet things . . . then his glimpse of her body gleaming in the firelights, her sitting on the hearth beside him. A tender, intimate scene . . . and then that timid little hand on his knee."[13] The danger alluded to by Coffee may well have been a reference to possible censorship by the Production Code admin-

istration of any overt sexual contact, the romanticizing of premarital relations, and miscegenation.[14] It appears that DeMille heeded Coffee's
advice; the final scene eliminates any direct physical action and simply
implies it through the fade-out—a technique often used to circumvent
censorship.[15] The visual sexualizing of Naturich, however, remains a
distinctly different approach to depicting the early Princess figure.

Because of the minimal use of dialogue, Naturich's entire personality is conveyed through her actions and implied by the star image of the
actress Lupe Vélez. DeMille chose Vélez for the 1931 film based on her
sexual screen persona as well as economic considerations (her reputation and popularity in Latin America and Europe would assure profits if
the film were released abroad). Associated with a fiery passion attributed
to her "Latinness," Lupe Vélez was often restricted to roles depicting her
as a sexual object for the white male lead, who fulfills his erotic fantasies
through her raced and sexualized body.[16] Though the film tones down
Vélez's persona as a vixen, it utilizes her Hollywood beauty and reputation to influence the impression that Naturich employs her sexuality to
solidify her position in Jim's life.

Filmmakers used Lupe Vélez's "aggressive, flamboyant, and stri-
dently ethnic" beauty and sexual appeal to convey a particular stereotype
of Latin women. As Ana López describes Vélez, throughout the 1930s,
"she personified the hot-blooded, thickly accented, Latin temptress with
insatiable sexual appetites on screen . . . and with her star persona. . . .
Vélez was, in other words, outrageous."[17] The Squaw Man does not exploit this image of Vélez to its full extent, but the depiction does overlap
with Vélez's later character, Slim Girl, in Laughing Boy (1934), whose
insatiable desires for material objects and excitement merge with her
passionate sexuality to create a deadly combination.

Based on Oliver La Farge's Pulitzer Prize–winning novel, Laughing
Boy focuses on the tragic story of two Navajos—Laughing Boy (Ramon
Novarro) and Slim Girl (Lupe Vélez)—who come from two different
worlds and attempt to make a life together. At a large powwow attended
by Navajos and Utes, Laughing Boy, a young, virtuous, and naive Navajo
from a remote area of the reservation, meets Slim Girl, an orphaned
Navajo who has been educated at a mission school and supports herself
as a prostitute. He is both attracted to and repulsed by her forward manner, her suggestive dancing style, and her unconventional beauty. Dis-
regarding cultural norms, Slim Girl dances inappropriately, intimidates

Laughing Boy with her overt flirtation and aggressiveness, and drinks whiskey. She "seduces the inexperienced Laughing Boy with moonshine and flirtation," and eventually, unable to forget one another, the two marry, against the wishes of his elders.[18] Unlike the young heroine of La Farge's novel, the film version of Slim Girl attempts, but fails, to fit into traditional Navajo culture. In the words of her mother-in-law, she has "lived the life of a white woman too long. Our ways will never be [her] ways." Laughing Boy, however, accepts her difference and attempts to accommodate her lifestyle by allowing her to work in town. Despite her love for Laughing Boy, Slim Girl yearns for the material objects, music, and excitement of a life in town, and she continues to see her white lover, George (William B. Davidson), who showers her with clothes, jewelry, and money. Slim Girl's two worlds collide when Laughing Boy travels to town to see her and finds her in the arms of her white lover. He attempts to shoot George but hits her instead. The film closes with a medium close-up of Slim Girl dying in Laughing Boy's arms.

The film capitalizes on Vélez's Hollywood persona by contrasting Slim Girl's vivacious and sensual personality, which metonymically connects to Lupe Vélez, with other Navajo women who are shy, modest, and traditional in their lifestyle. She is, in sum, "outrageous," and the narrative and cinematography depict her as a sexual fetish—colorful, bedecked in bright, shiny jewelry, and exuding sensuality and vivacity. An early scene, set during the large gathering of clans, positions her most overtly as a fetish. She asks Laughing Boy to be her partner in a traditional dance, but he refuses her and leaves the area. Undaunted, she flirtatiously approaches him, and the following exchange takes place within a choreographed scene that highlights her pursuit, their attraction, and his hesitancy:

> SLIM GIRL: "What's the matter, you don't like me?"
> LAUGHING BOY: "I came here to sing, not dance."
> SLIM GIRL: "But I want to dance with you."
> LAUGHING BOY: "But I don't want to dance with you."
> SLIM GIRL: "But I want to dance with you!"

As this exchange continues, Slim Girl lowers her eyes and advances toward him as she speaks; ending inches from his face, she gazes up at him. He, in turn, responds and moves backward, away from her.

SLIM GIRL: "Are you afraid of me?"
LAUGHING BOY: "I am not afraid of you. I could squeeze your
   neck as easily as I can squeeze a chicken."
SLIM GIRL: "Sometimes that is fun too."
LAUGHING BOY: "What do you mean?"
SLIM GIRL: "There are no girls like me in your north country, are
   there?"

SLIM GIRL: "You have never seen anyone like me before, have you?"
LAUGHING BOY: "No, I have never seen anyone like you."
SLIM GIRL: "Then perhaps there are other things you don't know."

At this point, Laughing Boy has stopped backing away from Slim Girl,
and a close-up frames their faces inches apart. The night scene allows
the moon and firelight to reflect off Slim Girl's abundant jewelry, her
glossy lips, and her shiny hair. Laughing Boy's slow response reflects his
attraction and wonder. She asks him again to dance and he agrees, but
her seductive dancing style infuriates him. He complains, "That is not
dancing! . . . You move like a snake; that is not good." Disturbed, he
leaves to go pray, but unable to forget her, he yearns to marry her.
   Slim Girl controls the physical exchange described above as well
as the conversation's sexual innuendo. She easily twists the momentary
violence directed at her through Laughing Boy's reference to a chicken
into an invitation for sexual pleasure. His mention of squeezing her neck
signals his unease, which also surfaces in his constant stepping back and
away from her. The film repeatedly underscores Slim Girl's power over
men. Intimidated by her sexual aggression, which exceeds their own,
they need to dominate and possess her as a way to control it. The desire to do her physical violence, which Laughing Boy suggests verbally,
manifests itself in George, who beats her because she wants to return to
Laughing Boy. Both also, however, love and desire her effervescent quality, and George wishes "to do everything to make [her] happy."
   Slim Girl's strength threatens the patriarchal order of each of her
relationships, especially that with Laughing Boy, whom she effectively
feminizes throughout the film. She pursues him, seduces him with whiskey, and then makes love to him; he remains at home while she goes
into the American town. Slim Girl also controls her own finances and
future. The money she demands as wages from George goes to increas-

ing Laughing Boy's herds. In sum, her forceful nature, in conjunction with her seductive actions, sensual and shy at one moment and overtly sexual at another, creates an image that elevates her from a woman to a dangerous object of desire and also of fear—a fetish.

The term "fetish," which emerged out of colonial history to define African religious objects of power, has at least three primary models— anthropological, Marxian, and Freudian. Both Karl Marx and Sigmund Freud applied it to particular manifestations in Western society. Marx equated fetishism with capitalism and the exchange of people and objects as commodities of value. For Freud, the fetish was linked with sexual fear of castration and the transference of that fear onto objects and, in many cases, the nonsexual parts of a woman's body. According to Hal Foster, "All define the fetish as an object endowed with a special force or independent life." The male act of gazing at the woman as a fetish detaches her from reality and redefines her as an object of consumption and possession—"an icon, displayed for the gaze and enjoyment of men." Feminist film theorists, following Laura Mulvey, have remarked upon the ways in which a viewer's relationship with film exacerbates the fetishistic relationship of transference, glamorizing the female body and making it exotic, until it is larger than life and spectacular. In this sense, cinema goes beyond the woman's "to-be-looked-at-ness, [it] builds the way she is to be looked at into the spectacle itself."[19] While fetishism includes the act of idolizing a woman, transforming her into an object of worship and desire, it also revolves around the fear of that object's uncontrollability and latent threat—ability to castrate or take away male power.

The film *Laughing Boy* constructs Slim Girl through the physical body and reputation of Lupe Vélez as a sexual fetish; race and culture also play a role in Slim Girl's formation as a fetish. This overlay bolsters the underlying fear of sexual difference inherent in fetishization with the stigma of racial degeneracy attached to the sexualized Indian woman. Within the narrative, her cultural difference—a mark of Whiteness or American cultural assimilation—contributes to her sexual exoticism for Laughing Boy, while her racial difference attracts George, who calls her a "slant-eyed little squaw," marking her physically ("slant-eyed") and rhetorically ("squaw") as nonwhite. Although genetically Navajo, she is a metaphorical mixed-blood because her white cultural background dominates her Native heritage and keeps her on the periphery of Navajo society—she is never accepted fully by them as Navajo. In fact, she states that American culture "makes two of me" and that "the white man spoiled that [Navajo] life . . . there is a mountain between us."[20] The result of the overlapping of the sexualized Latina with that of the exotic and sexualized Indian maiden conflates the stereotypes within the narrative as well as within the larger social discourse on race. While the narrative suggests that the consequence of circumstance perpetuates Slim Girl's experience as a "fallen woman," it also implies that her inherent sexuality—when drawn out by the immoral aspects of American culture—finds its natural fit in the occupation of a prostitute and the wild "bad girl" figure. In effect, the film positions her body as the site for male pleasure, physical mastery, and fetishized absence controlled by the underlying societal "unpleasure," or fear of her and defense against her. Such contradictions typify the complexities of colonial discourse.[21]

Similarly, in 1929, *Frozen Justice* presents Talu as a "faithless" wife of an Eskimo chief.[22] Film reviews describe her as "a half-caste Eskimo girl whose white blood causes her to hunger for the fleshpots of civilization"; as "torn between the two diametrically opposite temperaments—that of her Eskimo mother and that of her white father"; as a "fiery wench, who because she is a half-caste is heartily disliked by the other females"; and as a "velvet-eyed wanton . . . garbed in furs" with a "love of white women's finery." The descriptions conflate Talu's sexuality and racial heritage, implying that the roots of her problem are her mixed heritage, insatiable appetite, and promiscuity. *Variety*'s October 30, 1929, review, which assumes a racist position uncritically, goes further by remarking on the sexual aggressiveness of all the Native women in the film: "All desirable women residents of the Eskimo village [go] to a ship party tossed by the white sailors while their husbands and male relatives are ceremoniously chasing away the story devil and not looking. . . . The way these Esk [*sic*] women carry on with the sailor boys, all getting stewed and lovable . . . speaks not so well for Eskimo morals."[23] The implication is that all Native women are normally overtly sexual.

While the various ideas promoted by these reviews suggest that mainstream American viewers held differing opinions on whose blood caused the young woman's immorality, all depict the young mixed-blood as sexually active, attracted to material wealth beyond her status, and dangerous. Like Vélez, Lenore Ulric (Talu) was often cast as a "femme fatale, and was billed as 'the magic mistress of a thousand emotions,'" with the result that her screen persona and the character meld.[24] And, as with Slim Girl five years later, an overlay of textual description with the actress's persona contributes to Talu's sensuality and dangerous image.

These descriptions of Talu hint at a number of dangers associated with the hybrid fetish–femme fatale figure. Neither the femme fatale nor the fetish is a subject of power, but each carries a threat of power that, when the two merge, hints at a latent danger to masculine constructs of power. When combined in a racialized figure that symbolizes the social taboo of miscegenation, the threat expands to encompass not only the patriarchal order but the racial purity of white society as a whole. Diegetically, Slim Girl's most destructive power manifests itself in her ability to manipulate men and in their violent response. For example, because of his intense love for Slim Girl, Laughing Boy's normally pacifistic and gentle nature turns murderous when he sees her with George. This narrative outcome, however, must have appeared less dangerous to the Production Code office than did the Sexualized Maiden's desire for and acquisition of material wealth.

Director of the Production Code Administration Joseph Breen wrote on December 4, 1933, in a memo regarding *Laughing Boy*, "This is a story of a notorious Indian prostitute who, after seducing him, marries a fine, clean, upstanding Indian Boy and continues with her prostitution, using the money thus obtained to stock a farm with cattle and sheep and to obtain for herself and her husband certain tid-bits of luxury not common among Navajo tribes. It is a sordid, vile and dirty story that is definitely not suited for screen entertainment and, of course, is completely and wholly in violation of our Production Code." By March 22, 1934, Breen had modified this view. In a report to Will Hays, president of the Motion Picture Producers and Distributors of America, he wrote, "Inasmuch as the moral values of the story are all on the right side (the girl dies at the end of the picture, her death being brought about directly by her confused ideas of morality) we believe the picture to be an honest and effective transcription of the original story."[25] The 1933 communication indicates that the figure's representation holds a danger for the viewing society at large because her moral judgments and immoral activities twist the ethics of capitalist society; she uses her body as a commodity to achieve material wealth, but in a morally unsuitable fashion. Breen's note does not indicate what a suitable means for a woman to achieve wealth might be, nor does he clarify whether a woman's earning the family money is the root of the problem. The disturbing rhetoric of the 1934 communication highlights a key component in all of the Celluloid Maiden productions—that those in control of the studios and production ethics see justice in her death. In effect, these two segments indicate Hollywood's wariness of particular types of women and a need to control these "outrageous" women or defetishize them through death.

The Production Code office frowned upon the undermining of accepted moral and sexual norms, including the "ideals of female chastity and fidelity in marriage," according to Lea Jacobs's work on the fallen woman figure in pre-1934 Hollywood. As Jacobs points out, however, it also protected and even promoted the reproduction of images of immorality and infidelity. The fallen woman to which Jacobs refers is a white heroine who rises in class and wealth through sexual transgression. The Native American woman never seeks to rise in class per se, but she aspires to the material wealth of western European culture and exhibits the sexual tendencies of the fallen woman. Unlike her white counterpart, though, who, according to the code, must in the "most extreme cases . . . be left destitute and alone," as Breen's comments above make clear, the Native woman's only fitting punishment is death.[26] Thus part of the underlying message appears to be that a nonwhite woman's miscegenation or desire to obtain the trappings of western European culture are more taboo than prostitution and class ambition. The racist implications of such assumptions are made clear in her punishment, the severity of which is grounded in her race, not her actions. The continual reproduction and modification of this figure and her inevitable punishment ensure that she stands as an iconic image of racial degeneracy and sexual fetishism gone wrong, as well as a symbol of difference.

In all of these pre-1940 examples, the young Native woman's racial background plays a role in her construction as a sexualized and sometimes fatal figure. The mixed-blood woman bears the stigma of a racial degeneracy most often caused by white contamination of Native purity. This perceived taint twists the innocent sexual forwardness exhibited by the Princess figure into a disturbing and dangerous power. The very racist reactions to the Native woman seen in the Production Code records highlight the conflict between the intent of the film and the demands of the censors. The narratives, often written to promote a sympathetic image of Native Americans or to illuminate mainstream concerns about miscegenation, contrast with this presentation of the woman as a potentially violent, materialist, and sexually promiscuous woman.

Certainly, the films present a negative image of Native American–white relations, in line with late-1920s and early-1930s federal Indian policy and mainstream reaction to the policy. On one hand, this era witnessed a growing romantic image of Native culture, liberal movements pushing for cultural pluralism, and growing cultural guilt over the devastating effects of assimilation policy on Native communities (see chapter 1). On the other hand, while the Roosevelt administration's Indian policy recognized cultural pluralism, Congress supported it "only as long as Indian reform did not hinder recovery [from the Depression] in white society. Hollywood reiterated Washington's policies by portraying Indians as a separate nation not compatible with white civilization."[27] By playing on the stereotype of the sexual Indian woman who does not fit into Native culture because of her material "white" ways, nor into western European culture because of her racial heritage, the films seem to concur with the "separate and incompatible" assumption. As a result of these two differing sentiments, the films convey a degree of uncertainty about the basis for the figure's social dysfunction.

CHARACTERISTICS OF THE 1940s SEXUALIZED MAIDEN

Specific characteristics and trends from the early films discussed above are manipulated or reinforced in the 1940s Sexualized Maiden, resulting in the coalescing of five primary traits: beauty, mixed-blood heritage, out-of-control sexuality, marginalization in white society, and deadliness to men. The ambiguity surrounding the genetic origins of the young woman's moral downfall and overt sexuality vanishes by the 1940s. Her Native heritage now carries the full burden of her social and moral depravity, as well as her femme fatale–like power over men. Her desire for material wealth and the tendency, described above, to blame her yearning on the interference of white society in Native culture also disappear, replaced by a consuming and lethal passion for a white man. The films exhibit an overt racism directed at the Sexualized Maiden that, while sometimes critiqued within the film, displays disturbing masochistic undertones that will escalate by the 1950s. The 1940s character's pinup girl figure barely contains a flamboyant and exuberant personality, reminiscent of Talu's and Slim Girl's, and the overall image reflects a chaotic and uncontrolled energy. These changes, along with the tendency exhibited in the earlier films, reviews, and Production Code communications to conflate nonwhite race with promiscuity and immorality, form the basis for the 1940s figure, resulting in a visual manifestation of the merged psychological fears of racial Others and female sexuality.

The four Sexualized Maiden films I will discuss — *Northwest Mounted Police* (1940), *My Darling Clementine* (1946), *Duel in the Sun* (1946), and *Colorado Territory* (1949) — are variations of the western format. As such, they may be read as doing particular historical work within the revived western genre and the pre– and post–World War II eras. The western, already a feature genre in the silent period, all but disappeared from class A status — large scale, high-end productions — by the mid-1930s. The incongruity between the nation's economic predicament and the genre's myth of the frontier theme of American expansionism may have facilitated this decline. The vision of a progressive and mythological history may have seemed invalid to a nation trying to recover from the moral, economic, and social turmoil caused by the Depression.[28] But by 1936, Americans sought to redefine "their own culture and to create standard beliefs and values within the society" reflective of the new America that had emerged out of the devastation. And with the rekindled pride in America and the "surge of Americanism sweeping the country" while Europe headed toward war, the renaissance of the A western promoted the sense of American exceptionalism and idealism representative of the moment. A westerns such as King Vidor's *Texas Rangers* (1936), Cecil B. DeMille's *The Plainsman* (1937), James Hogan's *The Texans* (1938), DeMille's *Union Pacific* (1939), and John Ford's *Drums along the Mohawk* (1939) once again promoted the rugged individualism of the American hero and the manifest destiny of American nation building.[29] Others, like John Ford's revisionist look at the western structure, *Stagecoach* (1939), a film that presents each character as a reflection of class or culture within a complex and contradictory community, explored the western format as a microcosm of American society. Together with outlaw westerns such as *Jesse James*, these films set the tone for the genre in the 1940s.[30]

The Sexualized Maiden films fall roughly into four categories of the western: the historical epic, the classic, the cult of the outlaw, and the melodrama epic.[31] Although they share common elements, including the same racializing tendencies inherent in the western's ideology of the myth of the frontier and manifest destiny, the Sexualized Maiden films stand as individual artifacts of an era because of their interpretation of the western formula and the maiden's role in the narrative. With the exception of *Duel in the Sun*, the films position the Sexualized Maiden figure as a secondary character and her story as a minor narrative. Even so, her placement within the western underscores her racial and sexual difference and symbolizes the degenerate extreme in comparison to a white feminine ideal. As Thomas Schatz explains, the western's "essential conflict between civilization and savagery" emerges in any number of oppositions, including "cowboy versus Indian," "social order versus anarchy," and "schoolmarm versus dancehall girl."[32] The Sexualized Maiden's difference situates her within the "savage," "anarchist" half of the binary. Her mixed-heritage background complicates this, however, because it suggests that the danger to civilized (white) society from the "savage" is not an external threat but one already within the "blood" of the community.

The Sexualized Maiden's representation gauges the levels of racism woven into the narrative, whether the film critiques or seems to condone racism. With this in mind, the following analysis focuses on the individual films within their particular subgeneric formulas, taking into consideration press reviews and production information to underscore the trends that bind her as a figure across the western genre as a whole and the differences caused by the films' various approaches. These trends inform the larger thematic focus of this chapter—the variation on the problem of the conflation of sexuality and race—and enable a better understanding of the Sexualized Maiden's grounding in racial and colonial ideology.

DeMille's *Northwest Mounted Police* (1940), a historical epic, offers a temporal starting point for tracing the Sexualized Maiden figure's manifestations in 1940s film. According to Richard Slotkin, historical epics were expensive prestige films that were "relentlessly 'progressive' in [their] reading of history" and mingled "images of war as historically necessary or heroic with wishful scenarios of war-avoidance that have a contemporary reference." Products of the pre–World War II climate and the renaissance of the western, they attempt to describe "the political issues of war and peace" by relying on familiar racial figures of an enemy "identified by turns as savage and brown-skinned, fanatical and allied with non-Whites, and . . . corrupt." In addition, and important to this analysis of Louvette—the Sexualized Maiden figure of *Northwest Mounted Police*—the narratives use "gender signals as a key to the interpretation of morality."[33] In other words, gender shapes the moral and social norms of the characters.

DeMille's film, set in the Canadian wilderness and based on the 1885 Métis uprising led by Louis Riel against the British, opens with a preface that makes the film's colonialist sentiments clear: "Two great nations, one under the American flag, the other under the British crown. . . . Two vast territories, newly opened for civilization, each policed by its own great organization—the plains of Texas by the Texas Rangers; the wilds of Canada by the Northwest Mounted Police." In addition, the underlying belief that the civilization can exist only with vigilant policing and controlling carries with it the assumption that those opposed to the process represent the uncivilized and the unruly. The "theme of the story, the uniting of the two men on the border" and the "friendship between the United States and Canada," teams a Canadian Mountie, Jim Bret (Preston Foster), with a Texas Ranger, Dusty Rivers (Gary Cooper). Together they attempt to apprehend the Métis rebels and defuse the rebellion by making the Métis' allies, the Indians, "adhere to their peace treaty with Great Britain."[34] Initially at odds in their missions and both vying for the blond nurse April, the men join forces when April's brother Ronnie is kidnapped by his Métis lover Louvette (Paulette Goddard), daughter of the rebel leader Corbeau. The combined efforts of the Texas Ranger and the Canadian Mountie succeed in capturing a rebel wanted for criminal activity in the United States and in preventing a "war that might have torn Canada to fragments."[35]

DeMille's rendition of the historical epic casts Louvette as a savage and fanatical enemy of the civilizing mission of the great nation. Her alliance with the Indians and her manners equate her with colonial figures of savagery. Her mother's blood connects her to the tribe physiologically, while her status as a Métis rebel connects her to the tribe politically, because of the Métis' need for Indian warriors to ensure their defeat of the Mounties. Though the film carefully positions the Indians as manipulated by their mixed-blood relatives, it also reinforces an age-old stereotype of Indians as bloodthirsty savages and enemies of the white colonizers. For example, in one scene, Chief Big Bear (Walter Hampden) sits behind a pile of bloody Mountie jackets around which his men perform a war dance. Likewise, Louvette's mother, who killed three husbands, embodies the violent femme fatale figure of the American Indian Queen. In addition to her familial and political connections to these savages and "savage actions," Louvette lacks the morals and refinement attributed to members of civilized culture, and her character flaws include treachery and thievery. These traits make her a threat to civilization, a point reinforced by her fluctuation between cultures and political missions: she works for the rebellion but loves one of the enemy. Her uncontrollable temper leads her to strike a bargain with the Indians to kill the Texas Ranger. The ambush fails and results in Ronnie's death.

Louvette is the most extreme and animalistic of all the 1940s Sexualized Maidens, and these qualities are construed as signs of her Native heritage and racial inferiority. The story notes from the DeMille archives suggest that the script conception team originally saw her as "an authentic and rabid Métis," but DeMille modified this:

> I see a tough son of a bitch, you know, who is a half animal, and a magnificent one, crafty as hell, beautiful as hell, and unconsciously a terrible destroyer. I see a gorgeous black panther, something that is death; and yet anybody will go to it and stroke it and pet it and love it. . . . Men are afraid of her. . . . The fact that her father or brother or somebody is in trouble—she would defend that because it's her own, not because it is going to save the Métis. . . . Maybe there was a question as to whether her father was Scotch or English, but there's no question about her mother, because her mother was so and so, who killed three husbands.[36]

The rhetoric fetishizes her as a sleek and desirable animal. But it also defines her in terms of disease, deadly animals, and a murderous Indian mother whose actions reflect onto Louvette's own crafty and deadly personality.

The script team continues its composite of Louvette, suggesting that "this black panther can't keep her mitts off that kid [Ronnie]. She likes white meat. First of all, he represents a side of life that she can never reach." In addition, Louvette's description as "dark and vital" reinforces the internal darkness she inherits from her mother, while her "dark hair of an Indian" and "relatively fair" white skin distinguish her as a mixed-blood.[37] Her mixed-heritage further codes her as untrustworthy. As a

Mountie says to Ronnie, "Never trust a blue-eyed squaw. She is a thief as if it's second nature." After she kidnaps Ronnie, he calls her a "sneaking she-wolf" and a "dirty squaw," reinforcing the conflation of animal and Indian stereotypes with deviance. Through these quotes, a composite emerges of a femme fatale with no real control over her destructive nature; indeed, Ronnie's comment that she is the "sweetest poison that ever got into a man's blood" proves prophetic and literal, as her love results in his death.

As a mixed-blood femme fatale, Louvette undermines the traditional opposition between white men and women in the western genre. Women in the historical epic and in the traditional western "incarnate the Christian moral principles essential to a civilized order" and are "set off against the 'male' propensity for violence." Gender roles tend toward rigidity, with the visual landscape or background aligned accordingly: schools and towns as women's spheres of influence, and open plains and Indian wars as men's.[38] Like the typical western outlaw or Indian, Louvette disrupts these roles. Rather than symbolizing order, education, and morality, she embodies their opposites. Assuming the "male" position, Louvette controls Ronnie, navigates the world through violence, and represents the unruly aspect of the wilderness/civilized dichotomy. In addition, the film contrasts her both visually and morally to April, who stands for the civilizing force in the wilderness and embodies gentleness, refinement, and education. April is shown setting a broken leg, serving tea to Dusty when he comes to town, and carrying herself with decorum. Louvette, in contrast, is aggressive, uneducated by white standards, and unrefined.

DeMille confirms the women's polarity in a scene midway through the film in which April comes to Louvette's cabin to ask for her help in warning Ronnie about his impending arrest for desertion. The two figures are positioned next to each other in a medium long shot that emphasizes their differences. April wears a prim, blue, form-fitting dress buttoned to the neck with a big white collar, and a black cape over her head. Her movements are sparse and her physical bearing calm. Louvette, in contrast, depicts chaos. Her unbuttoned, multi-colored shirt falls off her shoulders; she walks angrily around the cabin, tearing at meat with her bare hands; and she throws her knife at April, who calls her a savage.

Although Louvette is not the only "savage" in the film, her sexuality, femme fatale threat, and mixed heritage elevate the level of disruption to the social and moral norms defined by the western genre. The genre tends to reduce Native Americans and women, according to Douglas Pye, "to functions in a symbolic world centering on White male characters and embodying White (and particularly Anglo-Saxon) male visions of national and gender identity." The western love triangle complicates these gender functions by contrasting two types of women. John Cawelti describes this as a triangle between the white hero and dark and light women. The light woman, like April, represents the virtues of civilization and the tamed wilderness, while in most cases the dark woman (often signaled by dark hair or her profession as a dancer or prostitute) "is a feminine embodiment of the hero's savage, spontaneous side. She understands his deep passions, his savage code of honor and his need to use personal violence." Often a reference to James Fenimore Cooper's dark-haired mulatta heroine Cora in *The Last of the Mohicans*, the dark woman's passion symbolizes her taint—her mixed-blood heritage—and her "passionate and spontaneous nature." If, as in the case of Louvette, her parentage involves a Native American ancestor, then her darkness intensifies with the overlay of the savage, who in the western often connotes "the bloodthirsty Indian or the lawless outlaw which is the irreconcilable adversary of the hero and the townspeople."[39] In the case of *Northwest Mounted Police*, the characterization of Louvette ensures that the "dark" woman carries the burden of all that is dangerous and tainted on the frontier.

Positioning Louvette as an insidious and covert threat to civilization allows the film to support superficially the pre–World War II industry trend of representing Native Americans as allies, not enemies. In addition, it maintains the themes of manifest destiny and antiassimilation, which run through most of DeMille's westerns, without going against the industry trend. By the mid-1930s, according to Angela Aleiss, "increasing conflict in Europe . . . began to influence Hollywood politics and consequently to reshape minority images even before America's entry into the war. Previous Westerns could boast of conquest, but a national campaign to purge the land of its Indian inhabitants smacked of fascist genocide. At the very least, the Manifest Destiny theme painted a racially intolerant picture of American's frontier heroes." *Northwest Mounted Police* was one of a number of prewar films that attempted to promote a sense of national unity through racial brotherhood by portraying Indians as allies rather than hostile enemies. Indeed, as Aleiss points out, the Indians remain aligned with the Canadians and Americans and against the Métis villains at the close of the film.[40] The film's attention to historical accuracy and extensive research into Cree costume, language, and weaponry also suggest DeMille's attempts to move past earlier stereotypes of Native Americans.

This pro-Indian bias, however, overlooks Louvette's status as a mixed-blood. Her threat resides in her feminine power, but the inclusion of her Indian heritage complicates such a conclusion, because her savagery, which makes her an enemy and a threat, comes through her mother's Indian blood. Unlike Slim Girl's or Talu's, Louvette's immorality and taint do not reflect the effects of miscegenation or the disruptive influences of western European culture on Native culture, though her status as a rebel does. The film's successful displacement of racial enmity onto a gendered structure results in a discourse on the dangers of miscegenation to the purity of white society and the threat of certain types of women to a patriarchal order.

This technique recalls the overlay of race and immorality in DeMille's earlier depiction of Naturich, whose passions drive her to murder and result in a tarnishing of her Princess status. But it also appears to reflect contemporary attitudes about minorities. The Production Code Administration supported the film, and Joseph Breen enjoyed it tremendously, taking issue only with a strongly suggestive love scene between Louvette and Ronnie. In order to sidestep a full rejection of the film, DeMille had the scene edited out to "end with a two foot wipe," which procured a fast transition into the next scene. The film received good reviews, reaching top-ten feature film status in 1940 and earning an Academy Award for editing. In sum, mainstream industry personnel and reviewers seemed undisturbed by Louvette's characterization, indicating that such depictions of women of color were acceptable at the time. According to Ana López's study on the Good Neighbor films produced in Hollywood for market in the United States and Latin America between 1939 and 1947, a plethora of films were marketed that similarly played up the "innate" sexuality of Latinas. Stars such as Lupe Vélez, Dolores del Rio, and Carmen Miranda were depicted, in contrast to Germans and Japanese, as "nonthreatening, potentially but not practically assimilable (that is, nonpolluting to the purity of the race), friendly, fun-loving, and not deemed insulting to Latin American eyes and ears."[41] In contrast to these racially stereotyped but assimilable portrayals, DeMille's Sexual-ized Maiden symbolizes pollution of white and Native culture, suggest-ing that a deeper racial anxiety exists in the case of white-Native mixing than it does in Latin-white relationships.

The Production Code Administration carefully monitored the ste-reotyping of Latin American women during the prewar and war period, and Hollywood cast the Native American man "alongside the military hero" in a "deliberate move to convey racial cooperation." This was part of the Hollywood film industry's "conscious effort to bring about greater understanding between various racial and ethnic groups in America, and among the many nationalities and races allied with the United States." But there seemed to be no industry censorship of the overt racial stereo-typing of, or violence to, Native American women or Japanese, an in-dex, perhaps, of the rising racism and interracial conflict in the country. Exemplifying racist policy of the period, under Executive Order 9066, Japanese Americans were interned in camps across the Southwest from February 1942 through the end of the war. Racial tensions between white and black factory workers in Detroit in 1943 erupted in "hate strikes" that "culminated on 21 June, when 25 blacks and 9 whites were killed and another 800 were injured." In Los Angeles that same month, escalating violence between Latino youth and white servicemen turned into the violent "zoot-suit riots." In the military, African American troops were segregated from whites while Native Americans were expected to "excel as soldiers" because of their supposedly innate scouting skills. In sum, the "end of World War II marked the close of one of the most in-tense periods of American bigotry."[42]

The A western, on hiatus during the war, reemerged in 1946, Hol-lywood's "biggest year ever in terms of box-office revenues."[43] Altered by the effects of the war and the country's internal social and cultural changes, the postwar westerns incorporated particularly "adult themes" and reflected the psychological trauma felt by the nation in films that critiqued racism, traditional moral assumptions, and the white hero's role in the American western drama. "Three new elements," according to Fenin and Everson's study of the western, "made their bow in the genre as a result of the postwar gloom and 'psychology' that settled on American films. They were, in order of their appearance, sex, neurosis, and a racial conscience. All had been used as plot elements in the West-erns before, but they had never succeeded in establishing themselves as *integral* parts of the simple and uncomplicated Western tradition."[44] The postwar Sexualized Maiden films were no exception to this rule. They presented an often sadistic brutality born of racism, which DeMille's *Northwest Mounted Police* seemingly promoted, in three types of westerns—the classic, the melodrama epic, and the cult of the outlaw.

John Ford's *My Darling Clementine* (1946), rated one of the top ten films of 1946 by the National Board of Review, falls into the category of the classic or neoclassic western. Such westerns, according to Richard Slotkin, knowingly use and adapt "traditional and relatively 'archaic' styles and story-structures." The classic western takes place in the historical West of approximately 1860–1890, emphasizes the establishment of law and order, and presents an essential and ritualistic conflict between civilization and savagery. These elements are constructed into various oppositions, mentioned earlier but worth repeating—"East versus West," "social order versus anarchy, individual versus community, town versus wilderness, cowboy versus Indian, schoolmarm versus dancehall girl"—and are manifested on any number of levels, including externally in the landscape and internally in the community. The western hero's "physical allegiance to the environment" ambiguously conflicts with his "moral commitment to civilization" and his role as a "promoter of civilization," and he maintains a tenuous existence on the edge of both. Ford's 1946 film, based loosely on Stuart N. Lake's book *Wyatt Earp, Frontier Marshal* and an earlier film, *Frontier Marshal* (1939), uses the stylized language of the western as a template for exploring a community founded on social and racial difference. As in the classic western, however, he ultimately opts for the acceptance of an established white order.[45]

Set in Tombstone, Arizona, in 1882, the film tells the story of Wyatt Earp's (Henry Fonda) temporary stint as marshal, his friendship with Doc Holliday (Victor Mature), his revenge on the Clanton clan for killing his brother James, and his love for Clementine Carter (Cathy Downs), Doc's ex-fiancée. *My Darling Clementine* complicates the framework of this story in two important ways. The film presents double heroes and parallel love relationships as opposing reflections of the American idyllic myth of regeneration, and it offers a complicated social view of America based on racial conflict, violence, and decay.[46] Wyatt Earp and Clementine Carter represent the promise of a "harmonious community," which embodies "an optimism that is very much of its immediately postwar moment."[47] Earp, as the traditional western hero, rides into Tombstone to avenge his brother's death and stays on as marshal long enough to do so, ridding the town of its villainous Clantons and disruptive drunken Indian and helping to inaugurate the church. He falls in love with Clementine Carter, a Boston nurse who has come west in search of her fiancé Doc Holliday. Rejected by Holliday, she falls in love with Earp, stays on to establish a school, and promises to wait for Wyatt's return. As the civilizing force and symbol of the East, education, and refinement, she is juxtaposed to Chihuahua (Linda Darnell), the mixed-blood saloon girl who stands for degeneracy, immorality, a wild and savage West, and a threat to civilized order. Similarly, Doc Holliday is the East to Wyatt's West—but his personality is forged from a disillusionment with the American ideal that creates a noir-style fallen hero character whose lifestyle threatens social harmony.

This paralleling of characters, though not unusual in westerns, takes on a psychological edge in *My Darling Clementine*, because of the portrayals of Doc and Chihuahua, that hints at the popularity of the film noir influence emerging in film at the time and signals the darkening cultural attitudes after the war. According to Thomas Schatz, "Hollywood's *noir* films documented the growing disillusionment with certain traditional American values in the face of complex and often contradictory social, political, scientific, and economic developments." Certainly, elements of noir color Doc's and Chihuahua's existences. Doc's tuberculosis, gambling, and rejection of his Boston medical practice and fiancée Clementine reflect his diseased character and his disillusionment with law and society. His pairing with Chihuahua signals acceptance of a dark inner nature that they share and that manifests itself outwardly, toward society, through destructive behavior. Together they inhabit the racially coded and violent underside of society, existing "outside the safety and comforts of American middle-class life" and as indices of the society's violence. Doc, like the hero of noir, "encounter[s] a *femme fatale*: a seductress, a deadly dame who will fascinate [him], drag him into deep waters and then, as if by some eternal law, perish herself."[48] This is Doc and Chihuahua's story, and, in fact, her sexual indiscretion with another man—Billy Clanton, who killed Wyatt's brother—leads her to betray Doc and ends in her murder.

In a move that indicates a need to underscore Chihuahua's moral darkness as linked to her multiracial difference, the film engages tropes of savagery as well as sexuality. Like Louvette, Chihuahua "carries the ethnic stigma of inferiority, and with it the customary traits of the Western 'bad girl'—sensuality, self-indulgence, vanity, willfulness, and moodiness." And, as Robert Lyon's analysis suggests, the cinematography—particularly "huge, softly lit Hollywood close-ups"—emphasizes this and presents her as an ethnic fetishization of the western's stereotyped "bad girl." She is "explicitly erotic, sexually active and not above a little infidelity." She also cheats at cards, lies, and displays aggression toward Clementine. The characterization of Chihuahua goes much further than this, however, engaging overlays of racial stereotyping that effectively position Chihuahua as a sliding signifier of Mexican inferiority and colonized Native America. Her name, Chihuahua, alludes to an area of Mexico and the type of Mexican cattle the Earp family herded across the country to Tombstone. In the saloon, she sings about cattle, metonymically linking herself to them. Her clothing and adornment—long, multitiered "Mexican" skirts, off-the-shoulder blouses, large flowers in her hair, and a sombrero—code her ethnically, as do her use of Spanish and her interaction with the Mexican kitchen staff. These are visual and aural markers of her Mexican ethnicity, which is also connected to her questionable occupation as "the idol of the miners and queen of entertainment," a phrase used by Harry Brand, director of publicity for the film.[49]

A more complicated structural move underscores her Indian ancestry and connects her to the film's only other Indian character. This occurs through Earp's telling Chihuahua, "If I catch you doin' that again [cheating], I'll run you back to the Apache reservation where you belong," and dunking her in the horse trough. The incident follows a scene in which she interrupts his poker game by flirting with him and cheating at cards. There is no other reference to Chihuahua's Native background, but this moment in the film links her to an earlier one in which Wyatt Earp's actions against another Native American earn him the title of marshal. Shortly after arriving in town, Earp and his brothers go for a shave but are interrupted by Indian Charlie's shooting from the saloon. Taking it upon himself to rid the town of their drunken Indian, Earp climbs into the saloon through the upstairs window and emerges through the front door, dragging the man with him. He unceremoniously dumps Indian Charlie at the feet of the mayor, shouting, "What kind of a town is this, anyway! Selling liquor to Indians! I put a knot on his head bigger than a turkey's egg. Indian, get out of town and stay out!" Earp's reprimand sets the Native Americans apart from the other disruptive forces in the film—Doc and the Clantons, for example—as the only characters verbally acknowledged by race. That Earp does not seriously hurt either character, does not handle them with the same level of physical violence he does other adult characters, but rather treats them as unruly Indian children, adds a level of paternalism to the scenes. As a result, the film positions Chihuahua and Indian Charlie beneath all of Tombstone's inhabitants, including the Mexicans working in the saloon's kitchen.

Chihuahua's mixed Indian and Mexican heritage and her actions also relegate her to the position of Indian within the western's structure, in which Indians are synonymous with savagery and the antithesis of white civilization. Thus the film also aligns her with the other forces challenging a civil society—the outlaw Clanton clan and the self-destructive and lawbreaking Doc. Chihuahua's connection to Doc, however, metonymically links his demise with her own; his self-destructive actions, illegal activities (he robs a bank), and his rejection of Clementine parallel her own. They are both "morally unworthy to participate in the ideal frontier community."[50] Chihuahua, one of only two female characters, continually fails to measure up to Clementine. Her non-white heritage, unruly behavior, and unsavory character traits exclude her from the white ideal represented by Earp and Clementine, and her death symbolically underlines this.

Ford's westerns are well known for their stylized characters and their exploration of the nuances of American cultural structures. His representations of Native Americans within the western structure are also well documented.[51] But *My Darling Clementine* is strangely unlike many of his other films. There is no literal Indian challenging the community's safety, as there is in *Stagecoach* (1939), *Fort Apache* (1948), and *The Searchers* (1956). Nor is there an overt commentary on Native-white relations, as there is in *The Searchers*, *Two Rode Together* (1961), and *Cheyenne Autumn* (1964). Ford's *Stagecoach* also has a fallen woman character, whom it pairs with Ringo, the outlaw hero, allowing them to ride off into the sunset together. This ending differs from that of *My Darling Clementine* precisely because of Chihuahua's race. The film does not allow her a happy ending with Doc because of Production Code regulations. Her race opens the door to a type of physical expression not often demonstrated with white women characters in westerns. The film accentuates Chihuahua's Indian racial heritage, in addition to her Mexican background, as if to justify or allow Earp's sadistic physical violence against her. Throughout the film, Earp usually controls his anger and his actions. Only in relation to Chihuahua does he temporarily lose control—and only after she taunts him suggestively and interrupts his poker game. Edward Gallafent posits that Earp's passionate response to her masks a desire that he cannot act upon because of her racial background and social status.[52] He may be correct, especially when we consider the history of colonial reaction to women of color and different sexual mores that often resulted in violence and rape. If so, then dunking Chihuahua expresses the internal conflict of a repressed hero regulated by moral and racial codes of honor.

Duel in the Sun, released the same year as *My Darling Clementine* (1946), takes the moment of sadism exhibited in Ford's film and escalates it to extreme levels. An independent film produced by David O. Selznick and directed by King Vidor, *Duel in the Sun* dives into themes of racism, sexual violence, and insuppressible passion carried in the blood. The postwar years witnessed a deepening alienation of Americans that "accompanied socioeconomic booms, rapidly changing views on marriage, sexuality, and women in the work force." The film industry, including makers of westerns, picked up on the "fashionable intellectual and literary trends of the period . . . existentialism and Freudian psychology," fashioning characters who exhibit dark inner turmoil and creating more psychologically probing themes. And, as do the psychological westerns of the late 1940s, *Duel in the Sun* probes a character suffering from an internal torment characteristic of American society's own tumultuous attempts to cope with the post–World War II milieu. The film's "strong psychosexual themes" challenge the limits of film decency and walk a thin line between subverting and supporting American ideologies of racial and sexual boundaries. Termed pessimistic and scandalous, nicknamed "Lust in the Dust," and ruled as tasteless as *The Outlaw* by the press, the film emerges as the most sexually overt, sadistic, and erotic of the 1940s Sexualized Maiden films.[53]

Falling into the categories of melodrama and western epic, *Duel in the Sun* twists the western by positioning a mixed-blood girl, Pearl (Jennifer Jones), at the center of the genre's system of oppositions and adding a distinctly melodramatic tone. The familial environment into which Pearl is placed pits eastern education and gentility, in the form of

Laura Belle (Lillian Gish) and son Jesse (Joseph Cotten), against western brutality, in the form of Senator McCanles (Lionel Barrymore) and
son Lewt (Gregory Peck). Though the family, in turn, is split by these internal oppositions, as a unit it represents the last vestiges of the old West,
symbolized by the senator's vast cattle baronage, which clashes against
the inevitable march of progress, represented by the railroad moving
across his land. The film also merges the western's misogynistic and racist tendencies with the melodrama's commitment to presenting the female protagonist's struggle against the social conditions that bind her.
As does the melodrama of passion, *Duel in the Sun* "explores a familial
world of subjectivity, of emotion and feeling, of problems of identity and
desire." Melodrama often represents social tensions as "sexual anxieties or conflicts." Such displacement emerges most clearly in the film's
presentation of Pearl's femme fatale sexuality as inherent in her Indian
blood and of her race as the cause for her internal struggle between
wanting to be a "good girl" and her innate "badness." Her loss of control results in "hysterical and 'excessive' responses to [her] entrapment
within the male order."[54] More so than the historical epic, classic, and
cult of the outlaw westerns, *Duel in the Sun* foregrounds racism and the
brutality that results from it as problems in American society.

The film narrates the story of Pearl Chavez, a mixed-blood girl
whose Indian mother (Tilly Losch) dances at the cantina and is a fla-
grantly unfaithful wife. Pearl's father, the fallen Spanish aristocrat Scott
Chavez, kills his wife and her lover; he sends Pearl to his ex-love Laura
Belle and her husband, Senator McCanles, prior to his hanging for the
murders. Though welcomed with open arms by Laura Belle and the
(good) son Jesse, Pearl receives verbal torment from Senator McCanles
and physical violence from the (bad) son Lewt. Torn between attraction
to the educated and refined Jesse and to the rogue Lewt, Pearl loses
her moral battle when Lewt rapes her. This pivotal moment transforms
Pearl from an innocent, albeit sexually provocative, young girl into an
erotic woman by unleashing the full power of the sexuality she inherited
from her mother. A sadomasochistic relationship unfolds between Pearl
and Lewt, and she falls in love with her rapist. Lewt's neurotic need to
control Pearl but not be controlled by her results in his refusal to marry
her, his killing of Sam Pierce (Charles Bickford), the man who wants
to marry her, and his shooting of Jesse, who tries to take her to Austin.
Pearl, emotionally tortured and spent, nurses Jesse back to health and

then goes off into the desert to kill Lewt, who is hiding from the law. The film ends with a tortured scene in which Pearl and Lewt shoot each other, she drags herself up a desert mountain toward him, and they die in each other's arms.

Pearl's transformation from an innocent young girl to a femme fatale who murders her lover reflects her inability to resemble the ideal placed before her by her father, Laura Belle, and Jesse. These three characters, who represent the various civilizing forces in the West, want her to become a "good girl"—an educated and refined woman who not only does not challenge the patriarchal order but assimilates into white society. The racism she encounters in Lewt and Senator McCanles, who continually remind her of her skin color and Indian heritage, make it impossible for Pearl to fit into this order. Lewt's racism and need to dominate her strong-willed personality manifest themselves in violence. Unable to control her future, her sexual urges, or the violence she encounters, Pearl psychologically splits, and her dark side emerges in the form of the femme fatale—a figure that articulates the "fears surrounding the loss of stability and centrality of the self, the 'I,' the ego."[55]

The racial ideology of the film connects the femme fatale's threatening persona to Pearl's mother, who embodies the stereotype of the oversexualized racial other—in this case, the Indian woman. Pearl's dark coloring and sensuality link her visually to her mother. Their physical and emotional similarities are established in the first minutes of the film, which also foreshadow Pearl's future. In the scene that introduces Pearl Chavez, a close-up shows her dancing to the music of the Mexican Hat Dance in front of an audience of enthusiastic young children. Her mother's lover approaches her on his way into the saloon, remarks "Like mother, like daughter," proceeds to eye Pearl suggestively, touches her arm, and says, "I'm commencing to think I like the daughter better." The scene cuts to an interior of the saloon he has entered and a long shot of a densely packed room full of motion, voices, smoke, and the music of tom-toms and trumpets. The camera captures Pearl's mother, a dark-skinned woman, performing the Orizaba—a more suggestive dance than her daughter's—on top of a bar surrounded by cowboys.[56] The camera responds to the energy of the place, moving between long shots that establish the size of the crowd of men cheering her performance and close-ups of the dance itself—swirling skirts, spinning figure, legs and arms flying counter to each other, a sexually charged performance.

These images are interrupted by an insert shot of Pearl's father playing cards. The men around the table rib him about his fancy ways and state that he is "not so fancy about [his] wife," suggesting her infidelity. A point-of-view shot moves from Mr. Chavez's tortured face to his wife, and the scene focuses on her movements and the crowd's reaction. The dance ends with Mrs. Chavez strutting across the length of the bar, not dissimilar to a catwalk, shooting off a cowboy's gun, and then falling into the arms of her lover, who kisses her. The two leave the bar followed by Mr. Chavez. The final scene in the sequence frames Pearl as she watches her father follow them and hears his gun as he shoots them. Like her mother, Pearl will be unable to control her sexuality, she will be driven to excessive displays of passion, and she will drive a man (Lewt) insane with jealousy, which in turn will result in both their deaths.

Pearl's psychological break comes much later in the film, after she has been living with the McCanles family for a while. Lewt sneaks into Pearl's room one night and rapes her. Jesse, who is leaving home (ordered away by his father for siding with the railroad and against the family business), walks in at the end of Pearl's rape. Pearl tries to explain herself and defend her name, but Jesse does not listen. She finally gives up, saying that she is trash like her mother. He disagrees but holds her ancestry against her anyway. In a passive-aggressive remark as damaging to her as Lewt's violence, he tells her that he loves her but that it is over now, and he leaves. This scene ends with Pearl repeating to herself, "Trash, trash, trash." The film cuts to Lewt serenading her on the fence and then to Pearl crying in her room. In a disturbing set of actions, Pearl is transformed from a hurt young girl into a possessed woman. A series of close-ups frame Pearl as she twists on her back in bed, crying, pulling her hair, and visibly wrestling with her grief. Lewt's music seeps into her room, and she sits up to listen. Her face still carries the look of anguish it did moments earlier, but her body responds with a very slight shimmy movement in the shoulders. She tries to stop her body, but, on failing, she smiles oddly with a crazed look on her face. Telling the departed Jesse, "All right, Jesse, you said you'd never forget," Pearl stands up, places her hands on her hips, and struts past the camera to the window. Throwing open the curtains to let in Lewt's music, she sits on the ledge and turns toward the camera.

This scene relies, in part, on the viewer's memory of the scene of her mother's wild, exhibitionist dancing and sexual abandon, and of

Duel in the Sun. King Vidor, Selznick International Pictures, 1946.

Pearl's own Mexican Hat Dance, which foreshadowed her future. Her shoulder shimmy, the transformation from tortured "good girl" to vengeful femme fatale, registers at the moment she embraces her inner darkness. Prior to the rape, Lewt's sexual passes arouse her, though she resists them; during the rape, her will collapses, and she responds. Her comment to Jesse that she is "just trash like [her] ma" reveals her inability to reconcile the differing parts of her soul—the erotic side, like her mother, that is fueled by music and sexual freedom, and the side yearning to be respectable, like Laura Belle and Jesse. Her comment also suggests the societal pressure she faces to condemn her mother and to throw away her free-spirited abandon for a restrictive place in a male-dominated world that defines womanhood by the Victorian Laura Belle. Jesse's rejection—his inability to accept that she did not encourage the rape—also reflects this ideology and promotes the idea that a violated woman is spoiled for all time.

No longer containing her sexuality, Pearl embraces Lewt's approach, and they play a cat-and-mouse game of seduction, passion, and rejection. Their relationship demonstrates a distinctly sadomasochistic edge that leads them to both love and hate each other. For Lewt, this manifests itself in racist remarks and abrupt splits with Pearl. For example, at a barbecue where Pearl expects Lewt to announce that they are "bespoken," his tenderness toward her turns to viciousness, as reflected in his question, "Why'd you have to go and tie on to me like that, least of all a bob-tailed little half-breed like you?" In part, the remark comes from his own need to please his father, who has just informed him that he will not have his ranch "turned into an Injun reservation." Lewt's respect for his father outweighs his desire to please Pearl and marry her.[57] Although he is unwilling to be tied down by Pearl, he cannot release her or allow her to find another man to love. In fact, he tells Sam—Pearl's new fiancé—"Pearl Chavez is my girl and she'll always be my girl just as long as I want her to be." Lewt punctuates his claim by killing Sam. The need to control and own Pearl catalyzes his obsession. In turn, these actions and statements illustrate that she also controls him.

The following scene demonstrates how abusive their relationship becomes and how unable they are to release each other. Shortly after Sam's funeral, Lewt, who has been on the run from the law, sneaks back to the ranch to see Pearl. As Lewt enters her room, she pulls a gun on him. The darkened room offers just enough light to illuminate the figures, Pearl in a white nightgown, her skin dark against the fabric.[58] As Lewt approaches the bed, the following exchange occurs:

LEWT: "One minute you're yammering because I don't love you enough, and when I go out and show you how much I do, you're wanting to plug me. Well you're my girl honey."
PEARL: "I was your girl."
LEWT: "Anybody who was my girl is still my girl, that's the kind of guy I am, you know, loyal. Ain't nobody going to take my girl, nobody, nobody."

He takes her gun and they embrace. This oddly tender moment ends abruptly with Lewt talking of going to Mexico and setting up a ranch. Pearl assumes she will go along, but Lewt coldly informs her that he can't be tied to her—a rephrasing of his earlier rejection. As she clings to him, he throws her to the ground and walks away, dragging her across the floor. He shoves her away and slams her face with the door as he leaves. The scene ends with Pearl, in her white nightgown, lying face up on the cold stone floor, crying. The moon shines down through a barred window, an effect that visually represents how her love for him imprisons her.

The only release from their mutual imprisonment and abuse lies in death. After Laura Belle dies, Jesse removes Pearl from the ranch with the intention of taking her to Austin with him and his fiancée, Helen; she will attend school there and become a lady like Laura Belle and Helen. However, an insanely jealous Lewt rides into town and shoots Jesse. Pearl nurses Jesse back to health and, when Helen arrives, leaves to find and kill Lewt. The film ends with their final reunion. Set in the hot, sun-drenched desert, the scene tracks Pearl's arrival at the base of the mountain where Lewt hides. He has been waiting for her, but when he comes out to greet her, she shoots him. A battle ensues with the two exchanging endearments and bullets. The camera follows the wounded Pearl's torturous ascent up the side of the mountain in her attempt to reach and kill Lewt. A shot-reverse-shot sequence juxtaposes Lewt dying to Pearl dragging her bloody body up the rocky mountainside. Urgency grips them when they realize that their wounds are fatal, and Lewt cries for her to hurry so that he can hold her one last time. She manages to reach Lewt, and just as they embrace and kiss, he dies. She gazes at his face and also dies.[59]

Their sadomasochistic relationship and their transgression of social taboos against such actions as murder, rape, and premarital and interracial sex are linked to their internal psychological darkness. In Lewt, this signals his morally unleashed ego, which in many ways celebrates the western hero tradition, but here marks his straying too far into the "savage" realm of the uncivilized. In Pearl, whose Indian heritage already positions her as a savage, it corresponds to "fears linked to notions of uncontrollable drives, the fading of subjectivity, and the loss of conscious agency."[60] To fit into the patriarchal and racial structures of her world, Pearl must exorcise or tame her inner, "dark" sexuality. In both cases, a thin line demarcates civilized and uncivilized or savage behavior; however, the film abstracts Pearl's "dark" sexuality through race, making her unknowable and uncontrollable power exponentially more threatening. That the film continually contrasts Pearl to a white feminine ideal, metaphorically presented by women in form-covering clothing, with pale white skins (a sign of their indoor lifestyle) and controlled passions, reinforces the impression that her sexuality exceeds the bounds of social convention. Because she is too sexual to be a proper wife, too dark to be a comfortable part of white society, and too passionate to be controlled with anything but violence, her position in the society and the family remains uncertain until defined by death.

Duel in the Sun challenged Hollywood boundaries by boldly exploring the ideologies inherent in categorizing Pearl as a racial and social outcast; nevertheless, it remained within the melodramatic and western paradigms. Thus, although the film illustrates the problems of the patriarchal order for women like Pearl, it fails to offer a viable solution. The film's killing of Pearl promotes the idea that society cannot afford to include someone like her. As a result, the film shows "that while white racism was a prevailing problem in American society, assimilation was still a dream among the politically liberal," even with Truman's appointment of the President's Committee on Civil Rights in 1946.[61]

Truman's motivation for civil rights had as much to do with America's international image as it did with internal racial strife. With the war came an industrial boom and large migrations of rural poor, including African Americans and Native Americans, to the industrial centers. Although the latter group's move from reservations to cities had begun after World War I, the Bureau of Indian Affairs' establishment of off-reservation employment centers in Denver, Los Angeles, Chicago, and Minneapolis escalated the migration during World War II.[62] But while economic necessity increased integration, racial equality followed at a much slower pace, with the "separate but equal" doctrine remaining politically entrenched until 1954. Along with racial strife, McCarthyism—fueled by rising fears of an internal Communist threat, the United States' push for world economic and political leadership under the Truman Doctrine (1947), and the rising protest movements in colonial nations contributed to a continued sense of internal anxiety. According to Richard Slotkin, the movies responded by "reverting to their generic maps in search of ideological reference points, which meant, for the most part, a return to the home terrain of the Western."[63]

As had Ford's and Selznick's, these films responded to the "conflicts of value and feeling that characterized the period from 1940 to 1960" by

encouraging "a richer exploration of the tensions between old moral assumptions and new uncertainties of experience." Many of the westerns
that advocated racial tolerance also challenged earlier stereotypes of Native Americans. Raoul Walsh's *Colorado Territory* (1949) was no exception, pointing out the problems of prejudicial thinking and promoting
a degree of integration within the parameters of the Production Code.
Stylistically, *Colorado Territory* is "indebted to *Duel in the Sun*" in its
psychological undercurrents, "fatalistic climax," and individualistic heroine.[64] The film adds to the earlier Sexualized Maiden film repertoire
by promoting a strong-willed mixed-blood heroine whose independent
nature is not suppressed by the leading man. More along the lines of the
cult of the outlaw western than *Duel in the Sun*, the film also positions
the outlaw and mixed-blood woman as its central couple.[65] Like many
of Walsh's female characters, and in direct contrast to Pearl, the heroine
Colorado "is comfortable in her own body and at ease with her feelings.
As surely as his male heroes, she is an adventurer who will ultimately
wind up side by side as an equal partner with a sympathetic man who
prizes her independent nature and has no wish to steal any part of it." An
unapologetically worldly woman whose own story parallels that of the
hero, Colorado returns to the source of her life—the land where she was
born and raised. As does the hero, she "lives over" her life as they traverse
the desert country, revealing her mixed-blood heritage as the source of
her circumstances.[66]

Colorado's story emerges within the narrative of Wes McQueen's
story. Wes McQueen (Joel McCrea), an escapee from Leavenworth,
heads west to start a new life. Pressured by an old partner to do one last
heist—a job that will allow him to buy a ranch and start an honest life—
he partners with Duke Harris (James Mitchell) and Reno Blake (John
Archer). He befriends Colorado Carson (Virginia Mayo), the young
half-breed woman involved with Reno, who has "fled to the mountains
to escape the unhealthy atmosphere of El Paso dance halls."[67] As Colorado tells Wes, her mother was Pueblo and her father white, and "it was
all right as long as Pa was living. After that it was either the Comanches
or the cowpokes. Don't know which was worse. You know, 'Let's go look
at the moon.' That was on clear nights. Rainy weather it was 'Let's go inside and pitch a little hay.'" After her father died, men "played her"; after
her mother died, she went to San Antonio to ride broncos but ended up
singing and dancing. She, like Wes, is a good person whose life expe-

riences have prompted her circumstances. Colorado proves herself by saving Wes's life when the rancher's young daughter, whom he has been courting, betrays him. Colorado and Wes run south with the money from his last heist, hoping to reach freedom and begin a life together in Mexico. They are tracked and eventually trapped by the sheriff's posse in an abandoned Indian cliff dwelling, the city of the moon. Pursued by the sheriff's posse, Colorado shoots at them deliberately to draw their fire, and she and Wes "die in a bullet-ridden embrace" not unlike that of Pearl and Lewt.[68]

The racial marking that so obviously resides in Pearl Chavez's skin color does not appear on Colorado; rather, her blond hair and light skin suggest that she is white. The film initially plays on this image, presenting her sensual figure, her suggestive manners, and her brazenly forward attitude as qualities of the western "bad girl." Like those of the Sexualized Maidens before her, Colorado's costume accentuates this image—tightly cinched belts, patterned skirts, and off-the-shoulder blouses that barely contain her bosom. Her open posture—legs spread—easy walk, and aggressive mouth add to the depiction of her as a "bad girl." As *My Darling Clementine* does with Chihuahua, *Colorado Territory* inserts Colorado's race into the narrative as an exotic addition to her story—an interesting touch, considering that, generally, Walsh's heroines' "worldly experience . . . needs no apologies."[69] Her racial heritage rarely comes up in the film: it is mentioned twice by Colorado herself, and once by Duke as a slur when he and Reno threaten to send her "back to the Indians." Thus the obvious insertion of her Indianness forces a link between her race and her sexuality. It also removes a veil of secrecy from her, adding honesty to her already likeable character. Her brief narration of her history clearly includes this information. She informs Wes of her dual heritage in the same few sentences that frame her early introduction to sex (see above). As a result, her mixed-race heritage becomes the ground from which her sensuality emerges and is forced into outright sexuality by Indian and white men. Through the remark "It was all right as long as Pa was living," this film, as does *Duel in the Sun*, places the responsibility for the social formation of women like Colorado on American society and on men in particular. Although not extensive, these momentary insights into Colorado's character point the viewer toward a possible metanarrative about racial inequality and social injustice.

While the film supports its mixed-race heroine by creating her as a sympathetic and likeable character, its placement of her within the landscape tends to reinforce images of Indianness that join the woman to the landscape and thus also reinforce the linking of her sexuality to that heritage. Colorado returns to her mother's land not because Reno takes her there but because "maybe there's more of my ma in me than I thought." Hiding out in the town of Aztec and in the abandoned cliff dwelling, the city of the moon, metonymically connects her to ancient Native places and peoples. The cinematography positions her on the landscape as a female power emerging out of it. She is "shown frequently standing astride an area from such an angle that she seems to dominate the land around like an earth mother." The landscape she embodies also takes on fearsome characteristics, particularly that of the canyon of death, where she and Wes die: "the Pueblo city of the moon, a gaping orifice with teeth in the form of Indian carvings," offers Wes McQueen "his last refuge."[70] And in this cave, Wes inscribes Colorado's innocence on the wall with a knife, linking her discursively to the place, its Native feminine connotations, and death. The Freudian connections to the dark and fearful might of feminine sexuality surface in this description. But additionally, the insertion of Colorado's Native heritage into this image of the womb-like spaces that devour men with their teeth overlays a psychological fear of the racial Other. This racial fear increases exponentially because Colorado, with her blond hair, appears to be an extremely white woman. Unlike the other Sexualized Maidens, whose dark hair is a visual clue to their Native heritage, Colorado's blondness covers her race, making it possible for her to pass as white.

At the height of Indian relocation programs and African American migration to northern cities, this image could be read as playing on the fear of racial infiltration and the loss of white purity. However, the strategies of pairing Wes and Colorado and of positioning the dishonorable intentions of his "good" white girlfriend next to the honorable qualities of Colorado suggest a questioning of American racializing assumptions. In addition, the film questions assumptions about interracial marriage and what determines a good partnership. The narrative depicts Colorado as a strong partner for Wes—a woman who aids him and stands on her own as well. Her race does not affect Wes or their decision to wed, and in this respect the film embraces interracial relationships. Through their death, however, it also demonstrates the inability of such unions to succeed in America, to withstand the onslaught of American racial antagonism, which the film represents by the posse.

TRENDS IN DEPICTING THE 1940s SEXUALIZED MAIDEN

As the analyses of these films illustrate, the representation of the Sexualized Maiden works within each film to specific ends, depending on the film's interpretation of the western formula and other generic influences. However, these Sexualized Maidens hold in common a number of characteristics, resulting in a type of figure in the 1940s that is different from its ancestors in the 1920s and 1930s and its offspring in the 1950s and 1960s. These include her very particular physical appearance and the racial and sexual stigmas she inherits from her Indian parentage. In turn, these traits enhance colonial figures of race and sexuality that inform her characterization as a femme fatale who at once attracts and repels.

The Sexualized Maiden of the 1940s appears as a voluptuous and sensual woman whose costuming and physical movements accentuate her erotic image. She temporally corresponds with film industry and 1940s popular culture images of the highly sexualized pinup girl. Often considered a "wartime phenomenon," the pinup, as Mary Beth Haralovich's work clarifies, "was an extensive part of American cultural life" in the 1940s. The pinup girl's emergence in fan magazines and movie advertisements, and the influence her image had on advertising, signaled changing attitudes about representing sexuality and "a return to a variation of the sensationalized representations of women" seen in the early 1930s. In particular, the early 1930s depictions emphasized "sensational aspects of sexuality in terms of clothing, body positions, and narrative enigmas about illicit sex." Similarly, the Sexualized Maidens of the 1940s are markedly more sensual, more scantily clad, and more suggestive in their poses than their mid-1930s counterparts, who reflected a tendency toward "less overtly sexual" images.[71] Corresponding to the increase in this type of imagery in film, the industry's most consistent censorship of the Sexualized Maiden character had to do with her revealing clothing and shot compositions that suggested sexual activity. The connection between the pinup girl body and the theme of innate sexuality triggers a visual and mental impression of the woman's type as a western "bad girl" or a prostitute. The Sexualized Maiden films result in a fetishization of the woman's body as an object from which men derive visual and sexual pleasure.

Unlike the pinup girl, however, the Sexualized Maiden adds a racial component to the fetishization that metatextually marks her historical placement within society as a member of colonized Native peoples. All have mixed Indian-white heritage (Louvette, Pearl, and Colorado) or Mexican heritage (Chihuahua, who may be white or assimilated, based on her lack of a stereotypical Spanish accent). Chihuahua's and Pearl's characterizations also include overlays of Mexican stereotyping through costuming that conflates the two ethnicities and implicates both in the women's social inferiority. With the exception of Pearl, all of the Sexualized Maidens are very light skinned, and two carry additional signs of their white heritage: Louvette's blue eyes and Colorado's blond hair. But within the films' narratives, this evidence of whiteness rarely signals their reception into western European culture—it only works to underscore their hybridity, exotic combination of racial and sexual difference, and tenuous social position within western European culture. At work here is the pathology of race in which phobia and fetish function together within the stereotype of racial difference. As Homi K. Bhabha asks, "Is it not analogous to the Freudian fable of fetishism (and disavowal) that circulates within the discourse of colonial power, requiring the articulation of modes of differentiation—sexual and racial—as well as different modes of discourse—psychoanalytic and historical?"[72] What Bhabha clarifies is the sexual and Freudian undertones that mark the racialized and colonized figure as a fetish.

The categorization of the Sexualized Maiden within the colonial order informs the process Bhabha describes. As Mary Ann Doane's work on race and sexuality in cinema explicates, this overlay of race onto sexuality works to position the raced woman outside the realm of sexuality as defined by Freudian psychoanalysis. The western European study of the psyche, as defined by Freud's work, relegates the white woman to the periphery of what is knowable from a male perspective. Doane explains that, in Freud's work on women and sexuality, "Women (and it should be stressed that these are *white* European women) and 'primitive' races function in a similar way and through opposition to buttress the knowledge of the psyche to which psychoanalysis lays claim—with the crucial difference that white women constitute an internal enigma . . . while 'primitive' races constitute an external enigma."[73] The cinematic representation of the Sexualized Maiden invokes these modes of difference with respect to the femme fatale, who wields sex as a man does, making her a threat to male sexuality and male dominance; her threat doubles with the added mark of racial ambiguity. As a result, race and sex are conflated and construed as proof of racial degeneracy while forming a fetishized object that promotes both lust for and fear of the racial Other, the Indian woman.

This brings us to one of the underlying themes of the Sexualized Maiden films: that the woman's sexual taint resides in her Indian blood like a disease. The idea that her blood carries degeneracy, which in this case emerges symbolically as an exaggerated sexuality, fuels the fear of racial tainting through miscegenation. Symbolically, she represents a moment of taboo passion between Native American and white lovers. As such, her hybridity signals a particularly disruptive combination that places the fault in the mother's own colonized past. As Abdul R. JanMohamed explains about western "fetishization of the Other," "All the evil characteristics and habits with which the colonialist endows the Native are thereby not presented as the products of social and cultural difference but as characteristics inherent in race—in the 'blood'—of the native."[74] The mixed-blood Sexualized Maiden carries this evil draped in a seductive form, which both entices white men and threatens the entire white patriarchal order. The use of ethnically European actresses for such parts adds a level of dangerous erotic Othering that results, as Mary Ann Doane explains in her analysis of the mulatta figure in cinema, in a "curious distanciation [that] attends the knowledge that one is watching a white pretending to be a black pretending to be a white."[75] Similarly, in the Sexualized Maiden films, the audience watches a white woman play out the results of miscegenation in the mixed-blood character. As the films make clear, the Sexualized Maiden's Indian blood taints her white blood and results in the destructive force that kills. Thus a white actress mimicking this transformation takes the racializing narrative further by visually enacting, or embodying, a psychological dread of interracial mixing and death.

On a cultural level, such "putting on" of Indianness and performing of colonial stereotypes of the degenerate racial Other include the white woman in the colonial process and place her in the position of the racially marked woman. The white actress participates in mimicking a process similar to that which confines her within the patriarchal order and determines women's roles in western society. As a result, the Sexualized Maiden serves to reproduce fears about white women's access to power through sexual liberation or interactions with men utilizing their sexual language. Within the context of the 1940s, such a conclusion is not unwarranted. During the early 1940s, up to 6 million women were recruited to work in the defense industry alone, increasing the "female workforce by more than 50 percent." The increased presence of the women's liberation movements in relation to increasing divorce and premarital sex rates postwar may have threatened many traditional ideas about women's roles in society.[76] Certainly, the rising interest in Freudian psychoanalysis, which analyzes such fears, may have influenced the depiction of women in these westerns as dangerously out of control and disruptive to traditional gender roles and patriarchal stability. The white actresses playing the racially exotic femme fatale are juxtaposed continually to white women characters, who, while strong, are not unruly. For example, *Northwest Mounted Police*'s April shows her conviction to travel into the wild north country as a nurse, but her decision stays within the bounds of her female occupation. Clementine crosses the country for Doc but gives up nursing for teaching, a more emblematic profession in the genre. And Helen in *Duel in the Sun* attempts to work as Jesse's equal but laughingly allows him to ignore her suggestions. Such contrasts to the Sexualized Maiden character and the actresses' putting on "race" allow the viewer, the white hero, and the actress to participate in erotic role-playing while reifying traditional gender roles and condoning the transgressive woman's punishment. The result verges on a sadomasochistic interaction between the white actress, her character, and the white male character.

The system that emerges in these trends depends on repression of unruly difference. Miscegenation compromises the Sexualized Maiden's white bloodline. Her savage past, working through its sexual manifestation, ensures her inability to navigate in and her exclusion from civilized (white) society. Her death, like that of all femmes fatales, castrates her sexual threat to the male order and eliminates her wildness.

Northwest Mounted Police, My Darling Clementine, Duel in the Sun, and *Colorado Territory* were expensive A westerns directed and produced by well-known and respected men in the Hollywood film industry. In addition, they utilized top and rising stars such as Gary Cooper, Henry Fonda, Paulette Goddard, Joel McCrea, Jennifer Jones, and Gregory

Peck. In short, they drew big audiences and helped ensure the industry's rise from its Depression slump and the western's place in history as an enduring American genre. These films continue to find their voice in film history and criticism; thus their impact cannot be underestimated. The films illustrate an often ambiguous reaction to racial integration and mixed-race relationships that sends a message advocating violence toward those who are deemed sexually and racially different. The overlay of sexual and racial difference that forms the Sexualized Maiden suggests how deeply ingrained our colonial history is in our national rhetoric. The stereotypes used to construct the Sexualized Maiden—the femme fatale and the wanton Indian woman—function to maintain a phobia and fetish about race that verge on sadistic fantasy, which even the films attempting to examine themes of race and sexuality continue to reinforce.

Four

The Only Good Indian
Is a Dead Indian

The Sexualized Maiden of the 1950s and 1960s

There's a dead Apache in here. Get it out.
  —Ed Bannon referring to his Apache lover, Nita, in *Arrowhead*

Hesh-ke in Apache means "the murderess," and so she is.
  —*Mackenna's Gold*

A squaw?!
  —Laurie's reaction to Martin's marriage to a Comanche woman,
  Look, in *The Searchers*

She started stepping out with younger men. I caught her once and I
. . . anyway she died young. Choked to death on her own vomit.
  —Tex Smith remembering his Cherokee wife, Flo, in *In Cold Blood*

THE QUOTES ABOVE, TAKEN FROM four films released between 1953 and 1969, illustrate the diversity in the representations of the Sexualized Maiden character during that time. Familiar stereotypes emerge in these epigraphs, as the films build on two of the basic components that informed the 1940s Sexualized Maiden figure: the femme fatale and the wanton squaw. Rather than adhering to the fairly cohesive set of characterizations of the figure's predecessor, however, these films highlight, alter, or eliminate aspects of the previous Sexualized Maiden. As a result, the group appears disjointed in its characterization, each film displaying different manifestations of racism and uses of the woman's body within the narrative structure. However, the films bear the marks of their eras' political and social ideologies about race, creating similarities that distinguish the 1950s films from those of the 1960s. In addition, although the group spans almost twenty years and various genres, its members adhere to similar racial formations based on sexual racism. The racial formations used in the 1950s and 1960s Sexualized Maiden films—the Native femme fatale, who poses a hidden threat to white society, and the fallen Princess—inform the character's place and role in the film and in the societal hierarchy portrayed by the film. They also unify the films into groups across the decades.

Clearly defined in Charles Stember's study of black-white racism in America, sexual racism refers to the "sexual rejection of the racial minority, the conscious attempt on the part of the majority to prevent interracial cohabitation."[1] The prejudice surfaces as an overlay of sexual and racial stereotyping onto power relations that are often fueled by the dominant group's fear of loss of power. Directly linked to sexual activity, sexual racism reveals a significant white hostility toward interracial unions, in part because the act of interracial sex deconstructs social taboos. Once those taboos are broken down and made inconsequential, political, social, and sexual hierarchies also disappear—or so the fear implies. Sexual racism informs all of the Celluloid Maiden films in some manner. In the Sexualized Maiden films, it surfaces through the treatment of the Native American woman by either the hero, with whom she is involved, or white society. It also manifests itself in the films' wielding of her race as an explanation for other characters' neuroses and for her treachery. The theme of miscegenation as a transgression that threatens to pollute American purity continues as the fundamental underpinning of these films. In addition, Americans as a social group remain idealized through white character types—non-Negro, non-Mexican, non-Jewish, non–western or non–southern European. In sum, sexual racism structures the racial formation upon which the films build their narratives.

The four Sexualized Maiden films of the 1950s and 1960s—*Arrowhead* (1953), *The Searchers* (1956), *In Cold Blood* (1967), and *Mackenna's Gold* (1969)—offer a lens through which to view the changing conceptualizations of race and race relations over the sixteen-year period. True to the early cold war and civil rights period, the 1950s films display an overt racist response to the Sexualized Maiden character, through language and actions that reproduce the physical results of extreme bigotry. The films also capture a sense of the country's heightened state of paranoia brought on by the threat of communism and by the escalating racial conflict emerging from the civil rights movement and desegregation policies. *Arrowhead* and *The Searchers* both cast the hero as an extreme racist whose paranoia results in an aggressive and abusive relationship with a Native American woman.

In contrast, the 1960s films characterize the shifting dynamics of the civil rights movement by inverting the dysfunctional relationship and submerging the issue of race in the film's structure. Thus, as African Americans and other racial minorities resorted to violence against a white-biased system, the Sexualized Maiden figure became the psychologically unstable instigator of violence, and the white hero or society the bewildered recipient. In keeping with the liberal idea that overlooking racial difference eases integration, the narratives of *In Cold Blood* and *Mackenna's Gold* outwardly appear to accept integration and interracial mixing, but the manner in which the 1960s films present the Sexualized Maiden reinforces easily identifiable stereotypes and racial assumptions. In sum, as the nation's various groups found different means by which to deal with the changing racial and social dynamics, so too did the film industry.

That the Sexualized Maiden films of the cold war and Vietnam eras registered the reaction to the character differently than did their predecessors is most clearly seen in the dynamics between the hero and the Native woman. Like the 1940s character, the later Sexualized Maiden may be a sexual partner to the white hero, but her ultimate relationship tends to be based on a power dynamic in which her sexual influence no longer drives men's actions. In other words, the sexual power exuded by the 1940s character diminishes considerably. The addition of a love component in the form of an affair or an unsuccessful marriage appears only as a mechanism in the plot that works to complicate and increase the psychological response of the hero and occasionally of the woman, inevitably resulting in the hero's rejection of her. Ed Bannon's hateful remark, above, illustrates this by reducing his lover Nita to a racial object: "There's a dead Apache in here. Get it out." In general, the films diminish the role of love, focusing more on the woman's value as a cultural commodity whose race plays a role in her objectification.

Along with its focus on the effects of racism on individuals, this group of films incorporates a fallen Princess type with the Sexualized Maiden character. The Sexualized Maiden's connection to the Princess figure emerges most clearly during the 1950s and 1960s, in a number of the characters that represent a degenerated Princess. The Princess holds a symbolic position in the western as the necessary link between American exceptionalism and American right to the land. Though she is an idealized and romantic character, western European culture keeps her at arm's length. The Sexualized Maiden, in contrast, destroys the symbolic possibility and idealized image of Native Americans, through her physical appearance in some cases and through acts of violence, treason, and base behavior in others.

In the 1940s, the Sexualized Maiden's mixed heritage caused a split personality, and her Indianness emerged in a symbolic representation of the taboo miscegenation act. In other words, the hypersexualized figure represented the physical action of mixed-race sex. In the 1950s and 1960s, the woman's mixed heritage and hypersexuality are not always the main issues; rather, the focus shifts to her "ignoble" Indian status. Two of the films—*Arrowhead* (1953) and *Mackenna's Gold* (1969)—rely on the femme fatale image to convey the Sexualized Maiden's inherent ignobility, danger to white society, and innate savagery. By so doing, they resemble the 1940s Sexualized Maiden films most closely. *The Searchers* (1956) and *In Cold Blood* (1967) shift the representation away from earlier models by introducing characters that might very well have been Princess figures had their physical attributes or their desire for "stepping out" with younger men and drinking not been emphasized.

As mentioned above, the films of each decade exhibit similar representations of race and racism through their use of narrative perspective and tone, through the level of racism displayed by the characters, and through the actions of the white hero. Approaching an analysis from the standpoint of decades illuminates the contrasts between the 1950s figures and those of the 1960s. However, pairing the films by their representation of the Sexualized Maiden as either a femme fatale or fallen Princess underscores the shifting construction and symbolic use of the figure within the decades and over time. This method highlights the hybridization of the Sexualized Maiden with the Princess figure that foreshadows the Celluloid Maiden of the 1970s and 1990s.

THE FEMME FATALE

The 1950–1960s Sexualized Maiden films adapt the blueprint of the 1940s Sexualized Maiden, whose five primary traits—beauty, mixed-blood heritage, out-of-control sexuality, marginalization in white society, and deadliness to men—surface in the form of a pinup girl figure. Progressively, over the next two decades, the Sexualized Maiden's mixed-blood heritage ceases to be a factor, as does her uncontrollable sexuality. Nita (Katy Jurado) of *Arrowhead* (1953) remains a close relation to her 1940s sisters, retaining the five characteristics mentioned above, with slight modifications. No longer controlled by an unconscious sexuality, she utilizes her physical charms to further a deadly political motive. Nita is a cold war femme fatale; beautiful and crafty, she embodies the threat of communism and the global uprising of peoples of color. Her secondary role within *Arrowhead*'s anti-Indian and anti-Communist narrative of containment "gives the story s.a. [sex appeal] touches" and elevates the racializing undertones of the film's anti-Communist rhetoric.[2]

Arrowhead, based on a novel by W. R. Burnett and the life of one of General Crook's chief civilian scouts, Ed Bannon, takes place in Texas along the southern wagon route to California. The film focuses on a moment in 1878 when the Apaches have agreed to turn themselves in to the cavalry officials for peaceful deportation to reservations far from their homelands.[3] Ed Bannon (Charlton Heston) warns the colonel that peace is impossible with the Apaches and that their promise is a ruse. The Apaches, under their leader Toriano (Jack Palance)—a young insurgent who has just returned home from a white school in the East—kill the colonel.[4] At first condemned by the other white characters as too extreme in his racism and mistrust of the Apaches and blamed for the colonel's death, Bannon is vindicated as a scout and a hero by the end of the film, when he outwits and kills Toriano. As a reward for his service, the cavalry reinstates him as a scout and puts him "in charge of directing the clean-up for all the remaining Apaches." A number of minor narratives complicate this central plot: Bannon and Toriano are presented as "doubles" separated only by race and ideological position, and Nita's roles as Bannon's lover and an Apache "Mata Hari" add intrigue and spice.[5] Both Apache characters threaten the government's agenda for removal and the settlers' safety; thus they must be contained.

The United States' cold war policy of containment of communism, administered through the Truman Doctrine, the Marshall Plan, and alliances within the North Atlantic Treaty Organization, attempted to retard the global spread of the political ideology of communism and to promote democratic capitalism instead. On the eve of 1950, the United States' successes overseas must have seemed a tenuous and momentary victory. In 1949, Mao's Chinese Communist army toppled Chiang Kai-shek's American-supported government, and the Soviet Union exploded its first atomic bomb. Shortly thereafter, the Korean War erupted (1950), and revolutionary movements in Indochina against the French and the Dutch, and in the Philippines against the United States, grew in intensity. Local uprisings in the colonial nations of Africa also increased, adding to the "general wave of anti-imperialist insurrection in the world," all of which appeared as "signs of a world Communist conspiracy."[6] But by 1953, the year of *Arrowhead*'s release, the government's cold war politics had succeeded in "effectively limit[ing] Communist expansion in Europe." Stalin's death and the Korean War stalemate eased tensions somewhat; however, while "military confrontation between the major powers [seemed] unlikely to yield advantage to either side," the wariness continued. "The stakes of superpower rivalry remained potentially unlimited," and, Slotkin suggests, "it was logical for each side to perceive any conflict, in any region of the globe, as directly affecting the bipolar balance of power." According to Slotkin, in this climate, the cold war competition "transferred to the 'Third World,' where underdevelopment and the disorders of decolonization provided a favorable environment for anti-Western and Communist political movements." The increasing focus on the third world included China and Southeast Asia, Africa, and Latin America, with emphasis on "anti-American and leftist parties" in Guatemala and Iran, which threatened the Western powers' access to oil and the United States' economic interests in Latin America.[7]

During these years, in addition to its global anti-Communist activities, the U.S. government supported internal policies such as disloyalty searches, anti-Communist bills, and the House Un-American Activities Committee's investigation of millions of Americans. As a result, a full-blown "red scare" infected the country, affecting every corner of the United States.[8] Westerns of the period expressed the conflicting moods of the country through a diversity of films, which steadily increased in production from 1948 to 1956—an average of thirty-six per year, or about 25 percent of industry productions.[9] The aura of conspiracy, the rhetoric of containment upon which cold war politics relied, and the presentation of America as world leader and Western hero easily transferred into various subgenres of the western, including cavalry westerns such as *Arrowhead*.

In his discussion of the allegorical uses of the western, Michael Coyne suggests, "Just as red protagonists in the 1950s pro-Indian Western were actually surrogates for Black Americans, the blood-crazed insurgents of anti-Indian Westerns (Ford's *Rio Grande* (1950), *Arrowhead*) were scantily disguised frontier equivalents of the communist threat."[10] While Coyne's conclusion simplifies the uses of the Native figure in these films to metaphors for other anxieties, it certainly applies to the Apaches and to Nita. Nita's sympathy for the Apaches' cause drives her relationship with the film's Indian hater, Ed Bannon. Her Indian blood and her spying allegorically signal her "redness," or communism, which in turn threatens America's security and political agenda.

Arrowhead depicts the Apaches as untrustworthy savages whose degree of cunning, like that of the Communist, must never be underestimated. As a spy for the Apaches and a member of the Cavalry community in her role as laundress and the hero's lover, Nita is doubly dangerous and represents an internal threat to white society at the fort.[11] The following banter between Bannon and Nita in scenes 76–78 takes place shortly after his arrival at the fort. It offers the audience its first substantial encounter with Nita, establishes her as a threat, and underscores the potential deadliness of the game they play:

NITA: "All this you did when you knew Nita was waiting."
BANNON: "Believe me, I could've done without doing it."
NITA: "Will Bannon say he's glad to see me now?"
BANNON: "Get us drinks. . . . You know where. What makes an
        Apache so pretty? Her Spanish blood?"
NITA: "Maybe her love for you."
BANNON: "That's her Spanish blood acting up."
NITA: "We drink."
BANNON: "Against the law for an Indian to drink."
NITA: "I drink in Spanish."

BANNON: "Mexican."
NITA: "Mexican-Spanish."
BANNON: "Mexican-Spanish-Apache. (*They drink.*) If only you
   were ugly."
NITA: "I love you, Bannon."
BANNON: "What you'd love is for me to tell you what Bannon
   heard in his mind while he was out in the field. Did he hear
   Apache drums, did he hear the singing of the wise men?
   How much does he know? Does he know what's going to
   happen tomorrow?"
NITA: "Bannon is wrong. My brother and I were cast out by the
   Apaches because our blood was not pure."
BANNON (*grins*):   "You're here for them to keep an eye on me.
   That's all right—I can keep an eye on them through you. It
   depends on which of us gives something away first."

This dialogue focuses on the various minority ethnicities that contribute to Nita's ambiguous identity, which, within the context of this exchange, offers a valuable cover for espionage. To everyone at the fort except Bannon, Nita appears Mexican-Spanish, and her brother's name, Spanish, reemphasizes that connection. In addition, one never sees Nita with Apaches; rather, the film associates her with them through her brother's actions—he "goes over to them"—and through this conversation with Bannon. But clearly, Bannon realizes that, even though she is a mixed-blood, her tribal heritage cannot be underestimated; it fuels her hidden anti-American sentiments. Thus, although her beauty and sexuality seduce him, his comment "It depends on which of us gives something away first" underscores his awareness of the dangers involved in their sexually charged spy game and his need to control both her and himself. Like Nita, Bannon cannot afford to give anything away.

Nita's sliding ethnicity and her relationship with Bannon also emphasize a colonial history in which Spanish conquistadors sexually conquered indigenous women of Central America, creating mestizos. Bannon keeps Nita as a sexual partner to control her actions and her access to information. This, in conjunction with his preoccupation with her race, rekindles colonial history. His continual referencing of her as Spanish-Mexican-Apache categorizes these ethnicities hierarchically, with Spanish at the top and Apache at the bottom of a social and racial scale in which he, like the Spaniards, is considered superior to the Indians. Read within the milieu of the global insurgency movements among brown-skinned peoples at the time of filming, the narrative's deliberate rhetorical maneuvering to focus on Nita's Apache heritage and her occupation as a spy suggests a connection between the Apache and third-world, brown-skinned anti-imperialists and Communists.

Although Coyne's argument that celluloid Indians represented the Communist threat in disguise has merit in the context of contemporary global politics, I contend that Nita and the Indians of *Arrowhead* also exemplify Native Americans and Filipinos in their continual political struggles with the United States, as well as other indigenous groups across the globe battling colonial rule. Bannon's wariness toward Nita underscores the idea that those racial groups that were rebelling against colonialism and imperialism were as dangerous a threat to America's global and internal war on communism as were the light-skinned Soviets. Certainly, the CIA's liaison at Paramount, Luigi Luraschi, found cause for concern. According to Lary May's study, Luraschi, who was "operating in tandem with the State Department's request for favorable portrayal of non-whites," felt the original script "presented 'a story which the Commies could use to their advantage in Asia,' for it served as an 'indictment' of America's treatment of Apache Indians."[12]

The rewritten version of *Arrowhead* takes Luraschi's criticism into consideration by restructuring the source of discontent to reflect the adversarial relationship between Bannon and Toriano, the Apache renegade, and by refocusing the racial hatred of the earlier film script into these two characters. The released version received mixed reviews from film critics in the 1950s, but most supported it, calling it an "excellent movie . . . authentic" and "superbly acted and directed,"[13] and the Production Code office felt no need to censor Bannon's racism. Only after the 1950s did film critics begin to tackle the overt racism and anti-Communist tone of the film. Nita's character, however, remains unexplored as a significant bridge between racism and communism.

Nita's carefully crafted femme fatale image suggests that the film uses her character to comment not only on communism but on inter-racial relationships as well. She is a composite of characters from at least two initial screenplay versions, originally titled *Adobe Walls*. Nita gets her Mexican ancestry and beauty from Maria, a young Mexican prostitute offered to the Bannon character for entertainment purposes, and her Apache heritage and murderous intentions from a "big handsome Apache girl," Alice, Mrs. Weybright's maid. Alice attempts to murder Bannon for killing her fiancé, not her brother, as is the case with Nita. Thus the film consciously composes Nita as a racial and sexual figure intimately tied to a vehemently racist hero. According to the shooting script, Ed Bannon knows the Apache, "their tricks—their lies—he lived with them as a boy until he sickened of their cruelty and ran away." The hatred Bannon feels for all Apaches "is as deadly as it is unrelenting." According to psychologist Joel Kovel, such extreme hatred often "implies a kind of love, or at least an inability to rid the mind of obsession with the hated other. And these obsessions are invariably tinged with sexuality: a preoccupation with, a deadly curiosity about, the sexual excesses of the hated group, etched in the imagination by the acid of a harsh moralism."[14] Nita becomes the potentially deadly sexual vehicle through which Bannon's "preoccupation with . . . the hated group" is exorcised.

The neurosis of such racism surfaces in their love-hate relationship in their final scene together. Bannon, out of self-defense, has killed Nita's brother and, in what seems a sign of grief, gets drunk before telling Nita. In retaliation, Nita attempts to stab him while he sleeps. Catching her, he comments, "The Apache in your family came out." He then turns his hatred on her by threatening her with life in prison—an extreme sentence for attempted murder but not, perhaps, for espionage. To avoid this fate, Nita stabs herself.[15] Bannon moves quickly toward her, just as she sinks to her knees. A look of profound sadness crosses his face, and it remains even as their final words are spoken. Nita snaps, "Don't touch me . . . I hated your hands on me . . . I failed . . . but my people won't. Even now the dance they make will protect them when you go out against them. My hope is that you are alive when they take you." As she dies, Bannon quietly addresses the sentry: "There's a dead Apache in here. Get it out." Throughout the film, Bannon displays moments of extreme tenderness that appear out of character with his Apache-hating role. The tone of this final remark, punctuated by the sadness in his face, suggests that he cannot reconcile his feelings for her and must racialize and dehumanize her. Her power to seduce him even while he distrusts and hates her speaks both to the power of the femme fatale image and to the complexities of racial bigotry.

Similar circumstances and racializations shape the Apache character Hesh-ke (Julie Newmar), the femme fatale figure in *Mackenna's*

Arrowhead. Charles Marquis Warren, Paramount Pictures, 1953.

Gold (1969), but subtle racism replaces the overt racism depicted in
Arrowhead. A "sultry, sensuous—but violent and unstable" "nymphoma-
niac," Hesh-ke is a threat to the hero Mackenna—the man who hanged
her brother and with whom she once had an affair—and his potential
lover, Inga. Columbia Pictures' description of Hesh-ke rhetorically links
her name to her social marginality: "Hesh-ke . . . is a name that means
'murderess' in Apache; thus, an outcast from her own people, she is a
double outlaw."[16] This explanation also implies that her naming creates
her personality. A long knife scar on her face mars her physical beauty,
and this, along with her name, symbolizes her innate savagery and her
status as an outcast. Her name and scar constantly remind the viewer
that, although her Apache heritage adds to her savage nature, the source
of her evilness is deep within her psyche. Thus Hesh-ke's femme fatale
persona is not a product of political beliefs, as is the case with Nita. Nor
is it the result of biologically tainted blood, as seen in the 1940s Sexualized Maidens. Her ultimate formation as a femme fatale remains unde-
fined beyond a metonymical connection to her racially defined body.

While the specter of communism molded Nita's portrayal as a femme fatale, Hesh-ke embodies the rapidly changing, sometimes explosive, and often violent tenor of the mid-1960s—the years of the film's inception and production.[17] During the decade, "race occupied the center stage of American politics in a manner unprecedented since the Civil War era a century earlier. Civil rights struggles and ghetto revolts, as well as controversies over state policies of reform and repression, highlighted a period of intense conflict." The peaceful sit-in protests of 1960, the Freedom Riders of 1961, and the movement for black voter registration all over the South illustrated the changing face of American racial politics and marked the beginning of a nationwide mobilization against racial inequality and white violence against blacks. These movements helped to initiate a "'great transformation' of the American political universe, creating new organizations, new collective identities, and new political norms." The government responded with a series of civil rights laws in 1964 and 1965. The various groups' challenges to "racial practices and stereotypes" helped to "usher in a wave of democratizing social reforms" like the Economic Opportunity Act (1964), the Voting Rights Act (1965), the Elementary and Secondary Education Act (1965), Medicare and Medicaid, and Aid to Families with Dependent Children (1965). But the government's failure to rigorously enforce the civil rights acts, to make fundamental changes to the structure of the political and social system, and to protect minorities from white violence resulted in an escalation of protests and ghetto riots across the country from 1964 to 1967. These included riots in Harlem, New York, in 1964; Watts, Los Angeles, California, in 1965; Chicago, Illinois, and Cleveland, Ohio, in 1966; and a total of "eight major uprisings, thirty-three 'serious but not major' outbreaks, and 234 'minor' disorders in cities across the country" in 1967.[18]

In addition to riots, racially based social movements emerged in increasing numbers and with broadened agendas, ranging from Martin Luther King Jr.'s peaceful protest organizations to more militant civil rights groups. The latter type included the Nation of Islam (popularly known as the Black Muslims), the Black Panthers, the Native American Movement, the American Indian Movement, and the Chicano movement's Brown Berets and La Raza Unida. Feelings of "disaffection from mainstream America had multiplied dramatically. Criticism of the war in Vietnam mounted, as youthful protesters rebelled against traditional respect for the 'system.' The civil rights movement took a more militant thrust and expanded beyond African Americans to other minority groups, while the feminist movement revived to challenge social values and the family structure itself." The mounting violence of the decade was not confined to protest movements. It also surfaced in political assassinations—of President John F. Kennedy (1963), Martin Luther King Jr. (1968), and Robert Kennedy (1968)—as well as "grisly murders" like those committed by the Manson "family" (1969) and government-sponsored war atrocities, most graphically illustrated in the My Lai massacre in Vietnam (1968). All of this leads Michael Coyne to comment that the "world's most affluent nation was one of the world's most violent."[19]

The Hollywood western demonstrated the unease and "patriotic uncertainties" of these times. Forced to compete with the daily violence depicted on the evening news, and to combat the box-office slumps caused by the increasing popularity of television, the film industry increased its depictions of realistic violence. Hence, according to Coyne, during the mid-1960s, the genre was "characterized by cynicism or pessimism and, increasingly, brutality."[20]

Mackenna's Gold's narrative and its depiction of Hesh-ke as an Apache femme fatale and a member of an amoral group of bandits led by a psychotic Mexican with dreams of grandeur exhibit the characteristics noted by Coyne. Set in the mid-1870s, the film relates the newest chapter in an age-old myth about Cañon del Oro (Canyon of Gold), protected by the Apaches but sought after by generations of non-Indians and, now, by young Apache warriors who "want the gold to support them in their fight against the white man." The Mexican bandit Colorado (Omar Sharif) and his gang of Apaches and Mexicans, which includes Hesh-ke, are searching for the canyon. Colorado needs the gold to finance his dream of immigration to Paris, where he can live as a gentleman. He takes as his hostages his old accomplice, Marshal Mackenna (Gregory Peck), who has memorized a map of the canyon, and a young immigrant, Inga (Camilla Sparv). Their odyssey across the desert is punctuated by skirmishes with the cavalry—led by the dishonest Sergeant Tibbs (Telly Savalas), who also desires gold—and local townsmen who temporarily join the group. This collection of "upright men" from Hadleyburg includes a preacher, a newspaper editor, two English homosexual lovers, and the legendary Adams (Edward G. Robinson), who was blinded by Apaches when he excavated the canyon's gold years earlier.

In sum, it is a story about "how money corrupts even the most sensible, intelligent and upright."[21]

The film is structured according to a racial hierarchy. It does not display the open racism of *Arrowhead* but relies on a ranking of characters in what appears to be a social commentary on racially violent groups and the corruptness of American society. Mackenna, the white hero, represents society's best. He is not perfect by any means—he is a gambler and an old friend of Colorado's—but, unlike the other characters in the film, he never succumbs to gold fever, and he refrains from overt displays of violence. Inga, the pure and prudish symbol of white womanhood, momentarily falls prey to gold lust but abandons the metal to make a life with Mackenna.[22] The pillars of the Hadleyburg community mentioned above fall in social standing as their desire for easy economic gain increases; their greed eventually leads to their violent deaths at the hands of Apaches. Colorado's bandits form the lower echelon of the economic and social scale, with the Apaches as the base.

Colorado, who is well groomed, intelligent, and the most refined of the Mexicans, borders on the psychotic. The Apaches are presented as more respectful of tradition than the Mexican characters but exceedingly savage in their torturing of whites and, as the film's character sketches depict, animalistic and either cunning, like Hesh-ke, or stupid. The script, for example, describes Monkey as follows: "[He] puts one in mind of a rhino, squat, ugly, powerful. In some ways he is more simple than Hachita, more elemental, brutish, a troglodyte. To eat, to ravish, to kill, these are all that life has to offer him." Hesh-ke, the Old Woman, and the Pima represent three stereotypes of Indian women that appear in westerns—the Sexualized Maiden, the hag, and the fat squaw. According to the script notes, the Old Woman "is Hesh-ke who has somehow managed to survive into somewhat premature old age." In other words, she represents Hesh-ke's future. The Pima, on the other hand, is "never more than dim, with a sluggish mind in her fat body, she is nonetheless aware that her only chance to survive lies in dog-like submission."[23]

The narrative positions Hesh-ke, because of her beauty and militancy, and Inga, because of her whiteness and purity, more prominently than the other women, but below the men in social status. The two women are continually juxtaposed to each other in shots that emphasize their similarities and differences. In a number of scenes in which Hesh-ke guards Inga, the camera frames the two in medium close-ups, highlighting their similar heights and frames. In each case, Hesh-ke's dark hair and skin are contrasted with Inga's blond hair and pale complexion. These scenes are extremely short and tend to punctuate longer sequences of action in which the women do not participate but simply observe from a distance. As a result, the inserted shots appear out of context, purposefully placed to highlight the women's racial difference, but similar standing, within a male hierarchy. Such comparisons of the white woman with the Native American woman appear frequently in westerns as symbolic oppositions between purity and impurity, morality and immorality, and civilization and savagery. The cinematographic representations of Inga and Hesh-ke reflect this tendency; in addition, however, the shots visually remind the viewer of Hesh-ke's physical threat to Inga, whom Hesh-ke attacks at every opportunity. Other such attacks occur in isolated cases in other Sexualized Maiden films—Louvette threatens April once (*Northwest Mounted Police*), Chihuahua attacks Clementine in a tussle (*My Darling Clementine*), and Colorado protects Wes from being attacked by his white girlfriend (*Colorado Territory*). In direct contrast to Hesh-ke, however, the Sexualized Maiden figures in these other instances do not try to kill the white heroine. *Mackenna's Gold* adds a constant and higher degree of threat to the white woman.[24]

Thus the 1960s Sexualized Maiden is linked to a tangible and violent attack on "the innocent members of American society," as symbolized by Inga, from an unexpected source—a woman of color. Within the context of the racializing undercurrents of the narrative and the milieu of the mid-1960s, Hesh-ke's character may be read as reflective of the often militant reaction against the established society by groups not previously associated with violent action—women of color, students, Native Americans, Chicanos, and Vietnamese. During the years between the film's production and release, college students throughout the country and in Europe protested against "the establishment" and the war. Large groups of Native Americans marched on Washington to protest treaty violations. In addition, while Native activists, women, and children participated in demonstrations across the country against treaty violations and for land rights, water rights, and fishing rights, others occupied Alcatraz Island off San Francisco—a siege that lasted two years and captured sympathetic media attention. Chicano farm workers under Cesar Chavez peacefully protested in California and were supported by large numbers of non-Hispanics in their efforts to secure living wages and better working conditions. Overseas, to the amazement of American military officials and war advisers, the Vietnamese proved a formidable foe, and increased American presence there failed to "turn the tide of war."[25] Many of these activists represented the lower social and economic strata of American society or, in the case of the Vietnamese, a counter to the Western imperial power structure. Thus, if Hesh-ke symbolizes the disenfranchised racial Other, she also represents the threat from below, the rising up of the downtrodden.

One particular scene, which takes place at a canyon lake, emphasizes this idea of the threat from beneath—the unseen or unfathomed radical element. A sequence of images frames the interaction of the four primary characters—Colorado, Hesh-ke, Mackenna, and Inga—reinforcing Hesh-ke's desire for Mackenna, his rejection of her, and her jealousy of Inga. In a series of murky underwater shots, the camera focuses on a naked Hesh-ke attacking Mackenna and Inga from the lake's depths. The darkness of the water and her skill allow her to travel a great distance below the surface without being detected by the other characters. In the first shot, she swims under Mackenna, grabs his feet, and pulls him under. It becomes clear that she is not trying to kill him only after she kisses him. As Mackenna struggles with her and ultimately rejects her, the scene cuts to a medium reaction shot of Colorado, sitting naked on the shore, laughing. The sequence cuts back to an angry Hesh-ke, who submerges and swims toward an unaware Inga. The shots move from an underwater view of Hesh-ke swimming to a medium shot of Inga going under, and back to Hesh-ke as she attempts to drown Inga. Mackenna arrives in time to save Inga.

This sequence is softened a few scenes later, when Colorado dumps Hesh-ke in the lake, but its powerful imagery remains as a reminder that even a naked and unarmed Hesh-ke is a very real threat to both Mackenna and Inga. The nudity and the dramatic underwater cinematography ensure the memorable quality of the scene.[26] They also subtly reinforce the racializing structure of the film. While the nonwhite characters unashamedly exposed their naked bodies to the viewer, the white characters remain protected by clothing, suggesting the stereotype of dark-skinned peoples as sexually more aggressive and available than whites. Similarly, the framing of Hesh-ke's dark-skinned body in a nebulous and dusky space underneath the white characters underscores the terror of unforeseen danger and drowning, but it also offers a racializing metaphor about society that situates minorities below the white elite. Through the sequencing of the scene, Hesh-ke appears as an immoral and violent racial Other who rises out of the depths to threaten the stability and tranquility of white America.

Hesh-ke's relentlessness and cold-blooded persona make her an effective femme fatale threat. She is an even less sympathetic character than the "terrible destroyer," Louvette, from *Northwest Mounted Police* (1940) and *Arrowhead*'s Nita. Thus she illustrates an extreme in the representation of the Sexualized Maiden in contrast to those of the late 1940s—Pearl Chavez in *Duel in the Sun* (1946), Chihuahua in *My Darling Clementine* (1946), and Colorado in *Colorado Territory* (1949)—who elicit some sympathy as victims of racism and miscegenation. Such sentimentality disappears by the late 1960s, and Hesh-ke's femme fatale qualities ensure a thoroughly negative reading of the Native American woman. Although Hesh-ke has supposedly been cast out of Apache society for amoral behavior, her actions continue to be linked with her racial heritage because of her skin color, Apache clothing, and connection to other minority figures. Though her individual deeds are depicted as the sum of all of this, they do not stand alone but are framed by the Apaches' torture of the townsmen, Monkey's continual attempts to rape Inga, and Colorado's psychotic behavior. Their actions warrant their violent deaths, and the film extends no sympathy at their passing. As a result of these depictions, an image emerges of nonwhites as unstable, volatile, and unsavory. Through such racial constructions, and in conjunction with Hesh-ke's metaphorical representation as the threat from below, the film dismisses the very real economic and political factors that led many of the 1960s activist groups to violence.

THE FALLEN PRINCESS AS SEXUALIZED MAIDEN

The image of the fallen Princess has long existed in noncinematic representations of Native American women. Rayna Green's findings in generations of music and literature reveal that the woman's "nobility as a Princess and her savagery as a Squaw are defined in terms of her relationship with male figures." Green argues that the act of sex determines whether a woman is a Princess or a squaw figure—the latter of which is described as unheroic, usually unattractive, and often the butt of jokes.[27] Though the film industry challenges this rigid qualification through its multifaceted depictions of the Celluloid Maiden, there are instances in which Green's findings apply precisely. Two pre-1950s examples, both Cecil B. DeMille characters, stand out as the beginnings of this trend: Naturich (*The Squaw Man*, 1931) and Hannah (*Unconquered*, 1947). In both cases, the woman's birth makes her a Princess character, but particular actions hint at her less savory, darker side. Naturich, as discussed previously, seduces Jim and murders his enemy, and Hannah beats the young white woman, Abby, whom her husband desires. Hannah's decidedly more aggressive and violent behavior, and DeMille's depiction of her people as savage reactionaries, ensures her unfavorable image and foreshadows the portrayal of Hesh-ke. But these sliding figures are complex: both women love their white husbands, perform heroic actions, and commit suicide. Although Hannah is more closely linked to the Sexualized Maiden image, she does not exemplify the 1940s type, because of her full-blood Indian heritage and her lack of visible sexuality. Nor does she lean toward later fallen Princess figures, because of her extreme violence. She does, however, signal the shifting hybrid trend of the 1950 and 1960s.

Two representations emerge between 1956 and 1967 that escalate the deconstruction of the symbolic Princess image through the use of Sexualized Maiden characteristics: Look in *The Searchers* (1956) and Flo in *In Cold Blood* (1967). Each of the films focuses on a different component of Green's squaw figure in such a way as to gloss over the woman's social status and lack of femme fatale qualities. *The Searchers* frames Look as a plump and comic figure; *In Cold Blood* depicts Flo as a promiscuous drunk. These two characters reflect the changing depictions of the Sexualized Maiden figure and its eventual hybridization with the Celluloid Princess.

The treatment of Wild Goose Flying in the Night Sky—or Look (Beulah Archuletta)—in John Ford's *The Searchers* clues the viewer in to the fact that she is not a Princess figure but, rather, a 1950s Sexualized Maiden. The young Comanche woman's plump figure and comical representation make her the constant butt of jokes and abuse, which in turn downplays, even negates, her desire to be married and her social status among her people. Look's position within the narrative structure works on one level as a "vulgar parody of the 'Indian marriage' theme that *Broken Arrow* invests with so much liberal sentiment."[28] On another level, the outright abuse she receives from her husband Martin (Jeffrey Hunter) moves beyond the humorous to the racially pathological, revealing a shocking aspect of Martin's generally gentle character. Look's small but important role expands Ford's exploration of the effects of sexual racism on a community and the contradictory applications of racializing logic to issues of miscegenation.

Based on the novel by Alan Le May, *The Searchers*, now considered John Ford's "masterpiece" and the "*ne plus ultra* of the genre," met with lackluster reviews in 1956 despite its success at the box office.[29] It has subsequently received critical acclaim for its cinematography, epic narration of "the American experience," and attempts to deal with the tensions of racism and miscegenation. Along this line of analysis, it has also been suggested that the film is Ford's attempt to atone for "the simpleminded racism of his earlier films" and that it is a vehicle through which he explores and exposes "the complex of thought and feeling that constitute racialist hatreds; shows how these develop and operate at the level of individual psychology and in the behavior of communities; and shows above all how racialist structures of thought produce a 'logic' which, if we accept and pursue it, traps us in cycles of violence and retribution without limits and beyond all reason." As a result, the film "goes further than other Westerns in dramatising and implicating [the viewer] in the neurosis of racism" and in forcing the viewer to confront his or her participation in the process.[30]

Set in 1868, *The Searchers* follows the epic journey of Ethan Edwards (John Wayne) and his half-breed nephew Martin Pawley in their quest for Ethan's niece and Martin's adopted half-sister Debbie (Natalie Wood), the sole survivor of an Indian massacre that claimed the rest of the family. Through a series of narrative frameworks that includes letters from Martin to his girlfriend Laurie Jorgensen (Vera Miles), parallel narratives, and tangential actions, the film "traces a network of racist loathing" of Indians "from Ethan, into White society and out to the implementation of government policy by the cavalry."[31] Supported in their efforts by the surrounding white community, Ethan and Martin spend seven years searching for Debbie, whom they eventually find living as one of the wives of the Comanche chief Scar (Henry Brandon). Ethan's motive throughout the film is to kill Debbie, whom he now considers defiled and no longer white because of her miscegenational relationship with Scar, while Martin's is to protect his "sister" from Ethan and to bring her home. Martin acts as a safety valve and witness to Ethan's racialist behavior, which fluctuates between heroism and extreme sadism, the latter of which Martin also falls prey to in his relationship with Look. The two men eventually rescue Debbie; Look is killed by the U.S. cavalry, freeing Martin to marry Laurie; and Ethan's motivation for finding Debbie turns to familial protection as he brings her home and places her in the Jorgensens' foster care.

Within the narrative structure, which is based on and attempts to probe a community's fear of miscegenation, "women are the motive for male activity (it's women who are being avenged, it's women the men are trying to rescue)."[32] As an Indian woman whose racial and tribal heritage connects her to that which threatens white women — the Comanche Indian man — Look falls outside this paradigm. Ford's careful representation of Look ensures this placement through a systematic devaluation of the Princess image that idealizes miscegenation and that was popular in pro-Indian westerns at the time. Three approaches are utilized to achieve this: the comic presentation of Look, other characters' reactions to her, and her positioning with respect to Laurie and Debbie.

Look is, as Douglas Pye points out, "from the outset a figure of fun — fat, comically modest and, in conventional terms, sexually unattractive." Although the elements surrounding Look add to this comic tone, she never acts the buffoon; rather, she carries herself with dignity. Accompanied in her first scenes by lighthearted music, Look's story emerges as a narrative contained within a letter from Martin to Laurie.[33] The sequence begins with Laurie reading Martin's letter to her family and potential suitor, Charlie McCorry (Ken Curtis). As she reads the following, the scene cuts to Martin bartering for a blanket: "At one of the agencies we outfitted with all kind and manner of trade goods, figurin' that'd make it easier for us to come and go. [Pause in Laurie's voiceover.] You'd laugh if I told you what was our biggest seller." At this point, Laurie's voice stops and the scene continues, illustrating Martin's actions with Look's music playing in the background. Look, a well-dressed young woman, eagerly watches as her father, who is dressed as a chief figure in a full breastplate and eagle headdress, negotiates her marriage price with Martin, who believes he is trading for a blanket. As Martin holds up items for their inspection, Look hopefully smiles at her father, who shakes his head, establishing her value and status. The two men finally settle on two bowler hats.

Ethan interrupts this scene and its music to usher Martin away from

The Searchers. John Ford, Warner Brothers, 1956.

the agency. As they ride off, discussing Ethan's newest lead on Scar—the Comanche chief who captured Debbie—the music becomes sober and the mood tense. Look emerges into the scene, accompanied by her music, only after Ethan asks Martin why Look is following them. Martin, believing Look follows him because of the blanket he purchased, tells her to go back. The mood shifts as Ethan informs a confused Martin that he has purchased a wife, not a blanket. Laughing, Ethan calls "Mrs. Pawley" forward to "join their merry group." At this point, Ford cuts back to a reaction shot of Laurie reading, "There's one more thing I got to tell you before you hear it from Ethan, how I got myself a wife . . . a little Comanche squaw." Laurie's displeasure is revealed in her exclamation "A squaw!" and her throwing the letter into the fire, to which Charlie responds, "A squaw, ha ha."

Ford cuts back to Look and the two men. The scene begins with the same lighthearted tone but quickly deteriorates into a violent situation. As Martin and Ethan sit around a campfire drinking coffee, Ethan continues ribbing Martin, who attempts to explain to Look, through Ethan, who speaks Comanche and acts as interpreter for the couple, that their marriage is a mistake. Out of frustration, Martin stomps off to lie down on his bedroll. Look follows and lies down on her own roll next to him, suggesting her desire to act as his wife. A long shot frontal view frames Martin as he angrily sits up and kicks Look out of what should be their marriage bed and down the hill. The scene cuts to a medium shot of Ethan sitting on a log, laughing uproariously. An audible thud sounds from the area where Look should have landed as Ethan jokes, "That's grounds for divorce in Texas. You're rough." The film cuts back to a long shot of Martin running down toward Ethan.[34] In anger, Martin tells Ethan to ask Look about Scar. At this moment, the light music and laughter stop, and the film's dark tone returns. The two approach and lift a terrified Look into the frame, interrogating her about Scar and Debbie. Look's fear shows in her expression and her continual movements away from the men. The encounter ends with Look gathering her blankets and exiting the scene.

The last framing sequence begins with Ethan and Martin studying an arrow of stones Look made, contemplating whether she went the direction in which it points or whether it is a sign for them regarding Debbie. The scene cuts back to Laurie reading the letter, in which Martin states they would "never know because the next day it snowed and we lost the trail." The men later find Look's body in a Comanche village, a victim of a cavalry massacre.[35]

As both Peter Lehman and Marty Roth have noted, Look's treatment in these sequences cannot be disentangled from the film's themes of racism and miscegenation.[36] She occupies the position of racial scapegoat for both white male and female sexual frustration. This is most clearly illustrated in the framing of her story within Martin and Laurie's relationship and in the context of Laurie's reaction to her and Debbie. Look is initially seen through Laurie's voice and Martin's words; thus she is positioned as Laurie's rival for Martin's attention. Laurie's indignant response — "A squaw!" — seems to be a reaction to being jilted for a woman she considers racially inferior. But Laurie's reaction to Look carries greater significance, as is indicated by a statement that she makes later to Martin about Debbie, who has been living as Scar's wife. Martin has just returned home, broken up Laurie's wedding to Charlie, and is about to leave again in a final attempt to find Debbie. In anger, Laurie asks, "Fetch *what* home? The leavings of a Comanche buck sold time and again to the highest bidder?" She adds that even Debbie's mother would have wanted Ethan to put a bullet in Debbie's brain rather than let her suffer the ramifications of rape by an Indian. Again, Laurie's racist outbursts stem from jealousy and thwarted sexual desire; however, her later statement also reveals that the fear of racial taint is so strong that even a soul as gentle as she advocates violence to a woman. Furthermore, her words connect Look and Debbie as Comanche squaws sold to the highest bidder. In Look's case, that bidder is Martin, who treats her as an unwanted piece of property and attacks her because he is frustrated that he married the wrong woman. Debbie never experiences such violence on screen. In fact, while violence to white women permeates the film through references and off-screen action, Martin's actions toward Look are the only instances presented visually to the audience, and they are rationalized by her status as a comic squaw figure—a "fat" and "sexually unattractive" Indian woman.[37]

Critics have commented on the seeming contradictions in these scenes between the comic tone and the overt violence, suggesting that the incongruity lies in Ford's discomfort with the material or the genre's tendency to treat Indian women in such a manner.[38] But, in fact, his choices make perfect sense. Ford's direction throughout the film suggests an understanding of racism as a neurosis that permeates a community, including the viewer. To illustrate this, Ford must reposition the overt racism exhibited by Ethan onto the two most likable and uncharacteristically racist figures: Laurie and her mixed-blood lover, Martin. Furthermore, Ford must project that neurotic racism onto an innocent Indian subject whose predicament parallels Debbie's to some extent. Thus, for Laurie's and Martin's reactions to be believable, Look must not be a typical Sexualized Maiden, that is, sexually aggressive, provocative, or dangerous; rather, she must be an atypical Princess figure.

The film first depicts Look as a Princess type by demonstrating her agency: she decides to marry and leave her family for Martin, and later she removes herself from an abusive situation. It downplays this agency through her comic presentation but does not eliminate it completely. Second, the film devalues Look's status through Laurie's initial remark—"A squaw!"—Martin's actions, and Charlie's and Ethan's laughter. This reduction of her value as a person to a racial object legitimizes, to some extent, their reaction to her. If she were a prototypical Princess, Laurie's remark and Martin's actions would be unthinkable, because in most pro-Indian westerns, the leading white male and female characters rise above the norm, seeing past issues of race to the Princess's innate value and social status. Third, and most important, the film contrasts Look's situation to Debbie's. Scar takes Debbie into captivity against her will but raises her as a member of the Comanche community and as his wife. Look, on the other hand, chooses to enter white society through her marriage to Martin, but she is not taken into the family fold; rather, she is rejected from it. In sum, the white characters exorcise their fear of Debbie's miscegenation by projecting it violently onto the body of Look.

For the most part, Look should be considered a Princess type: she is a chief's daughter; she is gentle and submissive; she displays no wanton sexual behavior; and she shows no violent tendencies. The film's display of overt violence toward her, in addition to its depiction of her as a comic character, however, characterizes Look as a 1950s Sexualized Maiden. *The Searchers*, as did *Arrowhead* in 1953, presents its racial aggressions without subtlety and with undisguised misogyny toward the woman of color.

More in keeping with late-1960s films such as *Mackenna's Gold* (1969), *In Cold Blood* (1967) applies subtle methods of racial stereotyping in its representation of Flo Buckskin as a fallen Princess type whose Sexualized Maiden tendencies result in her son's psychotic behavior. The film is based on Truman Capote's "nonfiction novel" of the same title, which recorded the murder of the Clutter family in Holcomb, Kansas, on November 15, 1959, by two petty criminals, Perry Smith and Dick Hickock.[39] Published in 1965, the year of the two men's executions, Capote's book attempts to document, through "observation" and materials "taken from official records" or from "interviews with the persons directly concerned" the events surrounding the "gruesome and mystifying crime."[40] Over the course of the "novel," Capote reveals that a burglary planned by Dick Hickock turned into a brutal massacre when the mentally unstable Perry Smith snapped because of Hickock's continued attempts to rape the Clutters' daughter, Nancy. An underlying social commentary emerges in Capote's attention to the childhood shaping of Smith's psychological instability, which points to a variety of environmental factors, including a dysfunctional family, abusive nuns and Salvation Army nurses, school bullies, and violent attention from "queens" in the merchant marine.[41] Capote embellishes these facts with a western-style narrative tone. Leslie Fiedler claims that, in keeping with a new 1960s "venture" in writing that exploited traits of the western, *In Cold Blood* "turns out to be an almost classic Western in theme, involving a white man and an Indian (Capote's Perry has a Cherokee mother, from whom he inherits his thick straight black hair and his 'iodine-colored' skin) bound together in a homosexual alliance against the respectable White world around them; and the scene is westernmost Kansas, more Far West than Midwest, Capote himself remarks, with cattle and Stetson hats and Colorado just over the horizon."[42]

This exploitation of western elements and tone transfers onto the film character Flo Buckskin (Sammy Thurman), Perry's (Robert Blake) Cherokee mother, champion barrel rider, rodeo princess, and promiscuous drunk, who evokes stereotypical memories of the western genre and the Celluloid Maiden.[43] Unlike Capote's novel, Richard Brooks's adaptation condenses the social causes leading to Perry's criminal behavior and repositions them onto Flo. Complex editing frames her as the underlying cause of Perry's psychotic tendencies. Thus, where Capote places the blame for Perry's psychological instability on a dysfunctional family and a flawed social welfare system, the film blames the mother.[44] It does this by emphasizing her Indian heritage through Mr. Smith's remarks and through its predominantly white cast. In a manner reminiscent of *The Searcher*'s handling of Look, the film's introduction of Flo evokes nostalgia for the Indian Princess stereotype and then deconstructs the image with scenes of Flo drinking and "stepping out with younger men."

Flo's role surfaces in two vignettes, presented as Perry's memories, and in his father's explanation of their family history to police. The three scenes are important to the viewer's understanding of how Perry Smith has become an unstable, brooding, romantic, "cold-blooded killer." The first scene begins with Perry Smith sitting in Dick's (Scott Wilson) car, strumming his guitar as they drive toward the Clutters' farm. Triggered by the sight of baby shoes hanging from Dick's rearview mirror, Perry flashes back to his childhood. The film cuts to a close-up of young Perry's face; the camera dollies back and pans right to focus on a man (Tex, played by Charles McGraw) sitting astride a cattle chute, then pans left to a young woman on horseback with a rope in her hands. As she starts forward, the camera pulls back to frame her ride toward the calf that the man let out of the chute. Behind her, "Tex and Flo" is written on the side of a truck. A series of short close-ups shows her technique as she ropes the calf, watched by the man and boy as well as three other children sitting to the side. The woman gets back on the horse and rides toward the man, who puts the young boy in front of her on the saddle, and the scene closes with the two riding around the ring.

The second relevant scene takes place during the murder investigation, just as Perry and Dick escape over the border to Mexico. Tipped off by Dick's last cellmate, Floyd Wells, about the identities of the killers, detectives visit Tex Smith, looking for information about Perry. The camera frames Tex standing in the cloth-covered doorway of his home in an ill-fitting raincoat. As the two detectives enter the space, the shot cuts to a close-up of a wall. Centered almost full frame is a rodeo poster from Dillon, Montana, "featuring Tex and Flo Smith." To the right is a medium close-up photo of Flo and Perry on her horse. The camera pulls back to reveal more photos, including one of Tex with Perry as a young man and one of Perry as a child. The photograph of Perry and his mother forms the backdrop as Detective Alvin Dewey (John Forsythe) hands Tex a photograph and asks if it is his son Perry. Tex answers, "Yup, that's him all right. Gets his looks from his mother, part Cherokee." Tex proceeds to explain, "I taught my kids the Golden Rule. . . . Our children were no trouble to us as long as we were together. . . . But she wanted the wild life, so she took the kids and run off, turned them against me. All but Perry. But I don't know what got into her. She started drinking, turned into a hopeless drunk. She started stepping out with younger men. I caught her once and I . . . anyway she died young. Choked to death on her own vomit." Tex concludes his reminiscing by telling the men that he took Perry with him "roaming to forget it all . . . how that boy loved me." The scene ends with the two detectives silently leaving the old man, without informing him of Perry's latest crime.

Flo's final scene follows shortly thereafter and again takes the form of a flashback. A series of intercut close-ups and point-of-view shots begins with Perry in the foreground of a Mexican hotel room, sifting through photographs as Dick and a young prostitute dance and drink behind him. The shots cut between Perry's face, Dick's, and the woman in rapid succession until they linger on Perry as he looks at two pictures—one of his mother on her horse and the other of the two of them. The pictures are similar to those seen at Tex's home and set at the same moment as Perry's original flashback. The images and background activities initiate

Perry's remembering, and the camera cuts to a shot of Flo, dressed in a slip, standing where the Mexican woman had been moments earlier. Another series of quick close-ups moves from Flo's face, to Perry's face, to Flo reaching down toward a man and pulling him into the frame to dance with her, and back to Perry with his pictures. The point of view shifts suddenly to a low-angle shot of Flo dancing with the man, cuts to child-Perry and his siblings watching, and back again to Flo's drink-blurred face. This toggling of images continues while Flo disrobes and the two fall onto the bed. As the children bow their heads to avoid watching their mother, Tex arrives. While the children watch, he hits Flo and then takes off his belt and whips her. Finally, Tex grabs Flo by the hair and begins to pour whiskey over her head and back. Finished, he looks at Perry, and the sequence cuts back to Perry in the present.

Clearly, the sequencing of the three scenes ensures the devaluation of Flo as a character and as a role model for Perry. The first scene establishes a happy family unit—Flo, Tex, and their four children—and Perry's place as the youngest and favorite. It also offers clues to the family's occupation within the rodeo circuit and the mother's beauty, grace, and skill as a roper. The happy memory indirectly creates a romantic composite of western symbols that includes the beautiful young Indian woman and the cowboy image. In the combination of Flo's youth, beauty, and children, she resembles a Princess figure rather than the Sexualized Maiden, who, in the past, was never depicted as a motherly character. The second scene narrates Flo's decline. The rodeo poster and her photos with Perry remain proof of the ideal Flo, but Tex's rendition of her contradicts these images. His comment that she desired "the wild life" emphasizes her agency in the process; according to the film, she is not the victim of social circumstances. The final scene, which includes the children, validates the father's description and justifies his actions. These images clearly connect Flo to the breakup of the family unit and depict her as a destructive force, but it is these scenes' placement in connection with another key scene that links Flo to Perry's mental breakdown.

This pivotal scene is edited into the narrative just prior to the last scene with Flo. Detective Alvin Dewey and another man sit in an unidentifiable room. Dewey holds a report titled "Murder Without Apparent Motive" while the man explains the psychological study's findings with regard to four killers: "They all had certain things in common. They all committed senseless murders, all felt physically inferior and sexually inadequate. Their childhood was violent, or one parent was missing, or someone else had raised them. They couldn't distinguish between fantasy and reality. They didn't hate their victims—they didn't even know them. They felt no guilt about their crime and got nothing out of it. And, most important, they told the police or a psychiatrist that they felt the urge to kill before they committed the murder. Their warnings were disregarded." The summary also describes Perry Smith. A motorcycle accident mangled his legs, and his disgust over Dick's constant references to sex seems to suggest his sexual impotence. The scene with Tex and the detective illustrates the violence, as does Perry's time in an orphanage, which he mentions to Dick in passing early in the film. And as the scene that follows this one confirms, Perry slides easily from reality into fantasy with little distinction between the two. This is the only scene of its type that references the psychological studies on psychosis that Capote discusses in the book. Hence, with this information in mind and the scenes' deliberate placement together in the editing sequence, the viewer cannot but connect Flo to Perry's psychosis. Nearer the end of the film, Brooks does include two quick moments that allude to some of the social factors that initiate Perry's psychosis—one of Perry flashing on his father with a gun just as he snaps and shoots Mr. Clutter, and one prior to his hanging, in which he tells of his father's own mental collapse after years of broken dreams. Though these scenes expand the viewer's understanding of Perry, their placement late in the film's narrative prevents their dispelling the conclusion that the Cherokee woman Flo is the root of Perry's mental dysfunction and the ultimate cause of the Clutters' murders. The subtle methods used to develop this racializing subtheme have much in common with those used in *Mackenna's Gold*, in which issues of race and racism are expressed through the visual structure of the film, and with *The Searchers*, which utilizes editing to similar ends.

Richard Brooks's and cinematographer Conrad Hall's noirish black-and-white styling of the film accentuates its psychological edge and adds a gritty urban quality to its realism. Typical of the increasing portrayal of realistic violence on screen, *In Cold Blood* appears to reflect the growing unease across America in 1967. Echoing the tenor of the moment, film critic Bosley Crowther asks about Perry and Dick, "Why did two who had originally intended robbery, and who had not committed murder before, suddenly come to the point of slaughtering four innocent people in cold blood? And what does this single explosion of violence indicate as to society's pitiable vulnerability to the kooks that are loose in the land?" The answer to his question lies, according to the film's visual narrative, at least in part in the degenerate racial Other amalgamated into the American populace. Max Kozloff points toward this in his analysis of *In Cold Blood*: "For here Capote has depicted the berserk but nondescript killer in the American crowd. Not the criminal who blends into the crowd, not the desperado who stands always apart from it, but the psychopathic individual who is *of* the crowd itself—or rather, the mob."[45] Though Kozloff refers to Perry and excludes race as a component, the film's editing and its use of the Native American woman as the root of this danger, as described above, include Flo and race in the equation.

The addition of Flo Buckskin's composite figure to a primarily urban crime thriller represents a cinematic shift, a crossing over of the Celluloid Maiden figure into nonwestern generic formats and the conflation of the two western figures that make up that figure.[46] Through the mid-1950s, the Celluloid Maiden figures fall on opposing sides of the noble/ignoble savage paradigm, symbolizing either the best of Native America and the ability to assimilate into western European culture or the worst of Native America and the failure to assimilate. Flo embodies the destruction of this model and the initiation of a hybrid of the two. But her shallow depiction as a recognizable Princess and Sexualized Maiden figure ensures her confinement within the western iconography of Native American women. In other words, and more so than in the case of Look, Flo never develops into a "real" person. Instead, the characters who remember and describe her for the viewer envision her only in simplistic and racially stereotypical terms: as a rodeo Princess, as a drunken "squaw," as a sexually aggressive Indian woman. Although her character is transplanted from the western to a contemporary urban setting, the generic western formulas and racial structures that define her into a characterization of old stereotypes—the Princess and the drunken Indian—remain firmly in place. Thus her Cherokee heritage and Native American background are underscored as negative elements rather than being celebrated or deemphasized.

The combination of contemporary setting and western conventions works to isolate and accentuate Flo's difference from the other characters even while she is an integrated member of society and pulls the ideological myth of the frontier into the urban present. Read within the context of the late 1960s, the rising urban presence of Native American and other minority voices, and the increasingly violent tenor of the American social landscape, Flo's representation signals the failing ideal of a racially assimilated America as symbolized through the Princess figure's union with the white hero. The film depicts her only as an alcoholic mother so out of control that she loses all she had—fame as a rodeo princess, a white husband, and an adoring family. In the case of *In Cold Blood*, racist reactionaries do not shatter the harmonious amalgamation of the white hero and the Native American woman. Instead, the Princess character self-destructs and destroys the ideal.

The representations of Look and Flo indicate that the ideal of America as it emerges in the Princess figure—the attainment of Whiteness and assimilation through marriage to the white hero—is unobtainable, that the myth is a fraud. Both women marry "good" white men but do not achieve the American dream through their marriages. Certainly this is true in Look's case, and Flo's alcoholism and desire for "the wild life" may be the result of her dashed dreams, or vice versa. Perry's reluctance to let go of his image of his mother as a Princess type whose connection to the frontier western experiences is captured in her rodeo pictures indicates this as an underlying possibility. The question arises, then, as to whether the inclusion of the racial Other in the American dream tarnishes it or the racial Other is tarnished by the American dream. Look's experiences lead to the conclusion that she has entered an already distorted society, while the implications presented through the editing of *In Cold Blood* point toward Flo as the cause of the debasement.

The manipulation of the Princess stereotype into that of the Sexualized Maiden subtly implies that Flo, like Hesh-ke, symbolizes an unseen threat to an innocent and vulnerable America. This notion of an unknowable danger within our midst runs through all the Sexualized Maiden films and signals a psychological fear of the racial Other that shifts over time. Tracing the ways in which the films present this anxiety also illuminates the changing political attitudes toward race. Both *Arrowhead* (1953) and *The Searchers* (1956) focus on race as a neurosis that affects whites, causing them to act violently against the racial Other. The films critique the racist hero differently, yet both depict the violence as a reaction to the Native woman and as somehow justified by her racial status, which the films accentuate. She is not considered an acceptable or desirable member of American society. Such treatment of race reflects the tone of the early 1950s, when conservative segregationist policy remained the national norm despite minimal governmental intervention.

In contrast, the 1960s films *In Cold Blood* (1967) and *Mackenna's Gold* (1969) invert the focus and deemphasize the racial rhetoric, directing attention inadvertently to the cause of the fear that drives racist action—the racialized Other. By downplaying obvious racism and constructing the character as maladjusted, these films blame the racial Other for her own violent or destructive nature. White America is not to blame for her deficiency. More clearly and directly than in the 1940s or 1950s films, but no less racializing, the 1960s films suggest that the woman's degenerate nature—Flo's alcoholism and Hesh-ke's murderous tendencies—not the racial social system, prohibits the women from successfully assimilating into white society. Such conclusions reflect the growing liberal consensus of civil rights legislation, which assumed that racial minorities, like white ethnics, if offered the same opportunities and conditions—that is, "the absence of formal discriminatory barriers, however much attitudinal prejudice may have existed"—should be able to integrate into mainstream society.[47] Like the bootstrap model, the ideology underlying this type of reasoning suggests that, with these opportunities in place, the failure to assimilate is the result of the minority's own deficiency or inability to "get over" the race issue.

The 1950s and 1960s films discussed above demonstrate a move away from the unified Sexualized Maiden figure seen in the 1940s to a hybrid that includes the full-blood woman, the Princess type, and the drunken squaw. The emergence of such an amalgamated character suggests an attempt on the part of the film industry to adapt the image of the Sexualized Maiden to fit the changing racial and political atmosphere of the country. The large temporal distance between the two femme fatale figures—Nita and Hesh-ke—and the differences in their representations from 1953 to 1969 suggest that, in the midst of minorities' racial backlash against whites, this character was an increasingly inappropriate choice. The development of the Princess type into the Sexualized Maiden in the mid-1950s westerns (Look) and across genres in the 1960s (Flo) indicates a move on the part of the filmmakers toward alternative representations of the character type.

Though the combination of the Princess and the Sexualized Maiden into one character may be an attempt to create a well-rounded and "real" Native woman, the use of easily identifiable characteristics results in the reemphasis of old stereotypes that reinforce the racial formations ingrained in the films. The shorthand storytelling process utilized in film narration relies on visual cues, including stereotyped ones, to efficiently present the viewer with enough information to understand the film's point. In the process, the combining of Sexualized Maiden traits with those of the Princess tarnishes the symbolism of the Princess figure, resulting in a depiction of the Native woman as an ultimately inappropriate status symbol for an assimilated America. Such representations of the Celluloid Maiden continue to be the norm in the 1970s and 1990s.

Clearly, one depiction is no more or less racist than the other. On the contrary, within the racializing process that constructs both figures as exotic Others, the amalgamation of images registers the inability of the filmmakers to adhere to the past dichotomy—the idealized Princess and the degenerate Sexualized Maiden—and their failure to find alternatives to it. The use of sexual racism as a structural component that orders the place of both the femme fatale and the fallen Princess in the narrative suggests their intensification of existing racial formations.

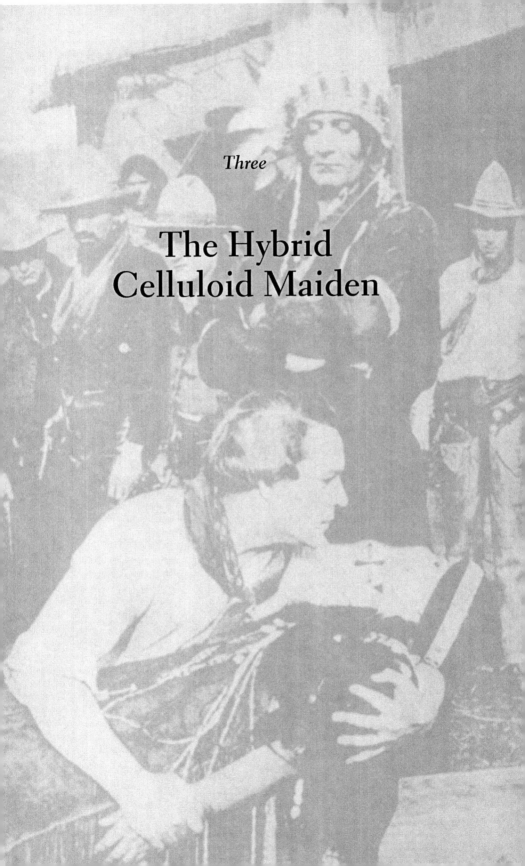

Three

The Hybrid
Celluloid Maiden

Five

Free Love and Violence

"Going Native" with the Celluloid Maiden in the 1970s

I reckon right then I come pretty close to turning pure Indian, and I
would have spent the rest of my life with Sunshine and her sisters.
— Jack Crabb in *Little Big Man*

A MANIPULATION OF FAMILIAR STEREOTYPES connected with
both the Celluloid Princess and the Sexualized Maiden, the hybrid Celluloid Maiden of the 1970s emerges as a symbolically modified offspring
of previous Princess figures. The quote above from Jack Crabb, or Little
Big Man, as the Cheyennes called him, about his wife Sunshine's potential to sway him toward "going native" hints at this change. Sunshine
and her contemporaries, unlike earlier Princess figures and in direct
contrast to their embodiment as assimilable Others, seduce the white
hero away from white American culture and "civilization." Exhibiting
popular countercultural and antiestablishment sentiments from the late
1960s and early 1970s, the revisionist westerns in which the Celluloid
Maiden appears present the figure as a beautiful and sexually uninhib-
ited woman who woos her husband further into "savagery" and the wilderness, either during their relationship or after her death. The woman's
diminishing role and her importance to the hero's embracing of Native
culture depend on a delicate mix of her status as a Princess type and her
framing as a sexually charged figure. Her sexuality is her filmic cachet,

but it often accentuates negative racial stereotypes about Native American women's sexuality. As a result, within the framework of the revisionist western, her image often undoes the positive intent of the filmmakers to refashion the western genre's racist portrayals of Native Americans.

The hybrid Celluloid Maiden characters that appear in *A Man Called Horse* (1970), *Little Big Man* (1970), *Jeremiah Johnson* (1972), and *The Man Who Loved Cat Dancing* (1973) share a number of identifiable traits linked to both the Princess and the Sexualized Maiden conventions. Her association with an exotic Native America, her commitment to the white hero and their family, her beauty, and her high social standing connect her to past Princess figures. But, for the first time in the tradition of the Princess figure, her social position does not rely only on her familial relationship to a chief; rather, the 1970s films modify this qualification to include the white hero's close male Indian friend.[1] Deeply embedded in the tradition of the western's discourse of conquest, these characteristics continue to link the Celluloid Maiden with the notion of a virgin continent, an untamed wilderness that awaits the white American hero. Reminiscent of the early silent-era Princess figure, the woman's sexual openness is accentuated and is underscored as a component of her Native heritage; this in turn ties her to old stereotypes about "primitive" cultures' being closer to nature and less restrictive than "civilized" cultures. Unlike her early predecessors, and more in keeping with the dangerous power of the Sexualized Maiden, the hybrid character captivates the hero and reinforces his rejection of white civilization and the "progressive" march of civilization.

Patrick McCarthy has suggested of the Indian woman in mountain men films that the "wild woman as seductress surfaces in the character of the American Indian maiden . . . [who] symbolizes the extent to which her bearded companion has already embraced the wilderness."[2] The films borrow this image, balancing the threat embodied in the woman's power to sway the hero from civilization by framing her as a Princess figure and a mother, and white society as corrupt, racist, hypocritical, and violent. As a result, the interracial couple's union and the hero's crossover into Native culture appear as stabilizing and positive choices for the hero. The 1970s Celluloid Maiden's sexuality, however, is a double-edged sword that becomes the mode of representation for her Otherness. The films' depictions of the character's sexuality through editing, cinematography, and scripting remind the viewer that the Sexualized Maiden's passionate nature overrides her other personality traits and promote her racial and sexual difference.

The hybrid Celluloid Maiden plays a small but symbolically pivotal role in the revisionist western's deconstruction and reconstruction of the myth of the frontier. In general, the myth relies heavily on the notions of white manifest destiny in the conquering of the American continent. These revisionist westerns, like the pro-Indian westerns of the 1950s, attempt to revise the classic western structure, which presents white culture as the icon of "civilization" and Native cultures as symbolic of "savagery." In their reconsideration of the "impact of westward expansion on Native Americans," these revisionist films portray Indians as representatives of civilization and whites as barbarians.[3] The 1970s films give the overall impression of attempting to approach Native American–white relations more realistically, and Native Americans more sympathetically, than had past westerns. Greatly influenced by the tumultuous 1960s and the Vietnam War, the films reflect through their white heroes a disillusionment with corporate and political America, racial inequality, and military violence. They illustrate unease with the previous paradigm and suggest a media culture in search of new ways to present or critique the national mythic genre and, in the case of the four films mentioned above, the Princess figure. Representing both the positive and negative images of previous Celluloid Maidens, the hybrid Celluloid Maiden stands firmly as the key character for deconstructing the myth of the frontier. In contrast, the white hero, whose defining metamorphosis into Indianness happens because of his reaction to her, emerges as a tangential participant. She symbolizes the white hero's moment of rebirth and self-awakening and his emergence as an amalgamation of two worlds whose roots are formed in Native America.

The Native woman's sexual and exotic allure is deeply entwined with the 1970s revisionist hero's acts of "embracing the wilderness" and "going native." On the most obvious level in these films, "going native" means abandoning white civilization and adopting the customs, costume, and worldview of the Indian. In effect, the hero switches identities, stepping into one that stands for everything his culture seems to have corrupted. The Native woman's sexual appeal makes this choice an easy one and gently paves the way for his transformation. Symbolically, because the Indian stands for the wilderness and a wild state of existence—a precivilized state in American lore—the hero's actions allow him to regress into a basic emotional, spiritual, and physical state of rejuvenation. According to Shari Huhndorf's work on this "cherished national ritual" in American culture, "going native" "articulates and attempts to resolve widespread ambivalence about modernity as well as anxieties about the terrible violence marking the nation's origins." Ideologically, because the hero usually returns to white society a better person in response to his regression into a primitive state and rebirth, "going native" means returning to the roots of American exceptionalism. In traditional genre westerns, the hero relives a moment in history at which conquering the American landscape and its wild inhabitants formulated and solidified an American identity and claim to the American landscape. In the revisionist western, however, by "going native," the hero emulates and participates in Native culture, thereby celebrating Native Americans and critiquing the process of colonization. Both result in the "metamorphosis of the WASP into something neither White nor Red"—a hybrid white-Indian who, ideally, retains the best qualities of both cultures.[4] The Celluloid Maiden is the defining element that eases the hero's transition into the wilderness, and their forming of a family unit binds the two together and holds the hero there, at least temporarily.

The Celluloid Maiden's death, which, as Richard Slotkin points out, "aborts the possibility of the hero's permanently 'going native,'" also catalyzes his temporary plunge into an emotional and psychological abyss where he embraces his internal wildness.[5] The hero's embracing of his internal "wilderness" raises the dangerous potential involved in permanently "going native"—losing control and reverting to primitive and base instincts. In other words, the hero resorts to a level of unbridled violence generally associated with the "savage reactionary," who aggressively resists the advancement of "civilization."[6] This can mean a triggering of momentary insanity, reclusive tendencies, and withdrawal from human contact. The western often uses the death or rape of the white woman as the catalyst for the hero's regression into savagery, his retaliation against Native Americans, and his regeneration into an American hero. The Celluloid Maiden films of the 1970s, however, invert the racial hierarchy in an embracing of Indianness and the use of the Native woman for this role.

The late 1960s and early 1970s was a time of national radical politics, both internally and externally. The United States' military intervention in Vietnam and Cambodia developed into the "greatest antiwar movement the nation had ever experienced."[7] Simultaneously, civil rights movements continued to demand changes in internal governmental policies, and among the voices raised were those of Native American activists protesting hundreds of years of treaty violations, mining company dumping and contamination of reservation lands, and overall destruction of land and culture by outside forces. Their faces were nationally visible through news coverage of fishing rights sit-ins in the Northwest, the takeover of Alcatraz Island in San Francisco Bay from November 1969 to June 1971, and Wounded Knee II, the standoff near Pine Ridge, South Dakota, in the winter and spring of 1973. Not all the coverage was pro-Native, but it raised mainstream awareness that Native Americans were active national citizens, not simply remnants of a vanished culture.

Such media attention and radical national politics not only inspired many Americans to think more critically about their country's political actions, past and present, but they also affected Hollywood's rendering of Native Americans. This change emerged most obviously in the politically vocal revisionist westerns that favored the radical politics of the era. These films attempted to depict a more realistic West than had previous films and tended to present Native American culture as an idealized alternative to a less than ideal American society. Although the Celluloid Maiden that emerges within the pro-Indian westerns of the time retains specific racist stereotypes, she indicates certain levels of liberalism, cultural pluralism, and racial integration. She does so during a moment in history characterized by uncertainty about America's future and disillusionment with the country's systems of power. The changes that emerge in her representation over the three years that span the release dates of the films also signal the changing dynamics of the film industry and a waning of the openly revisionist ideals. The hybridization of the Celluloid Maiden results in two different trends for the character that indicate the changing mood of the early 1970s. In the two films released in 1970, *A Man Called Horse* and *Little Big Man*, the Celluloid Maiden's connection to the land and spirituality—her ties to the myths of the Princess and earth mother—are accentuated and idealized. The latter two films—*Jeremiah Johnson* (1972) and *The Man Who Loved Cat Dancing* (1973)—eliminate such romanticizing and drastically reduce the character's screen time and voice.

THE SPIRITUAL EARTH MOTHER

Division and public action characterized the late 1960s and early 1970s, when a cluster of revisionist westerns—*Tell Them Willie Boy Was Here* (1969), *Soldier Blue* (1970), *A Man Called Horse* (1970), and *Little Big Man* (1970)—were released that used historical U.S. military actions against Native Americans as plot devices through which to critique current U.S. activities in Vietnam. According to Bataille and Silet, "At a time when 'flower children' were searching with Don Juan and Carlos Castañeda for spiritual awakening and protesters were decrying the genocide of Vietnam, new aspects of Indian existence became significant." Richard Nixon's escalation of warfare in Cambodia and Vietnam and his "stifl[ing]" of antiwar dissent at home added to an increasing air of "cultural despair among America's youth," which surfaced as the "hopelessness and romantic fatalism that pervades so many of Hollywood's 1969–1971 youth-cult films." The era's politics and open dissent reflected a "general revolt against oppressive, artificial, previously unquestioned ways of living" that permeated "every aspect of personal life." As Walter Zinn summarizes, it was "a time of upsurge" that included student rebellions against the establishment, antiwar demonstrations on a massive scale, women's rights activism, prison riots against the inhumane treatment of inmates and against the war, and Native American organization.[8]

In addition to the ongoing occupation of Alcatraz Island "in the name of all American Indians by right of discovery," Native Americans performed symbolic acts of political protest by taking over federal property, including Ellis Island and Bureau of Indian Affairs offices across the country. Protest camps appeared throughout the year on national lands such as Lassen, Mount Rushmore, and the Badlands National Monument. Less militant actions included the formation of pan-Indian organizations, pantribal conferences, and Native American newspapers to address issues affecting urban and rural Native Americans. The government responded on different levels. Pro-Indian policy emerged, symbolized by Nixon's gesture toward self-determination—the formal agreement to return Blue Lake to the Taos Pueblos on December 15, 1970, that vowed increasing political independence for tribes without termination of federal services or status.[9] Federal violence against Native American activists, including women and children, countered these executive gestures on many occasions, added to an already negative image of the country's domestic military actions, and offered parallels between the victims of American oppression at home and abroad.

The film industry, according to David Cook, responded to the mood of the era by "infus[ing] . . . the Hollywood Western with antimilitary, anti-colonial, anti-imperialist themes." Tapping into the visibility and media currency of contemporary Native American movements but focusing on the "vanishing American" figure, A *Man Called Horse* and *Little Big Man*, in varying ways, build on these themes. They present "Indian life as a valid counterculture—a more organic, life-enhancing existence than white society—from which the central character gains a new perspective on society and a new humanity." The two films do so through a now-familiar process in which "the White discovery of, and the renaming and adoption into, the tribal society of the American Indian" offers the viewer a glimpse into the alternative lifestyle of tribal peoples through the eyes of the white hero. Utilizing various techniques, the films present familiar themes of the western differently. A *Man Called Horse* relies on ethnographic details in portraying Indian culture; *Little Big Man* caricatures and lampoons American culture and white western heroes.[10] To validate tribal culture as an erotically attractive alternative, both films rely on romantic metaphors of nature and spirituality to frame the Native American woman as an iconic reference to popular youth and countercultural quests for alternative lifestyles.

Promoted as "the first authentic portrait of the American Indian set in a time of savage innocence and beauty," A *Man Called Horse* relays the story of Lord John Morgan (Richard Harris), who is captured by Sioux warriors while on a hunting expedition "in the American wilds in 1825."[11] The chief, Yellow Hand (Manu Tupou), nicknames him Horse and presents him as a gift to his old mother (Judith Anderson). Beaten and treated as a beast of burden, Morgan exists in a state of abjection until he realizes that, in order to survive, he must become one of the tribe, earn their trust and respect, and move up in status from slave to chief. This he does through methodical planning and deliberate action. With the aid of an interpreter, a captive Flathead-French mixed-blood named Batise (Jean Gascon), Horse learns the Sioux language and customs. Attracted to a young woman named Running Deer (Corinna Tsopei), who shares his attraction and whose status as the chief's sister will earn him his freedom if they wed, Horse woos her with his escape in mind.

To earn the right to marry her, he kills and scalps two Shoshone braves and submits himself to the Sun Dance ritual. His strategy works, and he marries Running Deer with the approval of the tribe. Their loving but short marriage ends when the Shoshones avenge the deaths of their two warriors in a raid that results in the slaughter of Running Deer, Yellow Hand, and others. Utilizing "superior" European tactics of warfare, Horse leads the remaining Sioux to victory, an act that wins him the title of chief and his freedom.

The opening scenes highlight Morgan's boredom with his own wealth, status, and lifestyle, and his search in the American wilderness for something to relieve his emotional and intellectual ennui. In contrast to the American mountain men he pays as guides for his trips, he appears the icon of civilization, class status, education, and refinement. The image hinted at through these depictions corresponds to what Leslie Fiedler understands as a basic component of a particularly American character who is essential to the myth of the frontier. Lord Morgan is what Fiedler would call "the White European refugee from civilization" who will be transformed by his encounter with the wilderness and, in particular, the Indian. In the case of A Man Called Horse, the Indian becomes "the abominable id—a projection of the bestiality white culture could not face in itself"—that will force the changes in John Morgan necessary for his maturation into the white hero. Indeed, Morgan's actions as the intellectually superior and physically equal white hero who rises to power and eventually saves the Sioux from annihilation by the Shoshones bears out this myth. For Fiedler, the union of the Native American man and the white European produces the males of "the New Race" of Americans.[12] But in A Man Called Horse, this metamorphosis hinges not on a Native man but on the Princess figure—Running Deer.

The film's thematic promotion of the superior white emancipator and its pseudoethnographic depiction of a "savage" lifestyle seem an improbable validation of Native American tradition as a countercultural option. Yet Running Deer's sexual and spiritual allure works within the larger narrative to ensure such a conclusion. The overemphasis on the harsh reality of tribal life and existence in the wilderness is contrasted with her compassion for Horse and her Princess image. The film portrays women as jealous, self-centered, and reduced through a life of hardship into "horrible old hag[s]" who are abandoned when their men are killed, but Running Deer emerges as the romantic virgin ideal who beguiles Horse "just before his spirit splits."[13] As a result, she initiates his transformation from "playing Indian" to "going Indian."

The breaking of Horse's spirit through his treatment as an animal initiates his entrance into a game of playing Indian in which his freedom depends on his ability to mimic the "savages" without becoming one. Or, as Armando Prats explains this type of maneuver, his "power to *become* Other must be balanced by the power to resist *surrender* to Otherness."[14] His calculated killing and scalping of the Shoshone raiders and his subsequent comment to Batise, "Now wife, then war party, then we go," illustrate that he adopts Indian custom and participates in their rites of passage not as a lifestyle change but as a motive for escape. At this point, even Running Deer remains a commodity in his eyes: "I bought her, didn't I?" He understands that, once he achieves the status of a brave by killing an enemy, he may "buy" Running Deer as a bride.[15] The critical moment at which Horse's equilibrium begins to teeter happens just after he offers the Shoshones' horses to Yellow Hand for Running Deer's hand and learns that, to marry her, he must prove his worthiness by withstanding the Sun Dance ritual.

In a sequence of scenes that director Elliot Silverstein "claims was inserted without his approval," Running Deer binds herself spiritually and sexually to Horse by uniting with him in a space that they reach during simultaneous vision experiences. It is through this action and during these scenes that Horse "*surrenders* to Otherness," embraces his new savageness, and "goes native."[16] The series of interconnected segments, which juxtaposes shots of Running Deer meditating with shots of Horse being tortured and becoming delirious, begins with a long shot of a white buffalo skin tepee and a naked Running Deer stooping to enter, but then quickly cuts back to Horse preparing for his ritual. Again, the view returns to the tepee, with a medicine man in the foreground and Running Deer's mother, Buffalo Head Woman, behind him and next to the tepee entrance. Cutting quickly to a dark red interior of the tepee lit as if by the heat of stones, the close-up behind and to the side of Running Deer focuses on a silhouette of her naked breast and upraised arm. As her mother opens the tepee flap, pours water on the rocks, and kisses her daughter's hands, the exterior light highlights more of Running Deer's body. The mother departs, and the editing cuts to a frontal shot of Running Deer as she sits engulfed in a bluish purple light with steam

A Man Called Horse. Elliot Silverstein, National General Pictures, 1970.

rising between her and the camera. The mood of the scene, established by the dim lighting and the haze, seems to suggest a primordial connection among the woman, ritual, and purification. The two camera angles create an erotic and voyeuristic moment during which the camera seemingly caresses Running Deer's skin and focuses tightly on her breasts and the sweat that covers her body. The composition of the shots and the attention to her breasts recall precinematic images of the Indian Princess and Pocahontas that so often depicted the maiden bare breasted. The manner in which the camera roams Running Deer's naked body also accentuates her eroticism, visually tying it through the sweat ceremony to an earthly, "Native" sexuality.

The sequence switches to Horse entering the Sun Dance lodge. A long scene takes place in which he tells the Sioux, using Batise as an unwilling translator, that he thinks very little of them and that one day he will be a chief. The turmoil this causes eventually subsides, and Horse is skewered in the chest and raised up to the roof, where he spins by the thongs that hold him. As he begins to go into a trance, he hears the

Great Spirit speak, and flashes of visions are intercut with close-ups of his swinging body. The fast-paced montage combines shots of buffalo, tall prairie grasses, and a woman running naked through the water toward him. The camera pulls back, behind Horse, who embraces Running Deer. The two communicate for the first time without language barriers, and he confesses both his physical need for her and his desire to escape. She confirms her knowledge and acceptance of these things. The tone created through the cross editing of these scenes and her naked body both in the sweat lodge and the vision space imply that the two are interacting within a spiritual space.

This crosscutting of individual shots of each is positioned in a progression leading to the shot of their united vision. The sequencing metaphorically implies their sexual union and connects Running Deer, as the medium of the vision, physically and spiritually to both the earth and to nonearthly powers. Although Horse's point of view prevails in the dream, the sequence suggests that Running Deer controls his vision and calls him into it. Her physical and spiritual connections to the land—relationships that Horse does not have—reinforce such a reading. Running Deer's metaphoric name and naked body link her to the plains landscape and the animals of the vision. Additionally, the spiritual qualities of the sweat lodge suggest her connection to other realms of the natural world and to the supernatural. Her movement from the physical plane of reality onto a psychic level where she interacts with another vision seeker implies her oneness with the universe. Clearly a reference to countercultural transcendental meditation and spirituality movements, these brief moments code Running Deer as the quintessential earth maiden who is mystically or spiritually connected to the world around her and to her lover. The vision scenes also seem to document Horse's realization that Running Deer and her way of life offer him the sexual, spiritual, physical, and emotional freedom that he was searching for prior to his capture. From this point onward, he calls her Little Freedom.

The visions, while out of character with the ethnographic tone of the film, signal Horse's embracing of the tribal way, which emerges in his growing feelings of warmth toward his wife and her relatives. The viewer realizes he has "gone native" when he turns on his only friend, Batise. Shortly after Horse and Running Deer's wedding, Yellow Hand's wife leaves him for another. Out of grief and shame, he consigns himself to an early death by vowing to never retreat in battle. As Horse watches his distraught wife's reaction to her brother's news, Batise celebrates it, because now Horse will be chief. Until this moment, Horse would have also rejoiced at the chance to move up in tribal rank and regain freedom. His deepening love for Running Deer and his growing respect for her tribal ways, however, emerge in his response: "For five years you have lived here and you've learned nothing about these people. All his death is to you is a means of escape!" Horse's compassion continues even after his wife's death; he tells his mother-in-law, whom he had considered "a horrible old hag," that he will be her son—a promise that ensures her survival. The film concludes with a shot of Horse bidding his wife's burial pyre goodbye that transitions into a long shot centered on the emergent hero as he leads his people to a new land. As many critics have pointed out, the film retains the white-hero-as-natural-leader figure; nonetheless, the sense of kinship he displays toward his wife's tribe replaces the moral vacancy of John Morgan and the arrogance he showed in the Sun Dance lodge. As a result, he emerges a better human being and a compassionate hero who crosses racial and cultural lines.

A *Man Called Horse* received mixed reviews, ranging from those who praised its ethnographic authenticity, to those who were grateful for its avoidance of "the white-race-is-the-cancer-of-history reproof that has marred much of the New Indian Lore," to those who felt it unfairly depicted Native Americans as savages.[17]

In contrast, Arthur Penn's *Little Big Man* "received the most positive responses" as "the present high-water mark in the treatment of Indians in the movies" and the "best of the lot" of the pro-Indian films.[18] Reviewers saluted the film's script (adapted by Calder Willingham from Thomas Berger's novel), the sensitivity with which the film presented Cheyenne culture, the acting of Dustin Hoffman and Chief Dan George, and the boldness with which Penn parodied American myth building. Reviewers' primary displeasure lay in the extreme length of the film and the difficulty with which it wed romanticism and realism in its attempt to recreate Berger's story for a youthful audience.[19] Part of its popularity lay in its allegorical references to American military activities in Vietnam, which tapped into American sentiments against the war. More specifically, the film "spoke to the genocidal policies of the U.S. high command (and, as we now know, the CIA) in Vietnam, and to the paranoid sense of imminent extinction that Kent State had fostered among America's youth."[20]

The film's satirical and "atypical comic tone, which softens its theme of genocide," its romanticized and idealized portrayal of Indian culture, and its themes of interracial harmony added to its appeal. This combination of elements registered the "political and social turmoil of this era, and reflected the consciousness of the movements of the time, the social attitudes they generated, and an overall reevaluation of America's morality and values." In sum, the film was a great success, and it continues to be viewed as a quintessential representation of the revisionist trend at its most radical.[21]

Little Big Man, told in flashback by Jack Crabb, or Little Big Man (Dustin Hoffman), when he is 121 years old and living in a veterans' hospital, relates his experiences on the western frontier between 1865 and the 1870s, a period of intense westward expansion, Indian wars, and anti-Indian sentiment. Jack's history as the "sole White survivor of the Battle of the Little Big Horn, popularly known as Custer's Last Stand" reads as a series of adventures and mishaps that allow him to migrate between the worlds of the Cheyenne Indians and the frontier whites. Like John Morgan, Jack Crabb spends most of this period searching for a home and an identity; he moves between his identities as the white Jack Crabb and the Indian Little Big Man. While in the white world, he moves through his "religious period," "gunfighter period," and "down and out period," trying on various identities and occupations with little luck. Unlike the traditional hero of the western, he never achieves the status of legend. Rather, as one who watches or participates peripherally in the making of the West, Jack is an antihero who seems unable to fully commit to or follow through on any particular decision. His most contented and fulfilling years are spent living with the Cheyennes, who find him as a child after the Pawnees kill his family and who teach him to be "a human being"—a Cheyenne. With them, he learns the importance of living in harmony with the natural world and the reality of white racial violence against Indians. What temporarily completes Jack and offers him the identity and centrality he desires is his time with the Cheyennes and, especially, Sunshine (Aimée Eccles).

The Celluloid Princess's connection to the land and a preindustrial, precivilized state are evoked by the narrative setting of the fron-

Little Big Man. Arthur Penn, National General Pictures, 1970.

tier West—a land still wild and untamed. *Little Big Man* presents
Sunshine as a hippie-like child/woman of nature enmeshed in the
landscape around her. Her name predates the earth and links her to
life. The sound of her breath precedes her, and we first see her lying
in the brush along a river, giving birth to her child in the middle
of a massacre. This scene integrates Sunshine with the land itself:
establishing shots (close-ups and high angles) frame her within the
underbrush, against the rocks, or isolated within the frame, holding her newborn. These tightly composed shots full of leaves, grass,
dirt, and water ensure that the viewer associates her with the earth;
in addition, her newborn baby, their mingled blood, and the surrounding warfare underscore the primal qualities inherent in her and
the wilderness. Her story, which begins with her child's birth in the
bush during a cavalry attack, ends with her and her children's violent
deaths in the snow during another attack that reenacts the Washita
River massacre by Custer in 1868.[22] The often violent cycles of life
from birth to death mark Sunshine's short life literally and metaphorically. She exists only within the landscape that codes her as a

child of nature ritually giving birth to children, whose deaths in her arms return them to the soil.

Sunshine is just a one-year moment (twenty-eight film minutes) in Jack Crabb's story, but she is a significant figure who replaces his missing white wife Olga (Kelly Jean Peters) and frames a new stage in his life among "the people" (the Cheyennes). During this time, Sunshine is present on screen for a total of thirteen minutes, during which she has either just given birth, is pregnant, or, "Indian style, [is] going off to have her baby." Through this constant connection of her with children and birth, and thus also sexual activity, the film renders Sunshine as a young earth mother whose fertility and beauty leave an indelible impression on Jack. He confirms her power over him in his first encounter with the daughter of his best Cheyenne friend, Shadow, and the woman who will become his wife: "I sat and watched that baby come into this world. 'Cept for her breathing that woman never made a sound, if woman she was. She didn't look more than a girl. I couldn't take my eyes off that girl and her baby." It is this experience of Sunshine's giving birth that first binds Jack to physical aspects of the natural world—in a sense, he is reborn with her child.

Sunshine's sexual activity and lack of inhibition—she does not seems fazed by Jack's voyeurism of her childbirth—are accentuated in the film as the linchpin in Jack's commitment to his life as Little Big Man and to "going native." In a humorous moment when they are camped with other tribes along the Washita River, Sunshine manipulates Little Big Man into sexually satisfying her three lonely sisters while she goes off into the snow to have their child. At first reluctant, Little Big Man finds it within himself to fulfill his wife's request. In so doing, he enacts Old Lodge Skin's (Chief Dan George) prophetic dream in which Little Big Man acquires multiple wives. A lengthy scene unfolds in which Little Big Man moves from one buffalo robe to another in an attempt to satisfy all three sisters' insatiable appetites. As Old Lodge Skin's dream had predicted, "it was a great copulation," and Sunshine, returning with their newborn son in her arms, remarks, "I knew you were a good man." This sexually charged moment results in Little Big Man's realization: "I reckon right then I come pretty close to turning pure Indian, and I would have spent the rest of my life with Sunshine and her sisters."

In hindsight, Jack Crabb pinpoints the moment in which he accepts

his inner Indianness and is seduced by the forces of nature, as represented by Sunshine and the act of sexual intercourse. Within the context
of the film's liberal revisionism, Sunshine's request and Little Big Man's
fulfillment of it surface as an endorsement of the 1970s' sexual revolution
and the hippie generation's support of communal living and free love.[23]
The unprecedented polygamous union Sunshine sets into motion, however, also seems to position her as sexually deviant and to stigmatize her
and her sisters as overtly libidinal. Her request, a successful component
of her exotic appeal, though titillating and perhaps sexually arousing to
some viewers, would seem abhorrent, or perhaps curious in an ethnographic sense, to the colonial imagination and the monogamous American mainstream. Thus Little Big Man's actions and his commitment to
Sunshine and her sisters after "the great copulation" illustrate his primal
instincts and his seduction by such forces of nature.

     This key revisionist moment in the film demands closer attention.
The construction of the scene deliberately rewrites both Cheyenne tradition and Thomas Berger's novel *Little Big Man*. In the novel, Little Big
Man complies with Cheyenne tradition by marrying Sunshine's sisters.
His initial reluctance to do so stems not from any Cheyenne taboo against
polygamy but from his training as a white boy. Traditional Cheyenne culture respected both monogamous and polygamous marriages, the latter of
which were seen as markers of wealth and high status; quite often, subsequent wives were sisters or cousins of the first wife.[24] The revision of this
cultural norm suggests an attempt to appeal to a broad demographic—one
that would resonate with both a countercultural concept of open sexuality and American ideologies about monogamy. The film also refashions
Sunshine from an occasionally sharp-tongued wife to an idealized, docile
girl child whose charm almost overshadows her sexual deviance.

     In creating the scene as it does, however, the film compromises
the revisionist position of the traditional western structure, as explained
above. The film assumes an inversion through its depictions of whites
and Cheyennes as extreme opposites, a revision of Berger's equal-hand-
ed representation. The Cheyennes, represented as peaceful, monogamous "hippie" types and icons of civilized people, are in "harmony with
nature, wise, tolerant, honourable and unrepressed." In direct contrast,
"white civilisation [sic] is alienated from nature," and whites are portrayed as "foolish, intolerant, mad, narcissistic, hypocritical, vicious,
and repressed." Additionally, Penn's scenes of the massacre of the Chey-

ennes—allegories for American actions in Vietnam, especially the My Lai massacre—connect the film's western European culture with acts of savagery and an uncivilized state.[25] Yet Little Big Man's acquiescence to Sunshine's request takes him one more step into a state of abandonment of all that is "civilized" and further calls into question the concepts behind the dichotomy of the myth of the frontier. This happens precisely because of the abnormality of the request in both white and Cheyenne cultures as they appear in the film. In addition, locating the act of "going native" within the culture categorized as "civilized"—Cheyenne—unravels the simplicity of the inversion model and embeds the concept of savagery within a basic community organization: the Native American family. Thus the film uses the Celluloid Maiden to reinforce the negative image of Native Americans as icons of savagery.

Both *Little Big Man* and *A Man Called Horse* rely on a visual and metaphorical equation in which the exotic sexual appeal of the Celluloid Maiden figure, enhanced through the casting of Greek and Asian actresses in the parts, catalyzes and completes the white hero's transformation.[26] The sexual bond between the hero and his Native wife also bridges the distance between the Native culture and the culture of the mainstream viewer through an established and recognizable process of marriage and family building. The combination of the exotic and the familiar forces a reassessment of ideologies that present racially and culturally stereotyped groups as substantially Other to a national mainstream while maintaining the allure of a "safe" difference. But, as Richard Slotkin points out, "The death of the Indian woman aborts the possibility of the hero's permanently 'going native,'" weakening the "symbolic exercises" of revisionism by continuing to engage the Native as the "cultural/racial Other" doomed to extermination.[27] Such is the case in both films. Sunshine's murder by the U.S. cavalry in front of Little Big Man catapults him into an utter state of abjection. He becomes a hermit and goes "as deep into the wilderness as [he] could get." This moment signals another level of his "going native," in which his only solace comes from the land itself—a metonymic connection to Sunshine. In *A Man Called Horse*, Running Deer's death results in Horse's ascendancy to the position of tribal leader, who must lead his beaten people farther into the wilderness in an attempt to stay their inevitable extinction. Yet both men ultimately leave their doomed Native families to return to their own western European cultures.

A tone decidedly darker than that of the earlier 1970s Celluloid Maiden films colors *Jeremiah Johnson* (1972) and *The Man Who Loved Cat Dancing* (1973), signaling a significant mood swing between the 1970 releases of *A Man Called Horse* and *Little Big Man* and the latter two films. While both *Jeremiah Johnson* and *The Man Who Loved Cat Dancing* are part of the cluster of revisionist films mentioned above in their referencing of the U.S. military, they do not incorporate actual battle scenes in their critique of the Vietnam War. More in keeping with another film of the cluster, *Tell Them Willie Boy Is Here* (1969), they focus on a hero whose past experiences with the military or the law psychologically alter his view of life and civilization. In addition, the earlier films' idyllic images of Native Americans, undertones of spiritual renewal, and rebirth of the hero as a better man are replaced by even stronger currents of dissatisfaction and withdrawal that surface in extreme violence. The Celluloid Maiden also changes dramatically. She emerges as a more realistic woman, but one whose voice the films silence almost to the point of erasing the character. Nonetheless, the Celluloid Maiden continues, perhaps more evidently than in the earlier two films, to act as the pivotal point in the hero's balance between insanity and sanity, savagery and civility. She also remains the force that eases him into a comfortable union with the wilderness and Indian society and validates his rejection of western European culture.

The change in spirit of these films seems to coincide with the increasingly pessimistic tenor of the moment. According to historians David Brody, Lynn Dumenil, and James Henretta, the United States' secret bombings of Cambodia in 1970 and President Nixon's increased military action, rather than the promised withdrawal of troops from Vietnam, did little to fulfill Nixon's "promise of 'peace with honor'" but instead "spawned a deep distrust of government among American citizens." The Watergate scandal, which began in 1972 and legitimized people's concerns about corrupt politicians and an out-of-control government, set in motion a "wave of cynicism that swept the country in its wake." Fueling the political turmoil, economic woes in the form of war debt, "spiraling inflation," rising unemployment, and an energy crisis that peaked during the 1973–1974 OPEC oil embargo against the United States, forced Americans to become aware of their vulnerability. As Walter Zinn points out, an increasing number of citizens, responding with hostility to "government and industry," "refused to identify themselves as either Democrats or Republicans," began "acquitting radicals" in court, and rescinded support of Nixon during Watergate.[28]

Coinciding with these changes, ongoing Native American radical political activities highlighted a tradition of internal colonial action by the federal government. Throughout the early 1970s, Native Americans continued to occupy abandoned federal buildings and public land in protest of the government's violations of treaty rights, sacred land, and religious freedom, and to stage sit-ins against police brutality toward Native Americans across the country. The takeover of Alcatraz Island ended in June 1971 with the removal of the remaining fifteen men, women, and children by federal marshals.[29] In 1972 and 1973, a number of other high-profile events increased public awareness of Native American issues and underscored Native Americans' commitment to changing the relationship between tribes and the federal government. These included the Trail of Broken Treaties, the takeover of the federal Bureau of Indian Affairs office in Washington, D.C., and Wounded Knee II. The Trail of Broken Treaties, organized by the American Indian Movement, brought six hundred to eight hundred Native Americans from all over the country to Washington, D.C., on November 2, 1972, to present a list of "20 civil rights demands" to the federal government.[30] On arriving in the capital, the group found its promised accommodations unavailable and thus took over the federal Bureau of Indian Affairs building. According to Duane Champagne, "After a week of occupation in which activists destroyed files, furniture, and Indian art, the government promised to review the 'twenty-point program,' refrain from making arrests, and pay the Indians' return travel expenses." Champagne adds that the occupation was a "great moral victory for the Indians," signifying the first time a national organization of Indians worked as a "united people" to face a confrontation.[31]

The victory formed a basis for continual declarations of sovereignty, including Wounded Knee II, a "powerful affirmation that the Indians of North America were still alive." Growing tensions between traditional Sioux on the Pine Ridge Reservation in South Dakota and the federally supported tribal government under Dick Wilson over abuses of power and violence against traditionalists resulted in a seventy-day siege of the town of Wounded Knee, from February 27 to May 8, 1973. Three hundred Oglala Sioux, many of them members of the American Indian Movement, came to the traditionalists' rescue. Declaring the town a "liberated territory," they worked with the community to rebuild houses, dig water wells, and fortify the area against further terrorism from Wilson's armed guards. In retaliation, well-armed FBI, federal marshals, and Bureau of Indian Affairs police surrounded the town. The altercation ended in an impasse, with a "negotiated settlement and withdrawal on both sides."[32] The national and international media coverage of the event and the subsequent judicial action against key American Indian Movement participants worsened the federal government's already tarnished image.

Jeffrey Wallmann's study of the era's westerns points out that the films' portrayals of civilization as "the oppressive enemy parallel the country's disgust at the war and disdain for the government."[33] Clearly revising the notion of an idyllic wilderness, *Jeremiah Johnson* (1972) visually documents the grandeur and awe-inspiring power of the Rocky Mountains and explores the violence of men's lives within that space. In the process, it records the reduction of a civilized man to a state of inescapable savagery and destabilizes the myth of the American Adam and an American Eden.[34] Just as "a growing portion of the nation's youth loudly proclaim[ed] its defection from everything," the hero in *Jeremiah Johnson* simply "drop[s] out."[35] Full of "youth-grabbing alienation," ex-soldier Jeremiah Johnson seeks solitude in the wilderness of the Rocky Mountains circa 1825.[36] Such a tone underscores the film's main theme, which, as Mick McAllister astutely points out, highlights "the failure of the Euro-American to understand and live within the American wilderness . . . the vision it presents is ultimately pessimistic, an urgent denial of the romantic daydream of escaping from white civilization into a new Eden."[37]

Sydney Pollack's film, based on the legend of an Indian fighter turned trapper found in both Vardis Fisher's novel *Mountain Man* and Raymond Thorp and Robert Bunker's biography *Crow Killer*, sets a slow pace through a brief period of Johnson's metamorphosis.[38] Over the course of his journey, Johnson (Robert Redford) learns the trapping trade, builds alliances with particular groups of Indians and other trappers, and acquires a white son (Josh Albee) and a Flathead wife (Delle Bolton). Depicted as a wandering soul, a man in search of an elusive peace, Johnson finds a moment of calm and happiness during his period as a family man. His hiatus from wandering comes to an abrupt end when Crow warriors kill his family in retaliation for Johnson's desecration of their burial grounds, which he has used as a shortcut to bring a search party through a mountain pass. His grief over the death of his wife, Swan, and son, Caleb, drives Johnson into a state of extraordinary violence against their killers. The remainder of the film depicts his degeneration into a man more savage than the Crows who hunt him.

Jeremiah Johnson's tale is, in good part, a tale of the American landscape, of an "American Eden," that offers a solace and security of its own kind but "exacts a toll on its inhabitants especially those not born to the land."[39] Johnson pays the price, and in the "process, he mentally becomes a feral man—an aberrational human form—and a cross between man and animal." In contrast, as an offspring of the wilderness, Swan accepts this "world in all its violence and beauty." Strong and silent, she symbolizes the world of the mountains; like the environment, she is a force with which Johnson must reckon, find peace, and love. Swan embodies the feminine attraction of the landscape that balances the violent reality of surviving in the wilderness and its seductive power over the white hero. In a sense, as Patrick McCarthy points out, she "further weds him to that which he already loves."[40] Through their union and her Indian ways, Swan slowly initiates Johnson into her world, her language, and her desires.[41] At the outset of the film, Johnson's reclusive tendency and antisocial attitude set him well on track toward evolving into the mountain man type his friend Del Gue (Stefan Gierasch) embodies: "exploiters of nature . . . degenerate cast-offs of white civilization . . . [many of whom] adopted the content of Indian culture, but most allowed the forms of those cultures, the violence of the Plains Indian life, to license and excuse their own willful, unbridled immorality."[42] Swan stays this process and, in so doing, becomes the Native American civilizing agent in the midst of Johnson's savage world.

Swan's heritage as the daughter of Flathead chief Lebeaux (Richard Angarola) follows the filmic tradition of the Celluloid Princess, yet her mix of Christianity and Native religion makes her a hybrid figure whose use of Catholic rituals binds Johnson, against his will, to civilization. Like Sonseeahray of *Broken Arrow* (1950), Swan is Johnson's Native American Eve and a representative of the "positive aspects of the American Indian."[43] The film underscores Swan's status as an Eve figure by introducing three other female characters—each the compan-

ion of a white man—prior to Swan's appearance in the film. Bear Claw
Chris Lapp (Will Geer) tells Johnson about Jack's woman and his own:
"[Hatchet Jack] was living with a female panther, two years in a cave . . .
she never did get used to him. . . . I packed me a squaw for ten years,
pilgrim. Cheyenne she were. Meanest bitch that ever balled for beads."
In addition, Jeremiah helps to bury the dead family of a white pioneer
woman (Allyn Ann McLerie) who survived a Blackfoot massacre only to
go insane. Her son Caleb, Jeremiah's adopted boy, goes mute from the
trauma. Through these depictions, the film economically presents three
figures that are both connected to Swan and contrasted with her.

The humanization of the panther through sexual innuendo associates it with the two other children of nature: the Cheyenne woman and
Swan, whose name also ties her to the animal world. The Cheyenne
woman's temperament and the reference to her as a whore—"balled for
beads"—symbolically link her to the promiscuous Native woman image, but in direct contrast to Swan. Swan's hybrid Christianity affiliates
her with the white woman, whose only solace is to keen over the graves
of her dead children. But as a child of nature, Swan lives in peace with
the very wilderness that drives the white woman insane. In sum, the film
presents her as the most centered woman and an ideal mate for Johnson. Married to a stranger and taken away from her people's homeland
into the land of their enemy, the Crows, she maintains a level of calm
and dedication that permeates their life together. While with Swan and
Caleb, Johnson appears content to curtail his wandering, build a house,
shave his beard, and learn her language.

Through Swan, the film appears to offer its audience the fulfillment
of the American Adam and Eve allegory. Such an ending would constitute a primary revision to the traditional myth of the frontier, in which
the white woman reins in the hero, settles down with him to start a
family, and with him sows the seeds of the American nation. A Native
American Eve adds a racial component to such a myth and suggests an
alternative to the creation of an American nation through the traditional
settler image. A multicultural and multiethnic unit, which appears content in its isolation from larger communities, replaces the white settler
town ideal. In addition, the couple's relationship to the environment,
based as it is on a hunting rather than a farming tradition, contrasts with
a mythology of America as built on the cultivation and taming of the
wild landscape. But the narrative eliminates such an ending through

Swan's abrupt death. Her death enacts a second revision—the depth to which the hero grieves and allows his inner savagery to rule his conscious life. Past heroes, such as Tom Jeffords in *Broken Arrow*, memorialize their Indian wives while continuing to pursue a "civilized" life; others, like Little Big Man, retreat temporarily into a hermit state; but Jeremiah Johnson turns into a killing machine. Without Swan, Johnson becomes a wild animal that wanders the mountains endlessly in a Darwinian game of survival of the fittest.

Although Swan plays a complex and pivotal role in Jeremiah's psychological development, her importance is deemphasized by the film and by critics who describe her as a mere sexual accoutrement for the white hero. The film narrative suggests that Johnson does not want a wife; in fact, Chief Lebeaux must present her to cover a social faux pas committed by Johnson when he unthinkingly out-honors the chief with a casual giving of gifts. This segment revises the romanticism of Vardis's narrative and the biographical information of Thorp and Bunker's work: in both, the Johnson character asks for the Flathead girl's hand in marriage. The change enhances the historic accuracy of the depiction of the fur traders who married Native women to forge alliances. In this case, however, eliminating the initial love interest reduces Swan to a commodity who has no choice in her future. Her image as a Princess type is consequently diminished. Two examples from the film's advertising also illustrate this type of reduction. In the film's press book, a photo caption reads, "Johnson and the Princess. The last thing he expected." The use of "Princess" clues the viewer in to her status, while the following quote from the press clipping files contradicts her Princess status with the heavily coded squaw image: "[The film] shows that our hero can work up a strong feeling for a squaw. It should be noted that this squaw of his [is] very good-looking and appealing no matter what standards of measurement you apply."[44] The first quote objectifies Swan by taking away her identity—she is not Swan but "the Princess." The rhetoric of the second quote is both sexual and derogatory. These descriptions are remarkably similar in sexual innuendo and tone to those Bear Claw uses to describe his own wife. In addition, these two quotes exemplify how Swan's personality and individuality are erased, a move enhanced in the film through her minimal and untranslated dialogue.

Like *Jeremiah Johnson*, but to a greater degree, *The Man Who Loved Cat Dancing* silences its Native woman, Cat Dancing—she has neither voice nor body in the film that carries her name.[45] Her story emerges only through gossip, partially answered questions, and fragments of conversations. Cat Dancing, however, remains important to the viewer's understanding of the white hero, to his temporary madness, and to the progression of the plot. In stark contrast to the three previous revisionist westerns, *The Man Who Loved Cat Dancing* takes place after the hero has "gone native" and suffered the consequences. As seen through the eyes of a white woman, the film focuses primarily on Jay Grobart's (Burt Reynolds) metamorphosis into a different person during the process of detaching himself from his Indian wife and falling in love with another Cat—the white woman Catherine Crocker (Sarah Miles). The film juxtaposes the two women, but because Catherine is present and Cat Dancing is absent, an uneven image of Cat Dancing takes shape in which her sexuality supplants her personality. The film leaves her a mute ghost that Catherine and Jay must come to peace with in order to start their life together.

As the film unfolds, the viewer slowly learns about the primary characters' motivations and history. Jay Grobart, an ex–military captain just released from prison, robs a train with three other men. Catherine Crocker, on the run from her oppressive husband (George Hamilton), inadvertently gets entangled with the outlaws, who take her along on their run. Grobart rescues her from rape by two of the outlaws—Dawes (Jack Warden) and Billy (Bo Hopkins)—and Catherine finds herself attracted to his "strength, his quiet, reflective manner," and, as time goes on, "his devoted love of the memory of his Indian wife."[46] Pursued by a posse that is led by Wells Fargo detective Lapchance (Lee J. Cobb) and includes Catherine's husband Crocker, the group eventually loses its members to death or abandonment until only Catherine and Grobart remain. The two continue farther into the mountain range, to the land of his dead wife's people. It appears that Grobart has robbed the train to buy back his two children from their Indian family. Grobart's son, Dream Seeker (Sutero García Jr.), and Cat Dancing's brother, Iron Knife (Larry Littlebird), refuse his offer and reveal the events behind Cat Dancing's death. With the posse closing in on them, Grobart abandons Catherine at the village and heads into the mountains. Dream Seeker, after witnessing Catherine's husband's treatment of her, takes her to Grobart. The two survive a gunfight with the posse that results in Crocker's death, and they retreat into the mountains.

Cat Dancing is mentioned briefly six times during this adventure, in a series of descriptions that leaves the viewer with the impression of her as a Sexualized Maiden. The first of these happens early in the renegades' run across the desert. The group, which includes Jay, his lifelong friend Charlie (Jay Varela), Dawes, Billy, and the captive Catherine, stops at the house of one of Jay's old sergeants. Catherine goes into the house with the man's wife to clean up. The wife, eager to learn more about Jay's "new wife" and surprised that Catherine is also called Cat—"That was his squaw's name"—relays tidbits of information about his former wife. Catherine learns that Jay "had to move out of the fort" because of Cat Dancing. She is told that Cat Dancing was "not really his wife" because they "never stood up in front of a preacher." She also hears that Jay is "just out of prison" for "kill[ing] a man on account of that squaw." Shortly thereafter, as the group camps for a night, the following brief exchange between Charlie and Jay adds greater dimension to Cat Dancing's image:

> CHARLIE: "You don't think of Cat Dancing no more. Jail take that all away."
> JAY: "Yeah."
> CHARLIE: "Nothing there, it's all gone back to ground."
> JAY: "She used to laugh, Charlie, black hair, like a child."

Further information emerges through Jay's answers to questions that Catherine asks as they travel together into the mountains. At one point, she hears him utter "Cat" while he dreams. When he awakes, she asks, "Was she very beautiful?" Jay answers, "Yeah." Later, after lovemaking, Catherine again raises the issue of Cat—"Can you tell me about it now? I mean, about Cat Dancing?" Jay states, for the first time, "She's dead." These four moments create a composite of Cat Dancing as beautiful, promiscuous, childlike, and captivating. Overall, she appears to be a Sexualized Maiden figure that surfaces in the hero's memory in vignettes reminiscent of poetry.

Through the first two-thirds of the narrative, the clues lead the viewer to believe that Cat Dancing caused Grobart's downward spiral from a civilized and upstanding white man to an outlaw. The narrative reveals that, as a young career army man, Grobart worked his way up to the rank of captain. He fell in love with a young Indian woman and "had to move out of the fort" because of her. It remains unclear whether army rules prohibited interracial unions or whether she was a prostitute—the sergeant's wife implies the latter through her tone and limited information about the "affair" between Cat Dancing and the murdered man.

The viewer does not learn the truth until Catherine and Grobart arrive at the Indian camp. The two are escorted to the tent of the chief, where Grobart explains his purpose for being there. "I have come to claim what was taken from me. My wife, Cat Dancing, was of the Shoshone tribe. My children were born after Sand Creek, and the Sioux and Cheyenne wars. When my wife died, Iron Knife brought my children here. I've come to get them." A young boy and girl are led into the tent, and the chief allows Grobart to talk with the boy, who refuses to leave his people to go with his father. At this point, Iron Knife asks the chief if he understands why Grobart went to prison. The chief, like the audience, Catherine, and the white characters, believes it was for "shooting the man who lay with Cat Dancing." Iron Knife tells another version:

> IRON KNIFE: "That man did not kill her. He [Grobart] killed her for lying with that man. But she was innocent. The man had raped her. The boy tried to tell him, but Grobart was filled with rage. He pushed the boy aside and he killed that man as he ran. Then, still raging, he came to Cat Dancing, but he would not hear her. He killed her there with his hands."
>
> GROBART: "No!"
>
> IRON KNIFE: "The boy saw Cat Dancing die. He saw you kill his mother."
>
> GROBART: "The boy speaks the truth. Your mother, your sister, was a faithful one."

Thus, near the end of the film, the viewer learns that Cat Dancing was a devoted wife and mother, a sister to a high-ranking member of the Shoshone tribe, and an innocent victim of racial and sexual violence. Most of the white characters assume that her race and location near the fort prove her promiscuous nature, and that this causes and justifies her death. In reality, her only transgression lay in her inability to stop her rapist, which resulted in her husband's temporary insanity—a jealous rage akin to the grief felt by Horse, Little Big Man, and Jeremiah

Johnson. So uncontrollable that he "would not hear" reason, Grobart proceeded to kill an unarmed man and the woman he loved.

The film also offers a parallel narrative that initially presents the hero's relationship with Cat Dancing as the cause of his degeneracy from an upstanding white man to a murderer and outlaw. Yet closer analysis reveals a number of twists to this subplot that retain the Celluloid Maiden figure as its focal point. Thus the film leads the viewer through a comfortable racist position and then reverses it. First, the hero enters a state of "savagery" because of his wife, but prior to her death. Second, the narrative initially blames the woman for the hero's transgression, but, in contrast with the earlier revisionist westerns, the film places the full burden of the Celluloid Maiden's death in the hands of the hero. Third, the couple lives on the border of "civilization," near the fort, rather than away from western European culture altogether. It is the maiden's death and subsequent transformation that lead him physically and metaphorically away from a civilized life and farther into the wilderness; in this way, the film resembles *Jeremiah Johnson*. Fourth, Cat Dancing—or her memory—molds Grobart into the type of man Catherine needs. Through his violence, the years of denial about the reality of his wife's murder, and his poetic memories and dreams of Cat Dancing, Grobart transforms into a new man. As the film reveals more details about Cat Dancing, each subsequent clue peeling away a layer of her racially coded image, Jay Grobart purges himself of her memory and, through his confession, his guilt. Simultaneously, Catherine falls in love with him because of his "devoted love *of the memory* of his wife."[47] With her growing knowledge of Cat Dancing, Catherine also changes, shedding her fine clothes, braiding her hair "Indian style," and learning to whistle as Cat Dancing's son does. The farther the two travel into the wilderness—Cat Dancing's homeland—the more compatible they become. In a twist on the previous revisionist westerns and more akin to past traditions in the western, the memory of the Celluloid Maiden initiates the transformation needed for the Adamic figure's journey into the wilderness to create an American Eden with a white Eve.

The Man Who Loved Cat Dancing, as do all of the films discussed above, "articulates and attempts to resolve widespread ambivalence about modernity" through the process of "going native." The film's pairing of Jay and Catherine, however, reinforces the racial hierarchy supposed by most of the white characters through its suggestion that the white woman provides a better union for Grobart than did Cat Danc-ing. The "going native" of the two white lovers and their status as the hero and heroine regenerate "the racial whiteness" ideology of the myth of the frontier while appropriating Indianness as the catalyst for their transformation into the Adam and Eve figures that will redeem white society.[48] As a result, the film illustrates a waning commitment to the anticolonial and revisionist ideals presented so forcefully by Arthur Penn in *Little Big Man* and Sydney Pollack in *Jeremiah Johnson*. Similar to *A Man Called Horse*, with its limited revisionist agenda, *The Man Who Loved Cat Dancing* continues to celebrate the formation of western cul-ture and the western hero. The film marks the end of the short-lived subgenre and the use of the Celluloid Maiden as a key figure in the deconstruction of the myth of the frontier.

Generally, the Princess's image surfaces most prominently during periods of intense national identity crisis (the turn of the century and the early cold war period) and when a symbolic rekindling seems most necessary. Revisionist westerns such as *Little Big Man* reject the white American hero by ridiculing him, in this case through the comic image of Jack Crabb/Little Big Man, while *A Man Called Horse* chooses a Brit-ish aristocrat in lieu of an American hero. Others, like *Jeremiah Johnson* and *The Man Who Loves Cat Dancing*, delve into the psychological instability of the hero. Such alterations of the western hero suggest un-easiness with the previous paradigm and a media culture in search of new ways to present or critique the national mythic genre, including the Native American woman. As they do with their heroes, these films remodel the Celluloid Princess to fit particular trends and mores of the 1970s. They attempt to portray a new and liberal Native woman by con-flating the morally pure and innocent Princess figure with a sexually aware and active woman. The use of already well entrenched symbols, such as the Sexualized Maiden and the Princess, complicates the figure but also creates a contradictory system of representation. Thus even the more liberal and risky presentations of the Celluloid Maiden, in *A Man Called Horse* and *Little Big Man*, do not differ that greatly from the more visually conservative depiction in *Jeremiah Johnson* or the rhetori-cally suggestive image in *The Man Who Loved Cat Dancing*.

The revisionist westerns represent varying degrees of commitment to voicing dissatisfaction with the political and social status quo and to reflecting the dissonance and growing ennui of the early 1970s. Each, to some degree, also hints at the changing attitudes in Hollywood about "how to make another kind of movie."[49] The vacillating use of "going native" in this small number of Celluloid Maiden films also indicates, to some extent, the latitude of the revisionist trend. The films, however, seem reluctant or unable to transfer such freedom to exploring the potential of the Celluloid Maiden figure as a revisionist symbol to the degree to which they do the white hero. Although she stands as a key character in deconstructing the myth of the frontier—a role of utmost importance—and she is an increasingly complex figure, the reduction of her filmic presence results in an overreliance on the audience's familiarity with the Princess and Sexualized Maiden stereotypes to flesh out the figure in a shorter amount of filmic time and space. As a result, the potential of the 1970s Celluloid Maiden remains untapped, trapped within the confines of a tradition of racializing images that promotes sexual exoticism over all else.

Six

Ghosts and Vanishing Indian Women

Death of the Celluloid Maiden in the 1990s

The 1990s saw the celluloid Indian back in the saddle, literally.
Multiculturalism became one of the buzzwords of the nineties, and
Hollywood filmmakers were ready to "set the record straight" on the
American Indian.

— Jacquelyn Kilpatrick

The complex forms of identificatory desire evoked by works
such as *Thunderheart* . . . and *Legends of the Fall* . . . suggest that
contemporary images of Native America have become even more
powerfully imbricated with the national Imaginary than in the past.

— Robert Burgoyne

THE CELLULOID MAIDEN REAPPEARS in the 1990s, after a hiatus
of seventeen years, in a number of films that reaffirm this figure's ability
to adapt to changing cultural trends in representing Native Americans.
The figure emerges in a diversity of roles—including an avenging ghost,
a political activist, and a mixed-blood Princess who crosses genres and
national film boundaries—that reveals the complexity of the figure. Although more contemporary and, in some cases, quite different from past
presentations, these uses of the figure stimulate cultural memories of

prior Celluloid Maidens through the films' reliance on, or reference to, previous modes of depicting the character as a Princess or a Sexualized Maiden type. As a result, a tension exists between the various films' multiculturalist and revisionist angles and the deeply imbedded system of stereotypes that continues to use the figure as a palimpsest upon which American national myths are reinscribed.[1] Thus, although the 1990s films use the Celluloid Maiden to promote a racially diverse narrative, to a greater extent, the character reproduces the social ruptures of an era when past national mythic identities and the ideologies of the western become antithetical to the nation's racial and cultural diversity.[2]

The contemporary narratives that incorporate the Celluloid Maiden rely on nostalgia marred by violence and racism in their articulations of the power structures involved in maintaining an American national identity and Native-white relations. Revisionist in intent, four films from the early 1990s promote a "realistic" image of the Native woman, and all reveal the underlying racial tension inherent in Native American–white relations. These traits clearly mark the efforts of *Thunderheart* (1992), *Silent Tongue* (1993), and *Legends of the Fall* (1994) to "'set the record straight' on the American Indian," or at least to rethink it and modify it in some way.[3] All exhibit revisionist disillusion with the myth of the frontier, which celebrates an idealized nation-building process. *Thunderheart*, *Legends of the Fall*, and the Canadian film *Legends of the North* (1995) critique the governing body of the nation-state—the corruption of the mythic ideal—at the same time that they celebrate the individual hero figure. *Silent Tongue*, the clearest western of the films, takes on the idealism of the genre itself through its portrayal of white men as an ineffectual force on the frontier and Native American women as effective reactionaries.

Through the efforts and contradictions that create them, these films participate in what Richard Slotkin suggests is a pattern of reciprocal influence in which politics shape the concerns and imagery of movies, and movies in turn question or promote current political and social attitudes.[4] Though not necessarily westerns, these Celluloid Maiden films, as a part of their revisionism, reference some aspect of the myth of the frontier that informs the genre. Their use of genre nostalgia and Hollywood western generic conventions also ties them to the Hollywood tradition of portraying the Celluloid Maiden. Their reliance on well-known visual metaphors in describing the Celluloid Maiden often contrasts

with their revisionist narrative ideology. The resulting conflict parallels
the tensions between conservative and liberal attitudes toward multiculturalism and the United States' national identity in the 1990s. *Legends
of the North* might be exempted from such a claim about U.S. films on
the basis of its national origin; however, the pattern of stress related to
the political moment in the United States in which revisionism resur-
faced in the 1990s also exists in this film.

The early 1990s witnessed the end of the cold war, the fall of the
Soviet system, the drawing to a close of the conservative Republican
presidential reign, and an increase in the United States' imperial behavior overseas, in places such as Panama and the Middle East. The sudden
collapse of the Soviet Union "left the political leadership of the United
States unprepared" for its uncontested position as world leader. The nation was overextended in military and economic aid to other countries
and unready to deal with such a monumental change. The fall of communism and the dissolution of the Soviet Union eliminated the United
States' external Other—the group used since the 1940s as a measure of
what Americans were not. President George H. W. Bush's "new world
order," a quest for a new political Other and a justification of global U.S.
government and economic investments, resulted in two wars—one in
Panama and the other in the Persian Gulf. Both reflected the country's
insecurity about its national identity and the belief in the need to reassert
international dominance. Certainly the Gulf War, in connection with
the ultraconservative religious mood of the nation, presented a message
of continued U.S. supremacy and established U.S. control over Middle
East oil resources.[5]

The resulting turmoil of the early 1990s culminated in an intense
questioning on the part of many Americans of their national past and
their imperial and neocolonial present. Howard Zinn explains that, in
the United States, a "citizenry disillusioned with politics and with what
pretended to be intelligent discussions of politics turned its attention (or
had its attention turned) to entertainment, to gossip, to ten thousand
schemes for self-help. Those at its margins became violent, finding scape-
goats within one's group (as with poor-black on poor-black violence), or
against other races, immigrants, demonized foreigners, welfare mothers,
minor criminals (standing in for untouchable major criminals)." On the
political scene, conservatives supporting Whiteness rhetoric and pro-
white national agendas countered liberal groups recognizing and cel-

ebrating a multicultural nation. Many critiqued the ongoing system of color hierarchy and ultraconservative political agendas that targeted peoples of color and the poor as responsible for national economic, social, and religious regression. They were, however, confronted by the rise of the religious Right, family values, and Bush's new world order. Such movements reaffirmed the ideology of America as the conquering hero and the world's policeman and echoed the ideological message of the myth, so prominent in the western film, that European-derived "civilization . . . really is *better* than all other civilizations, past and present." This conservative trend, which had its roots in the mid-1970s backlash against 1960s and 1970s liberalism, supported an increasing intolerance toward immigrants of color, illegal aliens, and the nation's racial poor; differing religious views and political orientations; and nontraditional "family values." Also in the early nineties, Native Americans and those of European descent in both North and South America mobilized against European and American quincentenary celebrations of Columbus's arrival in the New World.[6] Multiple voices were heard during this period both questioning and defending the colonial past, often resulting in heated debate and violence that indicated the depth to which the United States' identity remained tied to memories of conquest.

The Celluloid Maiden films register the effects of these debates and tensions in varying degrees in their revisionist narrative approaches and, in the case of *Silent Tongue* and *Thunderheart*, their diverse, contemporary portrayals of Native Americans and Native American–white racial power struggles. *Legends of the Fall* and the joint French-Canadian production *Legends of the North* maintain a more traditional and familiar approach to the Celluloid Maiden. They are, in outcome and style, similar to the much-heralded *Dances with Wolves* (1990), which, with its romanticizing of Native Americans, remains a hallmark of the 1990s revisionist movement and is remembered as the second western ever to win the Academy Award for Best Picture.[7] *Silent Tongue*, a western that follows more closely the approach of *Unforgiven* (1992)—also an Academy Award winner—challenges the conventions of the western and clearly questions the dominant racial and masculine order of the genre.[8] *Thunderheart* does not frame its narrative as a western; rather, it relies on the criminal investigation genre to inform its overarching narrative structure. Yet the film's location in the West, the positioning of Native Americans as the primary group within the narrative, and the narrative allusions to the western genre tie it to that tradition. This group of films offers a lens through which to view the legacy of almost ninety years of filmic presentation. In addition, these films maneuver the genre to speak to the political and media presence of Native Americans during the nineties, the demand for less racializing images in media, and, as Richard Slotkin suggests, the ongoing disillusionment of many Americans about the national government and "fundamental principles of national ideology."[9]

THE ACTIVIST, THE GHOST, THE HEALER, AND THE MARTYR

A chronological analysis of the 1990s Celluloid Maiden characters reveals a marked shift in their uses of the figure. The maiden metamorphoses from a highly revisionist and political manifestation of the Native woman as an activist against colonialism to a conservative martyr figure reminiscent of the silent-period Princess. Though *Thunderheart* and *Silent Tongue* focus on different eras in U.S. history, each creates a character who resists the white power structures manipulating her world. *Thunderheart*'s Maggie Eagle Bear and *Silent Tongue*'s Awbonnie embody the spirit of Native agency, their interactions with western European culture laying bare the often violent reality of the colonial experience for Native American women. In contrast, *Legends of the Fall* and *Legends of the North* retain a nostalgic tone most closely related to the silent-period films and display characteristics reminiscent of the various eras of Princess figures. *Legends of the Fall* relies on the "going native" theme prevalent in the 1970s films; *Legends of the North* reverts to a figure whose self-sacrifice harks back to the early depictions of the Celluloid Princess. The conservative construction of the Celluloid Maiden in these films is juxtaposed to the liberal agenda that underlies *Thunderheart* and *Silent Tongue*.

   Thunderheart is one of the most poignant of the revisionist works because of its contemporary setting and focus on Native activism. The film, Michael Apted's mainstream fictional remake of his documentary *Incident at Oglala*, places contemporary Native issues about land rights and political sovereignty squarely in front of the viewer.[10] It remains one of the few films that confront the audience with a realistic and complex picture of Native Americans, women's roles in tribal society, and the daily realities that many Native communities face. In addition, as Robert Burgoyne's work on *Thunderheart* and the national imaginary suggests, the film presents an internally colonized group pitted against the dominant nation from the point of view of the subjugated.[11] Thus this film undermines a particular idea of national unity by basing its narrative on examples of national discontinuity that result in political, social, and cultural differences.

Called to aid a murder investigation on the Bear Creek Sioux reservation in South Dakota, FBI agent Ray Lavoi (Val Kilmer), who is one-quarter Sioux, finds himself struggling between his loyalty to the bureau and western European culture and his awakening tribal identity. Well-trained in racializing poverty and nonconformity as signs of moral weakness, Ray initially blames the people of Bear Creek for their third-world status. Prompted by tribal police officer Walter Crow Horse (Graham Greene) to question his superior Frank Coutelle's (Sam Shepard) theory about the murder, Ray delves deeper into the incident, only to be drawn into a situation that forces him to confront the disturbing reality of Native-federal relations. As he learns more about the FBI-backed tribal government's "reign of terror" over the traditional and activist Sioux, Ray begins to wonder about his own heritage, to come to terms with his stereotypes about Indians, and to align himself with the traditionalists. Befriended by Walter, Maggie Eagle Bear (Sheila Tousey), and Grandpa Sam Reaches (Chief Ted Thin Elk), the traditionalist's medicine man, Ray begins to shed his white exterior and to take an interest in the problems of those living on the reservation. His interactions with Grandpa Reaches and Maggie initiate visions that link Ray to his Sioux heritage and bind him more closely to their cause. He eventually exposes the federal government's role in the terrorism, the uranium poisoning of the reservation's water source, and the murder at the heart of the film's plot.

Maggie Eagle Bear pays with her life for her political connections — her disruption of political order — and her interaction with Ray Lavoi. Her character is based on Anna Mae Aquash, an American Indian Movement activist who was allegedly killed by the FBI or by FBI supporters in 1976.[12] Maggie works for her people and against the dominant white culture represented by the FBI and Ray Lavoi. Her primary concern is to prove that the federal government has knowingly poisoned the reservation's only source of drinking water by illegally dumping uranium tailings into the river's source. A Dartmouth honors graduate, mother, and activist, and a force to be reckoned with, Maggie challenges Ray to "do his job," to investigate the many "suicides" and the "misappropriation of funds in school and health programs" on the reservation. In keeping with the reality of Anna Mae's death, the movie leaves the identity of Maggie's killer unknown, but the narrative implies that a federal plant within her community, the FBI, or the corrupt tribal government's vigilante squad aligned with the federal agents committed the crime.

Maggie's activism and militancy reach back into Celluloid Maiden history to revive the militant Native American Queen figure, whose resistance to encroaching Europeans is both sexually arousing and deadly. As discussed previously, the Native American Queen embodies the qualities of the feminized and premodern New World, including the danger awaiting the colonial forces there. As depicted in engravings and early accounts of colonial expansion, she figuratively represents the psychological reaction of the indigenous peoples to colonial action and the rape of their motherland, as well as the potential disruption of the colonial process. Her militant stance, with a "foot on the slain body of an animal or human enemy," suggests that she is capable of fighting back.[13] Similarly, Maggie's activities threaten the colonial order, in this case the U.S. government and the FBI. Though she is not a violent warrior like the Queen, Maggie's continual probing into the government's misconduct with the uranium mines, her relentless pursuit of justice for her people, who are being murdered, and her championing of Indian sovereignty cast her as a reactionary figure. Just as the Queen fought against the European invaders, she fights against the power structures that abuse the federal-Indian treaty relationship and for the rights of indigenous people. Within this context and because of the FBI's secret activities and infiltration of the tribal community, Maggie Eagle Bear's death, which recalls that of Sunshine's in *Little Big Man* (1970), symbolizes a history of governmentally sponsored military suppression of Native peoples and radically subversive elements in the nation's populace.

Thunderheart's narrative clearly criticizes the federal government's history of covert military intervention in tribal affairs for economic gain. Through Maggie's character, the film also highlights a tradition of Native community activism powered by women, including mothers and grandmothers. While some of this force gets channeled into education, symbolized in the film by Maggie's role as a teacher, a great deal emerges through political positions and organized demonstrations against treaty violations, destruction of sacred lands, and corruption in federal governmental programs that deal with Native American communities.[14]

Part of *Thunderheart*'s power lies in its open confrontation of several significant and controversial themes: colonialism, racism, and the violation of human rights. These are clearly summed up by various characters on both sides of the political struggle. Early in the film, Frank Coutelle explains to Ray that, while their assignment is a murder investigation, "it's also about helping people, helping people caught in the illusions of the past come to terms with the reality of the present." He explains this "reality" near the end of the film: "Let me tell you something. I feel for them, I really do, they're a proud people. But they're also a conquered people and that means their future is dictated by the nation that conquered them. Now rightly or wrongly, that's the way it works down through history." This patronizing, neoconservative perspective of U.S. dominance clashes with that of Jimmy Looks Twice (John Trudell), Maggie Eagle Bear, and the other traditionalists, who maintain their identity as a culturally and politically sovereign people. As Jimmy Looks Twice tells Ray, "We choose the right to be who we are. We know the difference between the reality of freedom and the illusion of freedom. There is a way to live with the earth and a way not to live with the earth. We choose earth. It's about power." Maggie Eagle Bear's position as an activist places her squarely in these cultural debates, and she initiates Ray into the power of the earth, reminding him at one point that evidence is not power: "Power is the rainstorm. That river right there—that's what I have to protect."

Thunderheart's narrative and its visual presentation connect Maggie to the land and water as its guardian. She fights against the uranium mines that are contaminating the water; she spreads offerings over the river and takes samples for testing; and she reminds Lavoi that the river needs her aid. Her death brings her full circle, back into the earth she protects. Well into the film, Ray and Walter Crow Horse go to the site of the first murder to investigate. The moon casts a pale light over the sand and rock formations of the badlands and the illegal, government-sponsored uranium mining pools. Startled by the sound of animals, Ray moves toward a shape in the sand. He finds Maggie partially buried, face down in the sand, only her denim jacket showing above the ground. Moaning with grief as he recognizes her, Lavoi turns Maggie over. Her

Thunderheart. Michael Apted, TriStar Pictures, 1992.

sand-covered face, tinted a pale blue, stares back at him while her open eyes reflect the light of the moon. Maggie Eagle Bear dies in the Black Hills, the Sioux's sacred land and the river's source, near the uranium mines she fought against.

Maggie's character embodies the contemporary activist and ecologist at the same time that it relies on elements from the hybrid Celluloid Maiden history. The only primary Native woman character, she is depicted as a love interest for the white hero, betrays her own people by aiding Ray, and is metonymically connected to the landscape, all of which invoke memories of the Princess figures. These elements are reinforced by the film's tendency to romanticize Indian spirituality. This aspect emerges most clearly in visions Ray has in connection with Maggie and Grandpa Reaches. A number of times, while on Maggie's property or just after having spoken to Maggie, Ray sees dancers in full regalia across the river. Walter informs him later that he has seen the old ones performing the Ghost Dance in preparation for war against the whites.[15] He also dreams of "running with the old ones" at Wounded Knee as white soldiers mow down the unarmed women and children. Grandpa Reaches stimulates Ray's memories of a childhood with his drunken Sioux father and a single dream of the old ones, but the majority of Ray's visions occur in conjunction with Maggie, who, through association, links Ray to the physical sites in the dreams. Such subtle references do not overwhelm the film's pro-Indian angle, but they do render Maggie a capitulation to Hollywood marketing. As John Walton suggests, she takes on the "favorable stereotype" of the earth mother, the "Ecological Indian," and the sexually attractive love interest.[16]

As mentioned above, Maggie's character is based on the American Indian Movement activist Anna Mae Aquash. The character's connection to this well-known woman and her much-publicized death is an important component of the film's pro-Native stance. The connection between the two women also underscores the human rights and anticolonial themes highlighted throughout the film. By overlaying the earth mother and other "favorable" Hollywood stereotypes onto the core representative of Anna Mae Aquash, however, the film undermines the potential of Maggie's character to effectively symbolize the resistance movement and replaces it with the Celluloid Princess. As a result, the political position characterized by Maggie within the cultural debates discussed early in the film shifts. She initially uses her Dartmouth training against the system — to investigate it and to empower her own people. But her commitment to Ray weakens the effects of these actions and repositions her on the side of the debate that Frank Coutelle supports. The character recapitulates to the colonial system and reverts from the Native American Queen figure to the Princess figure. This move cancels out Maggie's intentions to use the dominant society against itself. Thus the use of the Celluloid Maiden figure in the film weakens the film's political agenda and positions age-old stereotypes on contemporary images of Native American women.

Maggie Eagle Bear's sand-covered face, pale and tinted slightly blue, eerily reappears in Sam Shepard's *Silent Tongue* as the face of Awbonnie. Sheila Tousey plays the decomposing woman-ghost Awbonnie. Her distraught white husband, Talbot Roe (River Phoenix), ties her to the land of the living through his relentless vigil over her corpse. In direct contrast to most of the Celluloid Maiden films, *Silent Tongue* challenges the idea of the young woman who falls in love with the white hero by suggesting that such love and devotion are illusions of the colonial mind.

In addition, Shepard's film revises the connection between the Native woman and nature that plays such an important role in the Celluloid Maiden's tropic resonance.

The film enfolds the lives of three women—the Kiowa bone picker Silent Tongue (Tantoo Cardinal) and her two mixed-blood daughters, Awbonnie and Velada (Jeri Arredondo)—into the story of three white men who are bound to the women by violence and need. Awbonnie, whom Prescott Roe (Richard Harris) purchases from her father Eamon McCree (Alan Bates) for three horses with the hope that she will cure his son's melancholia, dies in childbirth. The heartbroken and selfish Talbot refuses to burn or bury her body, acts that would release her spirit; rather, he guards her decomposing form, battling the scavenging birds of prey and her angry ghost for its possession. Prescott travels across the desert in search of Eamon McCree to buy Awbonnie's sister Velada, be-lieving that she will halt his son's increasing insanity. Eamon refuses only because Velada—the "Kiowa Warrior Princess"—is the main at-traction of his traveling medicine show. Prescott kidnaps Velada, who eventually agrees to help for a large sum of money and many horses. As Prescott, Talbot, and Velada are preyed upon by Awbonnie's ghost, Eamon and his son Reeves (Dermot Mulroney) search for Velada, only to be hunted by Silent Tongue's people. Silent Tongue, so named when her tongue was cut out for lying to a chief, left Eamon and her girls to return to her people. But as one review points out, "Her brutal treat-ment at the hands of her own people is nothing to the way she and her daughters are treated by the new settlers."[17] Much like her daughter's ghost, Silent Tongue seeks revenge on the white man who forced her into marriage. As Eamon's nightmarish memories reveal, he came upon her in the desert while she collected bones, raped her while Reeves was forced to watch, and then took her as his wife.

Refusing an easy good/bad dichotomy between the Native women and their white husbands, Shepard's narrative hints at the affection felt by the white men for their captive wives. For example, Eamon covers the walls of his caravan with photographs of Silent Tongue and her daugh-ters. The images add a level of intimacy and tenderness to the relation-ship that contradicts the visions of Silent Tongue's rape and Eamon's callous economic selfishness with respect to Velada. Similarly, Talbot re-mains tender to his wife's shrouded body, holding it protectively, kissing its face, arranging its covering, and viciously attacking all that attempt to approach it, even when under siege by her femme fatale ghost. His own mental breakdown at her death clarifies the genuine intensity of his love. Like the Celluloid Maidens of the 1970s, the living Awbonnie acted as the white hero's anchor, allowing him to "go native" to a limited and safe extent.

While the film's insight into characters' emotional development leans toward the males, the women's activism refutes the western tradition of white-hero worship. The film achieves this in part by depicting the men as weak and atypical of the traditional western hero. In addition, the film underscores its revisionist agenda by giving the women agency through the acts of leaving or terrorism. Silent Tongue chooses to abandon her daughters and return to her people. She continues, however, to haunt her husband in his dreams. Awbonnie, depicted through Talbot's love as a Princess type during her life, metamorphoses into a femme fatale, much like Nita in *Arrowhead* (1953) and Hesh-ke in *Mackenna's Gold* (1969), whose physical connection to the hero turns violently against him. When Talbot thwarts her attempts to escape to the spirit world, Awbonnie's ghost carries on increasingly violent attacks on the bodies and minds of Talbot and Prescott Roe, until Prescott finally throws her body into the fire, an act that releases all parties involved. Prescott's actions allegorically suggest the need for white America to let go of its symbolic romantic notions of Native Americans. Early in the film, Awbonnie's ghost foregrounds the allegory by stating, "You keep me bound here out of your selfish aloneness." Her comment reinforces the traditional use of the Native American in western European culture as a symbolic racial and cultural Other that offers a psychological and political justification for the entrenchment of the American nation.

In keeping with the message above, *Silent Tongue* also inverts the traditional cinematic reliance on metaphorically linking the Native woman to images of nature. Although the beautiful Native woman remains tied to the landscape, stark and harsh images of the land replace all romanticism, as seen in Silent Tongue's bone picking, Awbonnie's physical decomposition, and the birds of prey that stalk Awbonnie's body. Nature takes on as violent a veneer as does the Celluloid Maiden. Reminiscent of the landscape in Cormac McCarthy's *Blood Meridian*, the desert of *Silent Tongue* never offers any oasis of beauty. Rather, the barren, dry land, punctuated by thirsty stands of trees, contains birds of prey, fields

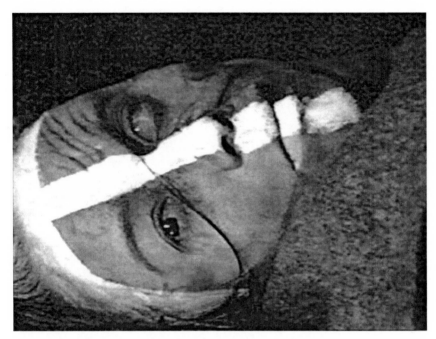

Silent Tongue. Sam Shepard, Belbo Films, 1993.

of sun-bleached animal bones, and a Greek-style Fury whose presence haunts and physically harms the living.[18] Like this space, Awbonnie's body carries the marks of life and death. Half of her white-painted face is decomposed, and her milk-white eyes are bright with passionate anger. Feathers, vulture wings, bones, and cloth adorn the tree where she lies. Because the viewer never encounters the living Awbonnie, her persona emerges from these images. As a result, Awbonnie and the land she inhabits invoke the memory of a vengeful, beautiful, and dangerous Native American Queen and the femme fatale, more reminiscent of the Sexualized Maidens of the 1950s than of the Princess figure.

The commitment of *Silent Tongue* to reworking the western forces the viewer to confront the colonial process head-on. Its "stylized allegory of the white man's brutalization of Native Americans" refuses to allow the viewer any lapses into romanticism or nostalgia about America's evolution as a nation.[19] Although the film relies on stereotypes, such as the Princess figure and the Native femme fatale, to shore up its characterization of Native American women, these do not consume the character.

Velada, the "Kiowa Warrior Princess" and rodeo queen, negotiates her own payment for helping Prescott Roe. Awbonnie, who "was [Talbot's] light," refuses the responsibility of that role, and her ghost takes her husband to task for his participation in her purchase and her death. The images of the Native American women fighting for their freedom are political and effective. The film's deemphasis of the Princess type in the characters of Awbonnie and Silent Tongue helps it push the boundaries of the figure more successfully than does *Thunderheart*.

The anticolonialist narratives in *Thunderheart* and *Silent Tongue* and the Celluloid Maiden's use within the films must also be placed within the context of the early 1990s' ultraconservative political atmosphere and the controversial quincentenary. The year of the quincentenary, 1992, marked a tumultuous moment in U.S. and Western history, a period that forced mainstream U.S. culture to reevaluate its historical narratives, its political heroes, and its heritage on this continent. Debates abounded regarding whether the quincentenary should celebrate Columbus and the "civilizing" of the Americas, the multicultural encounter, or five hundred years of indigenous survival in the wake of colonialism and genocide. A wide range of literary reactions illustrated the intense self-examination that academia and the American public underwent during this time.[20]

With respect to the post–cold war global political positioning of the United States, one is struck by the complexity of these quincentenary debates in relation to U.S. nationalism. During 1992, Americans witnessed the third-greatest period of U.S. immigration, a rise in anti–illegal immigration measures, and a decline in employment opportunities. As Walter Zinn suggests, events such as rising unemployment, U.S. economic expansion overseas, and the U.S. military action in Iraq culminated in insecurity, causing many Americans to question their position in their own country and their role in global economic politics. The works of Michael Omi and Howard Winant and of Lauren Berlant point toward the various strategies used by groups to express these identity crises, including masking racist political agendas in multicultural rhetoric. Within this milieu, the quincentenary was, in the words of Stephen Summerhill and John A. Williams, "no longer an innocuous ethnic celebration of Columbus' discovery of America, it had become a battleground for our entire view of Western culture."[21]

Thunderheart and *Silent Tongue* represent what appear to be respectful efforts by the filmmakers to explore and participate in the deconstruction of the colonial process and these debates. *Thunderheart*, in particular, relied heavily on the input of Native Americans and the continued collaborative effort between Apted and the Native American participants from his documentary *Incident at Oglala* (1992). Both *Thunderheart* and *Silent Tongue* challenge the tenets of the western's pro-white and pro–nation formation agenda, illuminating in the process a darker side of American history and the nation's continuing actions as a colonizing force. However, both films also show how difficult it is for those working with representations of Native Americans to divorce themselves from racializing stereotypes. Both Maggie Eagle Bear and Awbonnie represent the possible destabilization of the Celluloid Maiden figure and the concrete reality that Native Americans continue to demand an identity and voice outside the national whole. At the same time, *Thunderheart* resorts to invoking the Celluloid Maiden figure, and *Silent Tongue* the Native American Queen component of it. In addition, by placing its narrative in the past, *Silent Tongue* perpetuates the tradition of depicting Native Americans as historical relics of a mythic space. The inability to completely abandon tropic references is not unique to the film community; it emerged as a problem facing many Americans attempting to come to terms with the politics of the quincentenary.

On the whole, *Silent Tongue* and *Thunderheart* remain the most progressive of the revisionist Celluloid Maiden films. Perhaps as a sign of the waning influence of the quincentenary debates of 1992, subsequent films fail to maintain the level of commitment *Silent Tongue* and *Thunderheart* display in deconstructing Hollywood's presentation of Native Americans and the Celluloid Maiden figure. Only one year after the release of *Silent Tongue*, a decidedly more conservative and nostalgic approach to revisionism and the western surfaces in Edward Zwick's *Legends of the Fall*, setting the tone for *Legends of the North*.

The World War I family melodrama *Legends of the Fall* (1994), as one critic described it, throws "the golden shadows of the waning Old West . . . across the big screen with full reverential treatment."[22] The film celebrates an American individualism and isolationism born of the frontier landscape and shaped by antigovernment rhetoric. Like the revisionist westerns of the 1970s, *Legends of the Fall* weaves nostalgia for ennobled Native Americans and their spiritual connection to the world into its ideology. The film's hero, Tristan Ludlow (Brad Pitt), bucks the mainstream way of life. More at home working cattle, hunting in the wilderness, or defying authority than existing in the cultural mainstream, he tracks bears just to touch them, sails the world as a game hunter and trader among the world's tribal communities, and makes his living running bootleg liquor. The Native American character One Stab (Gordon Tootoosis) provides a point of reference through which the story unfolds and, with Isabel Two (Karina Lombard), is a pivotal influence on Tristan's emergence as a legend—a man more at peace with the "savages" of the world than with "civilization." Jim Harrison's novella of the same name, the basis for the screenplay, also includes these characters and attaches meaning to Tristan's father-son relationship with One Stab. The film, however, clearly emphasizes the Native American angle of the story to suggest that Tristan's wildness and inner savagery come from One Stab's influence, rather than, as is the case in the novel, from a hereditary link to his Scottish grandfather. The film also plays down Harrison's focus on demythologizing "our romantic notions of Cowboys and Indians," instead enhancing such notions.[23]

The "reverential treatment" accorded the Old West also applies to the film's reliance on stereotypical symbolism in its coding of the two primary Native characters. One Stab and Isabel Two represent the environment Tristan really belongs to—the vanishing world of the Indian West. While he loves his brothers and Susannah Finncannon (Julia Ormond), Tristan clashes with the civilized and educated world of the East that they represent. "He had always lived in the border lands . . . somewhere between this world and the next." It is this liminal spirit that binds him to One Stab and Isabel Two, who instinctively understand his wild nature and embrace it.

One Stab is a wise Cree Indian elder who outlives the family and is thus able to perpetuate its legend. The narrative opens with One Stab sitting in a tepee speaking these words: "Some people hear their own inner voices and they live by what they hear. Such people become crazy or they become legend." He is referring to Tristan Ludlow, the middle son of One Stab's friend Colonel William Ludlow (Anthony Hopkins). The film depicts One Stab as Tristan's spiritual guide and the man who feels Tristan's presence through his dreams. One Stab's voiceovers also link Tristan to the land and Tristan's periodic lapses into savagery to "the bear's voice he heard deep inside him, growling low from dark, secret places."

Similar to that of One Stab, the characterization of Isabel Two relies on the now-familiar traditional images of the Celluloid Maiden, with an emphasis on the Princess figure. In an interesting evolution of the figure, Isabel Two is not established as a Princess by any one particular scene; rather, the image emerges out of an accumulation of narrative vignettes that places her within the tradition of the figure. Demonstrating how deeply solidified the figure is in the American memory, the film economically presents the traces of Celluloid Princess ancestry in Isabel Two, clearly depending on the audience's genre memories of past figures. Much as the films of the 1950s and the 1970s do, *Legends of the Fall* confines the Celluloid Maiden to an extremely small though important position on the edges of the narrative, where her world centers on the white hero. Reminiscent of Sonseeahray in *Broken Arrow* (1950), Isabel Two has the gift of prophecy—at least where her life with Tristan is concerned. She knows she will marry Tristan, a fact she relays at age twelve to the newly arrived Susannah. The film's introduction of her as a child establishes her innocence and absolute devotion to the white hero. Isabel Two's reappearance as a beautiful and intriguing young woman, whom Tristan finds captivating, opens the door for the possibility of assimilation through marriage. The figure also carries traces of the 1940s Sexualized Maiden in her mixed heritage as the daughter of Paul Decker (Paul Desmond) and his Cree wife Pet (Tantoo Cardinal), who work for Ludlow. Her mixed-blood status carries no sexual or psychological stigma and does nothing to diminish her Princess persona. Rather, it works to underscore the liberal and antiracist utopia of the Ludlow ranch in contrast to the external world.

The structure set up by the film's coupling of Tristan with Native America and the power of the wilderness references the Hollywood trend seen in the 1970s Celluloid Maiden films. His ability to "go native" without falling too deeply into insanity or savagery depends on the Native woman—a Princess type—with whom he finds spiritual and psychological balance. *Legends of the Fall* symbolically establishes Isabel Two in this role by placing her in relation to the two white women in the film, Isabel Ludlow and Susannah. Isabel Two takes her name from Mrs. Ludlow (Christina Pickles) and thus is metaphorically connected to Tristan's absent mother through her name and to his spiritual father, One Stab, through tribal affiliation. Mrs. Ludlow's character does not develop beyond a cameo appearance here and there, but her return to the family ranch with a wedding gown for Isabel after years of absence establishes the girl as the family's choice to marry Tristan. The film does develop Susannah's character, and in fact she exists as the primary love interest for all the Ludlow boys. Susannah initially arrives at the ranch as Samuel Ludlow's (Henry Thomas) fiancée. She quickly captivates all the Ludlow men, who are starved for the presence of a cultivated eastern woman like their mother, and falls in love with Tristan. After Samuel dies in war and Tristan abandons her to exorcise his demons, she marries Alfred (Aidan Quinn).

Isabel Two's Native heritage makes her more capable of understanding Tristan's savage instincts and "the bear inside" than is Susannah, whose fragile eastern spirit continually clashes with Tristan's wildness. Isabel Two and Tristan marry and, according to One Stab, "It was then that Tristan came into the quiet of his life. The Bear was sleeping." Like *Jeremiah Johnson's* Swan (1972), whose Christianity worked as a link for Jeremiah between the wilderness and the civilization he abandoned, Isabel Two is well equipped for the position of cultural mediator. Her combination of "Western" education and Native grounding in the earth allows Isabel Two to keep Tristan anchored to the white world and to cultivate in him a certain level of contentedness, something missing from Tristan's relationship with Susannah.

Following in the footsteps of *Jeremiah Johnson* and *Broken Arrow*, *Legends of the Fall* tenuously hints at the idea of an American Adam and Native American Eve through Tristan and Isabel Two's union. But the film resorts to an interesting permutation on the Adam and Eve narrative by killing both the Native American Eve and her competitor, Susannah, the white Eve whose mental instability results in her suicide. This allows the film to continue the tradition of idolizing the white male hero, whose wild soul and individualism, cultivated out of his love for a Native American way of life, leave little room for domestication. In addition, within a discourse on race, Isabel Two's Native-white heritage suggests a new image of the American Eve—a more culturally and racially "white" one. She is a multicultural allegory for a changing American identity, which, on the surface, appears a seductive one. Yet multiculturalism carries a less than idealized meaning within the film's nostalgia for the waning American past and through its presentation of Isabel Two as a child raised in a primarily white environment and isolated from the racism she would have encountered in town. Multiculturalism looks more like an assimilative process than an interaction of culturally and racially diverse groups. Subtly, the film suggests that an egalitarian interaction of many different cultures and heritages, an idealized assimilated culture, is still unrealistic.

Comparable to *Legends of the Fall* in its romantic nostalgia for a mythic West, *Legends of the North* attempts to critique extreme white paternalism while maintaining a high degree of romantic attachment to the symbolism the Celluloid Maiden figure resonates in the earlier films. Here, too, one finds an insular community founded by a patriarchal leader who has abandoned the cultural system he sees as responsible for the demise of the Native American. The least revisionist of all the 1990s films, *Legends of the North* simply transfers the markers of change seen in *Legends of the Fall*, such as creating an educated, mixed-blood Princess, to a traditional martyr figure, as seen in the silent-period films. In so doing, the film forgoes any in-depth reworking of the figure.

Legends of the North takes place in the Yukon in the early 1890s. Aristocrat Charles Bel-Air (Georges Corraface) and his deceased father's guide, Whip (Randy Quaid), set out on a journey to find Esperanza, a legendary gold treasure. They find the gold guarded by a remote tribe of primitive Indians under the authoritarian rule of a white man, McTavish (Serge Houde), who fancies himself their "great white hope." As he tells Bel-Air, "These people were on the edge of extinction. And as their white father, I gave them a sense of themselves and their community." His commitment to them extends far enough to ensure their entrapment in his idea of how Native American culture must remain in order to survive. He keeps the tribe mired in the past, and all intruders—threats to the community's lifestyle—are either killed or married into the tribe as captive participants. His mixed-blood daughter, Kanata (Sandrine Holt), falls in love with Bel-Air as the two recite and enact *Romeo and Juliet* and *Wuthering Heights*. She rejects her Native lover for the white outsider, whom she helps to escape. Their journey across the frozen north toward freedom in the south ends in tragedy as she gives up her rations to ensure Bel-Air's survival. He illustrates his love for her by vowing to stay with her dead body, a gesture that fails when Whip finds him and takes him back to civilization.

The film returns to the silent period for its narrative structure. As in the early Princess films, the aristocratic white male leaves the East; France takes the place of the earlier films' East Coast or England. Bel-

Air journeys into the wilderness, where he must be rescued by the Princess figure. Kanata's character melds the Princess with the helper figure of that era, and for the first time in eighty years, the Princess does not marry the hero. Much as she did in *Iola's Promise* (1912) and *Red Wing's Gratitude* (1909), the Princess saves the hero when his culture clashes with her own. As in the romantic love narratives of the Princess films, the two lovers presumably would have wed once they reached civilization. Unlike the silent-period films, however, *Legends of the North* never quite melds its disparate elements into a satisfactory formula. It seems that the reliance on a *Romeo and Juliet*–style unrequited love theme, within a narrative that builds on the girl's exoticism, fails to hold the tensions found in the earlier films. Perhaps the structure simply no longer fits with the film's contemporaries, such as *Thunderheart* and *Silent Tongue*, and thus appears less successful. But it seems more likely that the addition of a white patriarchal and oppressive tribal ruler undermines the film's ability to maintain the tension between the vanishing American noble savage image and the manifest destiny of white cultural superiority.

The reliance of *Legends of the North* on the Princess as a martyr figure brings the historical trajectory of the Celluloid Maiden full circle, to its cinematic roots in the silent period. Kanata's mixed-blood heritage makes her a hybrid figure like Isabel Two. More overtly than does Isabel Two, however, Kanata retains the symbolic components of the first Princess figures, appearing as a beautiful and alluring chief's daughter whose yearning for western European culture can be achieved only through a commitment to a white male patriarchal figure—either her father or Bel-Air. The film's most obvious reversion to the silent-period figures surfaces in Kanata's self-sacrifice, which reaffirms the primacy of western European culture.

Kanata's high tribal social standing, her Native sensuality, and the exoticism of her tribal existence are enhanced for the contemporary audience and her white lover by their contrast with her Western literary training. Both *Thunderheart* and *Legends of the Fall* use this narrative tool to reduce the difference between the Native American woman and the white male and to highlight the Celluloid Maiden's aura as a contemporary woman—an intellectually equal partner for the white hero. *Legends of the North* takes full advantage of this mechanism to underscore Kanata's exoticism and difference from her peers, who, while they are equal in beauty to Kanata, never captivate Bel-Air's romantic imagination. One scene in particular brings this into focus. The newly arrived Bel-Air and Kanata are framed in a medium long shot, standing in the snow near the village meat-drying racks. Bel-Air, dressed in his mountaineering gear, recites *Romeo and Juliet* to a fur-swathed Kanata. Her costume fits the environment and reinforces the "Indianness" of their surroundings. The mise-en-scène carries on the tradition of juxtaposing the "civilized" white outsider to the "savage" and "primitive" Native girl, but Kanata's reciting of Juliet's line from memory jars the image. Bel-Air, along with the viewer, reacts strongly to this seemingly incongruous moment: a "savage" girl in an isolated Indian village with little or no contact with the white world knows this literary classic by heart. His delight at finding such a well-read and intoxicating woman increases as she informs him of her knowledge of other works as well. From this moment forward, they take on the roles of their literary counterparts, enacting the taboo relationships of both Romeo and Juliet and *Wuthering Heights*'s Heathcliff and Catherine. Kanata will go so far as to die as tragically as these well-known female characters of Western literature.

Though in some ways the Celluloid Maiden's education appears a progressive step toward creating a more equal union and a less "primitive" character, her training carries symbolic weight as intellectual advancement only because it comes in the form of Western liberal arts rather than Native-centered teachings. In the case of *Legends of the North*, the film's textual overtones are accentuated through the contrast of Kanata's education with her father's commitment to containing his people in a tribal culture of the past. The film has little to do with supporting equal opportunity for minorities and more to do with perpetuating a society governed through the unquestioned power of a white elite. McTavish molds a daughter who will fulfill his need for intellectual stimulation but will not threaten his primitive utopia. Unlike *Thunderheart*, in which Maggie Eagle Bear utilizes Western education as a tool against the colonial system, *Legends of the North* wields it as a sign of the civilized savage that validates colonialism in the process. The film reaffirms the ideological dictum from the turn of the century that the only way to save the Indian was through a Western education, which would prepare him or her for entrance into white society. Unlike in the early films, however, assimilation does not appear as an option or a goal in McTavish's world. Rather, the patriarchal white father isolates his Native "children" in order to teach them how to be better Natives. As a result, the film appears to capitalize on the demand for multicultural revisionist narratives, yet it does not commit to abandoning the racializing practices inherent in filmic stereotypes.

The revitalization of such a conservative Celluloid Maiden figure in *Legends of the Fall* and *Legends of the North*, which rely heavily on the Princess aspect of the figure, reinforces the figure's traditional symbolic boundaries. In other words, by eliminating the more progressive trends of the last twenty years, these films depict the Princess primarily as a romanticized ideal of the nation's historical emergence and racial hierarchies. Kanata's depiction, in particular, offers a subtle overturning of any attempt by the film to question the role of paternalism as a historical and contemporary colonial force. In addition, Kanata's self-inflicted death, as is the case with those of the silent-period Princess figures, relieves white America of its cultural guilt over the colonization process—as does the tribe's eventual killing of her father. Furthermore, the mixed-blood Princess nods toward a multicultural nation without challenging a white national ideal that relegates racialized minorities to the periphery of society, banishing them from its political and social center.

All of the 1990s films utilize the Celluloid Princess figure as their basic reference point, incorporating to some degree the traits of noble spirit, high social standing, a primary connection to nature and the American landscape's primordial essence, a tie to the American hero (symbolic of Whiteness), and racial exoticism. *Legends of the Fall* and *Legends of the North* retain the additional qualifications of innocence and purity seen in the 1910s and 1950s films, which dates the figure. Such a reliance on the Princess rather than the Sexualized Maiden aspect of the figure comes as no surprise, considering the importance of the civil rights movement of the 1960s and the 1990s' attention to creating more sympathetic and contemporary images of Native Americans. The move away from Vietnam-era liberalism and activism toward the conservative mores of the 1990s, however, also results in a revival of elements of the Sexualized Maiden that do not surface in the 1970s films but reach back to the 1940s, 1950s, and 1960s. The 1940s figures combine eroticism, sexual aggression, and femme fatale violence in the body of a mixed-race woman. The 1950s films eliminate the mixed-race component but add the woman's desire to kill the white hero. On the whole, the 1990s films appear less overtly anti-Indian and racist than their predecessors for three reasons. They adapt only one or two of the older combination

of characteristics; they eliminate the character's eroticism and sexual aggression; and they do not rely on sadism, as is the tendency of the older
films. As a result, the elements they do choose to include—mixed-race
parentage, femme fatale qualities, or Native American Queen–style resistance—seem to offer, but not guarantee, the possibility of a more complex
representation of the figure, as seen in *Thunderheart* and *Silent Tongue*.

The 1990s films all register some degree of uncertainty over abandoning the Celluloid Maiden as a palimpsest through which the nation's
"identificatory desire" for a mythic past continues to be considered.[24]
Certainly, the Celluloid Maiden figure's return from a countercolonial
symbol that throws white superiority into question to a symbol that reaffirms it indicates a waning commitment on the part of the film industry
to vigorously challenging racial inequality. This comes as no surprise,
considering the lackluster political commitment to addressing race in
the 1990s. The year 1992 marked the end of the Republican presiden-
cies and a move into a Democratic administration that ultimately failed
to resurrect a strong antiracism agenda for the nation. Rather, there
emerged a neoliberal project that sought to "rearticulate the neoconservative and new right racial projects of the Reagan-Bush years in [a]
centrist framework of moderate redistribution and cultural universalism."
Similarly, multiculturalism, which originally carried a liberal awareness
of racial structures and racial inequality in the United States, became a
buzzword for pacifying civil rights activists and minority groups.[25] The
resulting ineffectuality of the term reflected the political and social reality
of racial politics in the United States, as does the increasingly conservative
image of the Celluloid Maiden in 1990s films. The trajectory formed by
the 1990s films' changing applications of multiculturalism suggests that
the film industry continues to be influenced by external social indicators
when it deals with delicate issues of race. Whether a symbol of resistance
to, or acceptance of, the power structures involved in the colonialism historically present in Native American–white relations, the Celluloid Maid-
en remains a textual index and a telling metaphor for ongoing national
ambivalence regarding race, interracial mixing, and multiculturalism.

THE CELLULOID MAIDEN AS PALIMPSEST

This study of the representations of the Celluloid Maiden from the silent
period through the mid-1990s reveals the complexity of the figure and

its versatility as a metonym for interracial mixing and Native-white relations. It also highlights the continual remolding of the Celluloid Maiden
to resonate with subsequent generations, indicating the extent to which
our national myths continue to inform our sociopolitical present and
our strong commitment to maintaining such an ambivalent image. The
temporal distance of the 1970s and 1990s hybrid figure from the figure's
blueprint in the 1910s, coupled with the increasing tendency to rely on
genre memories of the subsequent adaptations, manifests itself in disuni-
ty between the ideological tenets behind the figure and revisionist intentions. Looking back over the past ninety years of images, one is struck by
how often the figure chafes against the most liberal aims of a film. The
variety of depictions of the Celluloid Maiden illustrates the difficulty of
locating this symbol within a mythic system of representation that is increasingly scrutinized and yet continually maintained. This may be the
reason the figure now emerges in cross-genre and Native-centered films
that reference the western but also attempt to move past it.

Although the Celluloid Maiden figure resists rigidity, offering instead a degree of latitude for change, even in its malleability it remains
contained within a particular racializing discourse of power, domination,
and exotic pleasure that fixes it within a cultural, historical, and racial
framework. Because the figure is constructed as an exotic Other, even
its most elusive presence ensures a film's inculcation into a colonial discourse based on racializing stereotypes. Thus the films never completely
reject the racial and colonial premises of American nation building and
the myth of the frontier. Rather, the ambivalence ingrained in the figure
allows it to continue as a palimpsest—a textual body erased and rewritten to fit each generation's idea of its place in American history and its
image of the role of the Native American woman within that history.

The individual components of the figure—the Celluloid Princess
and the Sexualized Maiden—underscore different manifestations of the
ambivalence toward Native Americans and interracial mixing. Embodying the concept of the noble red man, the Princess represents the best
of Native America and the idea of assimilation. Within the western's
colonial discourse on American nation building, she symbolizes the
notion of a virgin continent, an untamed wilderness that desires the
white male colonizer and the progressive march of civilization. The pro-
Indian films in which the figure emerges utilize it as a mitigating element between a liberal, utopian, mixed-race national image and the

reality of cultural violence against those who are racially and culturally different from a national white norm. Although she is a by-product of the early Celluloid Princess figure, the Sexualized Maiden harbors none of the romanticism of her predecessor. Rather, she stands for the dangers of assimilation and functions to maintain a phobia and fetish about race that verges on sadistic fantasy, which even the films attempting to examine themes of race and sexuality continue to reinforce. When, as in *The Searchers* (1956), *In Cold Blood* (1967), and the 1990s films, the two sides of the figure merge into a hybrid figure, a balance must be found between the different ideological foci. That balance appears to have moved over the course of the century toward the romanticism of the Princess. Nonetheless, the underlying ideology of the figure remains the same. This ideology involves the Celluloid Maiden's accentuated racial and cultural difference from the white hero and her ultimate death, which underscores the politics of conquest and the reality of the nation's racial hierarchy. In addition, while each generation of media adapts the tropic components, a fundamental and unresolved ambivalence remains clearly embedded in each revision.

Even with the wane, and perhaps disappearance, of the western, and with the rise of Native-produced films, a beautiful young Native woman cinematically represented by particular images who is physically connected with the white hero and dies rekindles a memory of the Celluloid Maiden. The inability to completely escape the evocation of the Celluloid Maiden as a symbol of white dominance, historical violence, political power, and desire for a particular national identity resides in the strength of the system surrounding the figure. The racial formation of the Celluloid Maiden, to borrow from Omi and Winant, relies on a particular "*interpretation, representation, or explanation of racial dynamics.*" These racial dynamics connect "what race *means* in a particular discursive practice and the ways in which both social structures and everyday experiences are racially *organized*, based upon that meaning."[26] The emergence of the Celluloid Maiden during moments of extreme national identity crisis and stress suggests the figure's ability to reinforce the familiar without completely alienating those trying to change the system; they too find value in its structure, as *Silent Tongue* makes evident. Additionally, the nation continues to rely on images from its myth of the frontier, particularly in times of war, economic stress, and changing population dynamics. One simply need recall President Reagan's reliance on a cowboy persona, the ongoing cowboy-Indian rhetoric used in international and urban warfare, and the backlash to legal and illegal immigrants of color to realize that the nation consciously relies on the power of such dynamics. Likewise, the death of the Celluloid Maiden provides a specific nostalgic image of a heterogeneous white ideal and justifies the ordering and controlling of unruly Others. The Celluloid Maiden, particularly the Princess persona, engages an idea of a multi-ethnic and multiracial state while allowing us to romanticize or ignore the racial politics of our historical past and present.

Perhaps the most obvious evidence of the figure's power and resilience resides in its emergence in a cluster of films released from the late 1980s through the 1990s. These include *Powwow Highway* (1989), *Black Robe* (1991), *A River Runs Through It* (1992), *Dance Me Outside* (1994), *Grand Avenue* (1996), *Smoke Signals* (1998), and *Naturally Native* (1999). Of this group, the two historical dramas—*Black Robe* and *A River Runs Through It*—remain most closely tied to the Hollywood tradition of depicting Native Americans in the past. *Black Robe* presents a Princess-type figure who, like the hybrid Celluloid Maidens of the 1970s, woos her white lover away from his own culture and his religion. In contrast, *A River Runs Through It* briefly introduces a young Native woman into an otherwise non-Native narrative as a sexually active flapper. In both cases, the women simply disappear from the narratives. The remaining films also reference, but do not fully develop, the Celluloid Maiden figure. They include films that are Native centered (*Powwow Highway* and *Dance Me Outside*) and Native written, Native produced, or both (*Grand Avenue*, *Smoke Signals*, and *Naturally Native*), and that highlight the racial realities in contemporary communities.

Dance Me Outside and *Grand Avenue*, the HBO production by Native American writer Greg Sarris, adhere most closely to the Celluloid Maiden figure. Of the cluster, only these two films kill off the young woman. *Dance Me Outside*'s Little Margaret (Tamara Podemski) appears in the first few minutes of the film as a young native Canadian woman whose poor judgment in asking a white thug to dance at a bar on the edge of the Native reserve results in her rape and death. She exists for no more than a few brief scenes, but her murder motivates the other young characters to avenge her death. The young women of the tribe eventually spearhead a national campaign against the young man's minimal sentence, but when the courts disregard their pleas and release him after one year, they kill him. Justine (Deeny Dakota) of *Grand Avenue* has a more substantial role as a teenage daughter in a dysfunctional family. Although, like Little Margaret, she is promiscuous, Justine does not die for her sexual activities per se, but when caught in the cross fire between rival gangs. Neither Little Margaret nor Justine appears consciously contrived as the Celluloid Maiden type, but their youth, physical look, interaction with non-Indian men, and sexuality trigger genre memories of past images in Hollywood films and their prescribed deaths.

The emergence of the Celluloid Maiden image in these films, whether intentional or not, underscores how deeply inscribed the figure and mainstream stereotypes are in American culture, and how successful the colonizing process has been in encouraging Native Americans to reaffirm such a figure. Native-centered and Native-produced films have the potential to disempower the figure by allowing the young girl to live and by creating more realistic images of Native women; certainly, the main characters in *Dance Me Outside* and *Grand Avenue* attest to this. But, even in their obvious retaliation against Hollywood stereotyping, the films contain the young woman in the figure through her typecasting or her death.

According to Robert K. Thomas's work on the internalization of colonialism by Native Americans, the legacy of colonialism is the interpolation of both the colonized and colonizing subject into the continual validation of the system.[27] This process results in a vicious cycle of internal and external racism. A case in point surfaces in the mainstream recognition of Irene Bedard (the voice of Pocahontas in Disney's 1995 release) as a Princess figure even in roles that do not utilize the figure, such as her character in *Smoke Signals*. It is simply her metonymical connection to Pocahontas, or her presentation as a beautiful young girl, that inscribes her as that figure. Bedard reenacts the conflict of such stereotyping in the film *Naturally Native* as the youngest of three sisters. Teased by her siblings for acting the part, she must confront the racism of that image when a date calls her an Indian princess and then attempts to rape her. His attack leaves her traumatized and in the hospital. This film, perhaps more than any other, demands that the viewer question the violence behind the Celluloid Maiden figure without fully enacting the figure. The young woman does not die!

The introduction of trauma as an alternative to death first surfaces in the Native-centered film *Powwow Highway*. A single mother of mixed-race children, Bonnie Redbow (Joannelle Nadine Romero) is framed for drug running, thrown in jail, and separated from her children. These experiences indicate her connection to the Sexualized Maiden figure, but she is also a Celluloid Princess in her goodness, honesty, and dedication to her children. The physical and psychological trauma she experiences foreshadows that of future Princess types: Pocahontas in the 1995 Disney film is left alone after her white lover leaves, and, as discussed above, Irene Bedard's *Naturally Native* character is hospitalized. While replacing death with trauma diffuses the racist and colonialist implications associated with the Celluloid Maiden figure, it does not erase them. Rather, a subtle shift occurs in these films that underscores Thomas's point about internal colonization. Even when it is an accurate description of the realities faced by Native Americans, the replay of violence onto the body of a Native woman who resembles the Celluloid Maiden reifies the figure.

A number of questions arise that need further investigation but are outside the limits of this work. In particular, over the last decade, the Native woman continually fades from the screen, seen mostly behind the main male figure or as an extra who creates a more realistic image of Native communities. While the early 1990s Hollywood films pay particular attention to creating more substantial Native male characters, why does the Native woman decline in her screen presence? The revisionist attempts of the 1990s pay no real attention to the Native woman. This leads me to wonder whether Hollywood simply cannot fathom the reality of a progressive Native female lead in these films, or whether the films are simply following social trends in relegating women and people of color to the role of accoutrement to the white hero. Second, a certain level of social sadism exists in reproducing the Celluloid Maiden figure. Why are the reproduction of this social violence against the body of a woman of color and the symbolic representation of a colonized people not challenged in the same way that similar representations of men of color have been? Third, what still legitimizes the use of this figure in the eyes of the viewing public? A number of films, including *Thunderheart* and *Silent Tongue*, attempt to get closer to the roots of these last two questions through their disruption of the Celluloid Maiden figure, yet even so, a satisfactory answer eludes them. Last, and in reference to the work of Robert K. Thomas and Homi Bhabha, how do we deprogram the effects of internalized colonialism and colonial rhetoric? How and when do we stop reinscribing violent silencing onto the body of the Native American woman?

As the first in-depth documentation of this particular depiction of Native American women in film, *Killing the Indian Maiden* offers a stepping stone for further investigations of the cinematic representations of Native American women. I have traced a trend in Hollywood of utilizing the Celluloid Maiden as a vehicle through which to explore and express the American ambiguity over Native American–white relations and interracial mixing. As my analysis shows, latitude for expression and manipulation of the figure exists, but her death remains a necessary component for "fixing," to borrow from Bhabha, the figure within the colonial and racializing discourse in which the films participate. In addition, this study's historical tracing indicates the significance of the Celluloid Maiden figure within American identity politics and an ongoing reestablishment of a particular American national image as a white patriarchal system of power. These findings, of course, lead to more questions than they answer, but the material presented here does offer a starting point for understanding how deeply imbedded the Native American woman is in violent and romantic images of American nation building.

Conclusion

Into the Twenty-first Century

THE BOMBINGS OF 9/11 and the "war against terror" plunged the nation into another era of national conflict, uncertainty, and questioning about what it means to be an American, what the nation's role is in the world, and what its political and social boundaries are. In the past, the United States relied on images of the frontier and itself as a frontier nation to answer such questions. According to Fredrick Jackson Turner, whose frontier thesis of 1893 set this notion into play on a grand scale, the frontier in American imagination is an economic, geographical, political, and psychological demarcation between East and West, civilization and savagery. He described the frontier as an ongoing and organic ebb and flow, progressing westward and incorporating a continual rebirth of social, economic, and political development. This idea, in turn, stamped its quintessential mark on America and its notion of frontier: as free land for the taking and as offering economic freedom; as a space in which the struggle to conquer the land and its savagery results in a distinct American character; and as spawning a particular nationalism and democracy grounded in aggressive individuality and a pioneering spirit.[1] The concept of the frontier exists today, influenced by Hollywood westerns, a domineering form of capitalistic democracy, and the nation's economic and political positioning as a world leader. The American frontier, now global in scope, provides new threats posed by "Indians" in the form of terrorism, illegal immigration, non-Christian religions, and the need for oil. Post-9/11, the Republican Party and President George W. Bush, as his father and Ronald Reagan had before him, resorted to using the Hollywood frontier and the western iconography of John Wayne to bolster American support for the war against terror. And, as in similar moments in past decades, a coinciding resuscitation of the western occurred in both film and television.

The western has a tradition of shifting and recreating itself to fit the needs of each new era of viewers. In keeping with this tendency, a new set of films reflects modern issues and a contemporary audience. While these updates are positive in general, the core treatment of the Native American has not changed in any substantial way. The production of such films as *Open Range* (2003), *The Missing* (2003), *Hidalgo* (2004), *Firefly* (2005), *Brokeback Mountain* (2005), and *The New World* (2005) and television miniseries such as TNT's *Into the West* (2005) suggests a desire to update the myth of the American frontier. Most of these films revise the western genre either through location or through a focus on alternative heroes and storytelling. *The Missing* places the white woman as the frontier hero. *Hidalgo* moves the frontier hero to the Middle East; *Firefly* sends the cowboy hero into space. *Brokeback Mountain* openly presents a homosexual relationship between cowboys. And *Into the West* attempts a sensitive retelling of Indian and white narratives of westward expansion. The variety of liberal approaches presented by these films implies a desire to widen the scope of the mythic frontier and of the American hero. Conversely, the focus of *The New World* on the John Smith–Pocahontas legend reaffirms rather than critiques the age-old themes of nation building and manifest destiny. These changes to the genre emerge in the development of the frontiersman and frontierswoman but not to any degree in the Indian. Four of the films that include Native characters—*Missing, Hidalgo, Into the West,* and *The New World*—continue to rely on standard generic figures and themes: the noble/ignoble savage, the sexualized young Princess figure, and the vanishing Indian.

While the total of six films and one miniseries in three years hints at a revival of the genre, the western may no longer be an adequate allegory for war and nation building, particularly when other genres seem more accessible to contemporary generations of viewers. Certainly, the film industry provides more immediate cultural commentary via war films such as *Black Hawk Down* (2001) and *Jarhead* (2005). Other genres that deal with these themes and issues—cross-racial unions, assimilation, and multiculturalism—resonate more with a youth culture bred on video games, comic books, fast-paced action, and science fiction. The *Star Wars* epics, the alien invasion scenarios, and the growing number of comic book adaptations come to mind. As the western does with the Indian, these genres provide a space for the Other, which defines it against the norm, and for violent extermination of it as a threat. The hero is also always identifiable in terms of standards well known by the American public, making allegiances between the audience and the appropriate character inevitable. In addition, a few prime-time television serials—*ER* (NBC), *Grey's Anatomy* (ABC), *Commander in Chief* (ABC), *Lost* (ABC), and *Gilmore Girls* (WB)—weave interracial relationships into their plots, providing contemporary stories of multicultural interaction. Rarely, however, is the mixed-race couple the show's primary focus; rather, it tends to occupy secondary narrative standing. The lack of truly multicultural programs and realistic character demography suggests that Whiteness and Eurocentrism continue to define American film and television standards, narratives, and casting.

Whether or not the western resurfaces as a primary national genre, the replaying of the stereotypes suggests that the Indian remains an important cultural icon. Certainly, the Celluloid Maiden still captures the national imagination across genres, as illustrated in the WB series *Smallville* (2002) and Terrence Malick's *The New World* (2005). Over the last thirty years, the cinematic trend has been either to diminish the narrative presence of the figure or to critique its symbolism. These two examples reverse this trend by reviving and celebrating the most basic components of the Celluloid Maiden.

Smallville introduces the Celluloid Maiden in season 2, episode 10. In this episode, a young Clark Kent—the burgeoning Superman and the show's hero—meets and falls in love with a young Native woman who, as the last of her people, must protect an ancient cave from developers. Kaila is a hybrid Celluloid Maiden with remarkable similarities to DeMille's 1940 description of the femme fatale Sexualized Maiden Louvette. A shape-shifter, she morphs from a beautiful young woman into a deadly wolf. Kent kills her while she is in wolf form to protect others from her savage attacks.

The New World rejuvenates the Celluloid Maiden as the focal character of a love triangle, a tactic not utilized so deliberately since *Duel in the Sun* (1946). Unlike the silent-period *Squaw Man* films and *The Man*

Who Loved Cat Dancing (1973), which force the white hero to choose between a white woman and a Native woman, *The New World* and *Duel in the Sun* position the Celluloid Maiden as the pivotal character between two white men. But Malick's Pocahontas is no lusty Pearl; rather, she is a child of nature, an innocent Princess figure reminiscent of Sonseeahray (*Broken Arrow*, 1950) and Sunshine (*Little Big Man*, 1970). Set in a romantic, Edenic landscape in which the young Pocahontas dances, romps in an impersonation of a deer, or simply lies in vast fields of grass, the film revives the concept of America as virgin land, pure, captivating, and for the taking. The cinematic attention to landscape and the limited dialogue accentuate the emotive quality of the young woman's actions and link her metaphorically to this fecund landscape. Pocahontas's love for Smith will result in her betrayal of her father's people and expulsion from their Eden. Smith's subsequent betrayal of her leads her to marry John Rolfe and, ultimately, to die in England.

Elements of the real Matoaka's (Pocahontas) life story filter through *The New World*, but this is no docudrama exploration of the historical figure. Rather, the construction of the fictional love triangle of Pocahontas, John Smith, and John Rolfe sets this film squarely in the Hollywood tradition of the Celluloid Maiden stories. Indeed, the film relies on the men's love for her various personas to underscore the metaphors of Pocahontas as the New World, colonialism, and conquest. Initially presented as a free spirit, unfettered by work or worry, Pocahontas illustrates the concept of the precolonial world as a place of childlike innocence, free of avarice and corruption. This is the America and the woman of Smith's infatuation. Her fall from grace leads to her life in the Jamestown colony, where Smith abandons her. A period of transformation into a European woman follows as her broken spirit, dampened by loss and depression, captivates Rolfe. It is this young colonized woman, whose link to nature is reduced to working in the plowed fields of the colony, who abandons her native land to travel to Europe. She will die there, and her son and husband will return to the New World to claim their place as Americans.

The visual power and strength of *The New World*'s symbolism and the critical acclaim the film received underscores, yet again, that American popular culture is not ready to release the Indian from its cultural iconography. Across genres, the Native American woman remains locked in iconography. The continuing visibility of the Celluloid Maiden in film and television reaffirms that American popular culture still uses the Native woman as a scapegoat in the complex web of power relationships based on gender and race. A brief survey of popular and consumer culture verifies that Americans continue to sexually exploit Native women through these stereotypes: Indian Princess Barbie dolls and Pocahontas Halloween costumes, sexy Native American calendar girls selling the latest in Indian fashion, the continued use of the Land O'Lakes maiden to promote butter, and OutKast's 2004 Grammy production complete with sexy "Indian" backup singers are only a few examples. Such "putting on" of Indianness is not new. Americans have a long tradition—from the Revolutionary period through the present—of donning Indian dress and playing Indian as a way of creating a sense of themselves as Americans. It is, however, a very real form of appropriation and racism that at its core assumes Native Americans are cultural artifacts to be manipulated by the public for its pleasure.[2]

The lived reality of stereotyping and sexual racism is much more frightening. During the 1960s and 1970s, the Indian Health Service sterilized Native American women without their knowledge in an attempt to lower birth rates among Indian families.[3] According to the National Sexual Violence Resource Center, the "average annual rate of rape and sexual assault among American Indians is 3.5 times higher than for all races." The Bureau of Justice Statistics reported in 2000 that, between 1992 and 1996, at "least 70% of the violent victimizations experienced by American Indians [were] committed by persons not of their race" and that the average rate of violent victimization for Native women was 98 per 1,000, "a rate higher than that found among white females (40 per 1,000) or black females (56 per 1,000)."[4] Two familiar stereotypes about Native women are inherent in these examples: the squaw whose overly active sexuality results in a brood of children for whom she cannot provide, and the Sexualized Maiden who deserves to be raped because she is inherently bad. Also implied is that men have the right to Native women's bodies—that, as women of color and members of a "conquered" people, Native women are sexually exotic property. These numbers and the reality that Native women find themselves measured against these stereotypes suggest that a cultural ambiguity toward Native American women still exists, and that it is often played out violently on their bodies. Such social sadism implies that this study of the Celluloid Maiden figure remains highly relevant. It also means that we in cultural studies, film studies, women's studies, American Indian studies—and we as American citizens—are failing in our attempts to produce long-lasting change in regard to racism, colonialism, and sexism.

Filmography

Across the Wide Missouri. Dir. William A. Wellman. Perf. Clark Gable, Ricardo Montalban, John Hodiak, Adolphe Menjou, J. Carrol Naish, Jack Holt, Alan Napier, George Chandler, Richard Anderson, María Elena Marqués. MGM, 1951.

Alice's Restaurant. Dir. Arthur Penn. Perf. Arlo Guthrie, Pat Quinn, James Broderick, Tina Chen, M. Emmet Walsh. United Artists, 1969.

Arrowhead. Dir. Charles Marquis Warren. Perf. Charlton Heston, Jack Palance, Brian Keith, Katy Jurado, James Burke, Miburn Stone. Paramount Pictures, 1953.

The Battle at Elderbush Gulch. Dir. D. W. Griffith. Perf. Mae Marsh, Alfred Paget, Charles H. Mailes, Lillian Gish, Robert Harron, Kate Bruce, Henry B. Walthall, Lionel Barrymore, Harry Carey. Biograph, 1914.

The Big Sky. Dir. Howard Hawks. Perf. Kirk Douglas, Dewey Martin, Arthur Hunnicutt, Jim Davis, Elizabeth Threatt, Buddy Baer, Steven Geray, Hank Worden, Henri Letondal, Booth Colman. RKO, 1952.

Black Hawk Down. Dir. Ridley Scott. Perf. Josh Hartnett, Ewan McGregor, Tom Sizemore, Eric Bana, William Fitchner, Ewen Bremner, Sam Shepard, Gabriel Casseus, Kim Coates, Ron Eldard, Thomas Guiry, Danny Hoch, Zeljko Ivanek, Jeremy Piven, Orlando Bloom, Steven Ford, Hugh Dancy. Columbia Pictures, 2001.

Black Robe. Dir. Bruce Beresford. Perf. Lothaire Bluteau, Aden Young, Sandrine Holt, August Schellenberg, Tantoo Cardinal, Billy Two Rivers, Lawrence Bayne, Harrison Liu, Wesley Cote, Frank Wilson, François Tassé. Goldwyn Pictures Corporation, 1991.

Bonnie and Clyde. Dir. Arthur Penn. Perf. Warren Beatty, Faye Dunaway, Estelle Parsons, Gene Hackman, Michael J. Pollard, Gene Wilder, Denver Pyle, Dub Taylor, James Stiver. Warner Brothers, 1967.

Brokeback Mountain. Dir. Ang Lee. Perf. Heath Ledger, Jake Gyllenhaal, Randy Quaid, Anne Hathaway, Michelle Williams, Valerie Planche. Paramount Pictures, 2005.

Broken Arrow. Dir. Delmer Daves. Perf. James Stewart, Jeff Chandler, Debra

Paget, Will Geer, Basil Ruysdael, Arthur Hunnicutt, Jay Silverheels. 20th Century-Fox, 1950.

The Broken Doll: A Tragedy of the Indian Reservation. Dir. D. W. Griffith. Perf. Gladys Egan, Dark Cloud, Jack Pickford, Alfred Paget, Kate Bruce, Dell Henderson, Guy Hedlund, Francis J. Grandon, Mack Sennet, Linda Arvidson. Biograph, 1910.

Broken Lance. Dir. Edward Dmytryk. Perf. Spencer Tracy, Robert Wagner, Jean Peters, Richard Widmark, Katy Jurado, Hugh O'Brian, Eduard Franz, Earl Holliman, E.G. Marshall. 20th Century-Fox, 1954.

The Caine Mutiny. Dir. Edward Dmytryk. Perf. Humphrey Bogart, José Ferrer, Van Johnson, Fred MacMurray, Robert Francis. Columbia Pictures, 1954.

Captain John Smith and Pocahontas. Dir. Lew Landers. Perf. Anthony Dexter, Jody Lawrance, Alan Hale Jr., Robert Clarke, Stuart Randall, James Seay, Philip Van Zandt, Shepard Menken, Douglass Dumbrille, Anthony Eustrel, Henry Rowland, Eric Colmar, Joan Dixon, William Cottrell, Francesca De Scaffa. United Artists, 1953.

Cheyenne Autumn. Dir. John Ford. Perf. Richard Widmark, Caroll Baker, Karl Malden, Sal Mineo, Ricardo Montalban, James Stewart, Edward G. Robinson, Dolores del Rio, Gilbert Roland. Warner Brothers, 1964.

The Cheyenne Brave. Dir. James Young Deer. Pathé, 1910.

Colorado Territory. Dir. Raoul Walsh. Perf. Joel McCrea, Virginia Mayo, Dorothy Malone, Henry Hull, John Archer, James Mitchell, Morris Ankrum, Ian Wolfe, Harry Woods. Warner Brothers, 1949.

Dance Me Outside. Dir. Bruce McDonald. Perf. Ryan Rajendra Black, Adam Beach, Jennifer Podemski, Michael Greyeyes, Lisa LaCroix, Kevin Hicks, Rose Marie Trudeau, Gloria May Eshkibok, Selim Running Bear Sandoval, Sandrine Holt, Tamara Podemski. Shadow Distribution, 1994.

Dances with Wolves. Dir. Kevin Costner. Perf. Kevin Costner, Mary McDonnell, Graham Greene, Rodney A. Grant, Floyd Red Crow Westerman, Tantoo Cardinal. Panavision, 1990.

A Daughter of the Sioux. Dir. Ben Wilson. Perf. Ben Wilson, Neva Gerber, Robert Walker, Fay Adams, William Lowery. Selig, 1909.

Drums along the Mohawk. Dir. John Ford. Perf. Henry Fonda, Claudette Colbert, John Carradine, Edna May Oliver, Eddie Collins, Dorris Bowdon, Jessie Ralph, Arthur Shields. 20th Century-Fox, 1939.

Duel in the Sun. Dir. King Vidor. Perf. Jennifer Jones, Gregory Peck, Joseph Cotten, Lionel Barrymore, Lillian Gish, Herbert Marshall, Tilly Losch. Selznick International Pictures, 1946.

Easy Rider. Dir. Dennis Hopper. Perf. Peter Fonda, Dennis Hopper, Jack Nicholson, Karen Black, Phil Spector, Warren Finnerty, Luke Askew, Sabrina Scharf, Robert Walker Jr. Columbia Pictures, 1969.

Fighting Blood. Dir. D. W. Griffith. Perf. George Nichols, Florence La Badie, Kate Bruce, Robert Harron, Francis J. Grandon, Alfred Paget, Dell Henderson. Biograph, 1911.

The Forest Rose. Dir. Theodore Marston. Perf. Marguerite Snow, William Russell. Thanhouser, 1912.

Fort Apache. Dir. John Ford. Perf. Henry Fonda, John Wayne, Ward Bond, Shirley Temple, John Agar, Pero Armendaríz, Irene Rich, George O'Brien, Victor McLaglen, Anna Lee. RKO, 1948.

Frontier Marshal. Dir. Allan Dwan. Perf. Randolph Scott, Nancy Kelly, Cesar Romero, Binnie Barnes, John Carradine, Edward Norris, Eddie Foy Jr., Ward Bond, Lon Chaney Jr. 20th Century-Fox, 1939.

Frozen Justice. Dir. Allan Dwan. Perf. Lenore Ulric, Robert Frazer, Louis Wolheim, Laska Winters, Ullrich Haupt, Tom Patricola, Alice Lake, Gertrude Astor. Fox Film Corporation, 1929.

Geronimo's Last Raid. Dir. G. P. Hamilton. American, 1912.

The Graduate. Dir. Mike Nichols. Perf. Anne Bancroft, Dustin Hoffman, Katharine Ross, Murray Hamilton, William Daniels, Elizabeth Wilson, Brian Avery. Embassy Pictures, 1967.

Grand Avenue. Dir. Daniel Sackhiem. Perf. Irene Bedard, Tantoo Cardinal, Eloy Casados, Deeny Dakota, Alexis Cruz, Diane Debassige, Jenny Gago, Cody Lightning, A. Martinez, Simi Mehta, August Schellenberg, Sheila Tousey. Home Box Office, 1996.

Hidalgo. Dir. Joe Johnston. Perf. Viggo Mortensen, Zuleikha Robinson, Omar Sharif, Louise Lombard, Adam Alexi-Malle, Saïd Taghmaoui, Silas Carson, Harsh Nayyar. Touchstone Pictures, 2004.

In Cold Blood. Dir. Richard Brooks. Perf. Robert Blake, Scott Wilson, John Forsythe, Paul Stewart, Gerald S. O'Loughlin, Jeff Corey, James Flavin, Charles McGraw, Sammy Thurman. Columbia Pictures, 1967.

Incident at Oglala. Dir. Michael Apted. Perf. Leonard Peltier, Robert Redford, John Trudell. Miramax Films, 1992.

The Indian Runner's Romance. Dir. D. W. Griffith. Biograph, 1909.

The Indian Squaw's Sacrifice. Defender, 1910.

Iola's Promise. Dir. D. W. Griffith. Perf. Mary Pickford, Dorothy Bernard, William J. Butler, Arthur V. Johnson, Charles Hill Mailes, Claire McDowell, George Nichols, Alfred Paget, Josef Swickard, Henry B. Walthall, Charles West. Biograph, 1912.

Jarhead. Dir. Sam Mendes. Perf. Jake Gyllenhaal, Scott MacDonald, Lo Ming, Kevin Foster, Peter Sarsgaard, Damion Poitier. Universal Pictures, 2005.

Jeremiah Johnson. Dir. Sydney Pollack. Perf. Robert Redford, Will Geer, Stefan Gierasch, Josh Albee, Allyn Ann McLerie, Charles Tyner, Delle Bo, Joaquin Martinez, Paul Benedict. Warner Bros., 1972.

Jesse James. Dir. Henry King. Perf. Tyrone Power, Henry Fonda, Randolph Scott, Nancy Kelly, Henry Hull, John Carradine, Jane Darwell, Donald Meek, Slim Summerville. 20th Century-Fox, 1939.

The Kentuckian: Story of a Squaw's Devotion and Sacrifice. Dir. D. W. Griffith. Perf. Edward Dillon, Florence Auer, D. W. Griffith, George Gebhardt, Harry Solter, Mack Sennett, Anthony O'Sullivan. Biograph, 1908.

Last Train from Gun Hill. Dir. John Sturges. Perf. Kirk Douglas, Anthony Quinn, Carolyn Jones, Earl Holliman, Brad Dexter, Brian G. Hutton, Ziva Rodann, Bing Russell, Val Avery, Walter Sande. Paramount Pictures, 1959.

Laughing Boy. Dir. W. S. Van Dyke. Perf. Ramon Novarro, Lupe Vélez, William B. Davidson, Chief Thunderbird, Catalina Rambula, F. A. Armenta, Deer Spring, Pellicana. MGM, 1934.

Legends of the Fall. Dir. Edward Zwick. Perf. Brad Pitt, Anthony Hopkins, Aidan Quinn, Julia Ormond, Henry Thomas, Karina Lombard, Gordon Tootoosis, Christina Pickles, Paul Desmond, Tantoo Cardinal. TriStar Pictures, 1994.

Legends of the North. Dir. René Manzor. Perf. Georges Corraface, Randy Quaid, Macha Grenon, Sandrine Holt, Serge Houde, John Dunn-Hill, Billy Merasty, Jon Baggaley, Aubert Pallascio, Linda Smith. Trimark Pictures, 1995.

Lieutenant Scott's Narrow Escape. Dir. James Young Deer. Pathé, 1911.

Little Big Man. Dir. Arthur Penn. Perf. Dustin Hoffman, Faye Dunaway, Chief Dan George, Martin Balsam, Richard Mulligan, Jeff Corey, Aimée Eccles, Kelly Jean Peters, Carole Androsky, Robert Little Star, Cal Bellini, Ruben Moreno. National General Pictures, 1970.

Lo, the Poor Indian. Kalem, 1910.

Mackenna's Gold. Dir. J. Lee Thompson. Perf. Gregory Peck, Omar Sharif, Telly Savalas, Camilla Sparv, Keenan Wynn, Julie Newmar, Ted Cassidy, Lee J. Cobb. Columbia Pictures, 1969.

A Man Called Horse. Dir. Elliot Silverstein. Perf. Richard Harris, Judith Anderson, Manu Tupou, Jean Gascon, Corinna Tsopei, Dub Taylor, William Jordan, James Gammon. National General Pictures, 1970.

The Man Who Loved Cat Dancing. Dir. Richard C. Sarafian. Perf. Burt Reynolds, Sarah Miles, Lee J. Cobb, Jack Warden, George Hamilton, Bo Hopkins, Robert Donner, Sandy Kevin, Larry Littlebird, Nancy Malone, Jay Silverheels, Jay Varela, Owen Bush, Larry Finley, Sutero García Jr. MGM, 1973.

The Massacre. Dir. D. W. Griffith. Perf. Wilfred Lucas, Charles H. West, Blanche Sweet, Eddie Dillon, Claire McDowell, Robert Harron, Lionel Barrymore, Jack Pickford. Biograph, 1912.

The Mended Lute. Dir. D. W. Griffith. Biograph, 1909.

Midnight Cowboy. Dir. John Schlesinger. Perf. Dustin Hoffman, Jon Voight, Sylvia Miles, John McGiver, Brenda Vaccaro, Barnard Hughes. United Artists, 1969.

The Missing. Dir. Ron Howard. Perf. Cate Blanchett, Tommy Lee Jones, Evan Rachel Wood, Jenna Boyd, Eric Schweig, Aaron Eckhart. Revolution Studios, 2003.

My Darling Clementine. Dir. John Ford. Perf. Henry Fonda, Linda Darnell, Victor Mature, Walter Brennan, Cathy Downs, Tim Holt, Ward Bond, Alan Mowbray, John Ireland, Roy Roberts. 20th Century-Fox, 1946.

Naturally Native. Dir. Jennifer Wynne Farmer, Valerie Red-Horse. Perf. Valerie Red-Horse, Yvonne Russo, Irene Pedard, Kimberly Noris, Pato Hoffmann, Mark Abbott, Collin Bernsen. Red-Horse Native Productions, 1999.

The New World. Dir. Terrence Malick. Perf. Colin Farrell, Q'Orianka Kilcher. Newline Cinema, 2005.

Northwest Mounted Police. Dir. Cecil B. DeMille. Perf. Gary Cooper, Madeleine Carroll, Paulette Goddard, Preston Foster, Robert Preston, George Bancroft, Lynne Overman, Akim Tamiroff, Walter Hampden, Lon Chaney Jr. Paramount Pictures, 1940.

Oklahoma Jim. Dir. Harry L. Fraser. Perf. Bill Cody, Marion Burns, Andy Shuford, William Desmond, Si Jenks, Franklyn Farnum, Edward Brady, Gordon De Main, Iron Eyes Cody, J. W. Cody, Artie Ortego, Ann Ross, Chief White Eagle. Monogram Pictures, 1931.

The Oklahoma Kid. Dir. Lloyd Bacon. Perf. James Cagney, Humphrey Bogart, Rosemary Lane, Donald Crisp, Harvey Stephens, Hugh Sothern, Charles Middleton, Ward Bond. Warner Brothers, 1939.

Open Range. Dir. Kevin Costner. Perf. Robert Duvall, Kevin Costner, Annette Bening, Michael Gambon. Touchstone Pictures, 2003.

Out of the Snows. Dir. Ralph Ince. Perf. Ralph Ince, Zena Keefe, Pat Hartigan, Gladys Coburn, Huntley Gordon, Red Eagle, Jacques Suzanne. National Picture Theaters, 1920.

The Outlaw. Dir. Howard Hawks, Howard Hughes. Perf. Jane Russell, Walter Huston, Jack Beutel, Thomas Mitchell, Joe Sawyer, Frank Darien, Pat West, Carl Stockdale. RKO, 1943.

The Plainsman. Dir. Cecil B. DeMille. Perf. Gary Cooper, Jean Arthur, Charles Bickford, Anthony Quinn, James Ellison, Victor Varconi, Granville Bates, Purnell Pratt. Paramount Pictures, 1937.

Pocahontas. Thanhouser, 1910.

Pocahontas. Dir. Mike Gabriel, Eric Goldberg. Perf. Irene Bedard, July Kuhn, Mel Gibson, Linda Hunt, John Kassir, Frank Welder, David Ogden Stiers, Russell Means. Walt Disney Productions, 1995.

Pocahontas, Child of the Forest. Edison, 1908.

Pocahontas: The Musical Tradition Continues. Dir. John Jopson. Perf. Regina Belle, Peabo Bryson, Céline Dion, Alan Menken. Walt Disney Productions, 1995.

Pocahontas II: Journey to a New World. Dir. Tom Ellery, Bradley Raymond. Perf. Irene Bedard, Jim Cummings, Donal Gibson, Finola Hughes, Linda Hunt, Judy Kuhn, Russen Means. Walt Disney Productions, 1998.

Powwow Highway. Dir. Jonathan Wacks. Perf. A. Martinez, Gary Farmer, Joannelle Nadine Romero, Amanda Wyss, Sam Vlahos, Wayne Waterman, Margot Kane, Geoff Rivas. Handmade Films, 1989.

Red Deer's Devotion. Dir. James Young Deer. Pathé, 1911.

Red Wing's Gratitude. Dir. James Young Deer. Perf. James Young Deer, Lillian St. Cyr. Vitagraph, 1909.

The Redman and the Child. Dir. D. W. Griffith. Biograph, 1908.

A River Runs Through It. Dir. Robert Redford. Perf. Craig Sheffer, Brad Pitt, Tom Skerritt, Brenda Blethyn, Emily Lloyd, Edie McClurg, Stephen Shellen, Vann Gravage, Nicole Burdette. Allied Filmmakers, 1992.

Scarlet and Gold. Dir. Frank Grandon. Perf. Al Ferguson, Lucille Du Bois, Frank Granville, Yvonne Pavis. J. J. Fleming Productions, 1925.

The Searchers. Dir. John Ford. Perf. John Wayne, Jeffrey Hunter, Vera Miles, Ward Bond, Natalie Wood, Pippa Scott, John Qualen, Olive Carey, Henry Brandon. Warner Brothers, 1956.

Silent Tongue. Dir. Sam Shepard. Perf. Richard Harris, Sheila Tousey, Alan Bates, River Phoenix, Dermot Mulroney, Jeri Arredondo, Tantoo Cardinal. Belbo Films, 1993.

Smoke Signals. Dir. Chris Eyre. Perf. Adam Beach, Evan Adams, Irene Bedard, Gary Farmer, Tantoo Cardinal, Cody Lightning, Simon Baker. Shadow-Catcher Entertainment, 1998.

Soldier Blue. Dir. Ralph Nelson. Perf. Candice Bergen, Peter Strauss, Donald Pleasence, John Anderson, Jorge Rivero, Dana Elcar, Bob Carraway, Martin West, James Hampton, Mort Mills, Jorge Russek, Aurora Clavel. Embassy Pictures, 1970.

The Squaw Man. Dir. Cecil B. DeMille. Perf. Dustin Farnum, Monroe Salisbury, Winifred Kinston, Red Wing (Lillian St. Cyr), William Elmer, Foster Know, Joseph Singleton, Dick La Reno, Fred Montague, "Baby" Carmen De Rue. Jesse L. Lasky Feature Play Company, 1914.

The Squaw Man. Dir. Cecil B. DeMille. Perf. Elliot Dexter, Ann Little, Katherine MacDonald, Theodore Roberts, Jack Holt, Thurston Hall, Tully Marshall, Herbert Standing, Edwin Stevens, Helen Dunbar, Winger Hal, Julia Faye, Noah Beery, Pat Moore, Jim Mason. Paramount Pictures, 1918.

The Squaw Man. Dir. Cecil B. DeMille. Perf. Warner Baxter, Lupe Vélez, Eleanor Boardman, Charles Bickford, Roland Young, Paul Cavanagh,

Raymond Hatton, Julia Faye, DeWitt Jennings, J. Farrell MacDonald, Mitchell Lewis, Dickie Moore, Victor Potel, Frank Rice, Eva Dennison. MGM, 1931.

Stagecoach. Dir. John Ford. Perf. John Wayne, Claire Trevor, John Carradine, Thomas Mitchell, Donald Meek, Andy Devine, George Bancroft, Tim Holt. United Artists, 1939.

Tell Them Willie Boy Is Here. Dir. Abraham Polonsky. Perf. Robert Redford, Katharine Ross, Robert Blake, Susan Clark, Barry Sullivan, John Vernon, Charles Aidman, Charles McGraw. Universal Pictures, 1969.

The Texans. Dir. James Hogan. Perf. Randolph Scott, Joan Bennett, Walter Brennan, May Robson, Robert Cummings, Raymond Hatton, Harvey Stephens, Robert Barrat. Paramount Pictures, 1938.

Thunderheart. Dir. Michael Apted. Perf. Val Kilmer, Sam Shepard, Graham Greene, Fred Ward, Fred Dalton Thompson, Sheila Tousey, Chief Ted Thin Elk, John Trudell, Julius Drum, Sarah Brave. TriStar Pictures, 1992.

Two Rode Together. Dir. John Ford. Perf. James Stewart, Richard Widmark, Shirley Jones, Andy Devine, Linda Cristal, John McIntire, Paul Birch, Willis Bouchey, David Kent, Woody Strode. Columbia Pictures, 1961.

Unconquered. Dir. Cecil B. DeMille. Perf. Gary Cooper, Paulette Goddard, Howard Da Silva, Boris Karloff, Cecil Kellaway, Ward Bond, Katherine DeMille, Henry Wilcoxon, Sir C. Aubrey Smith, Victor Varconi, Virginia Grey, Porter Hall, Mike Mazurki, Richard Gaines, Virginia Campbell, Gavin Muir, Alan Napier, Nan Sunderland, Marc Lawrence, Jane Nigh. Paramount Pictures, 1947.

Unforgiven. Dir. Clint Eastwood. Perf. Clint Eastwood, Gene Hackman, Morgan Freeman, Richard Harris, Jaimz Woolvett, Saul Rubinek, Frances Fisher. Warner Bros., 1992.

Union Pacific. Dir. Cecil B. DeMille. Perf. Barbara Stanwyck, Joel McCrea, Akim Tamiroff, Robert Preston, Lynne Overman, Brian Donlevy, Robert Barrat, Anthony Quinn. Paramount Pictures, 1939.

The Vanishing American. Dir. George Seitz. Perf. Richard Dix, Lois Wilson, Noah Berry, Malcolm McGregor, Charles Stevens, George Magrill, Shannon Day, Charles Crockett, Bert Woodruff. Paramount Pictures, 1925.

White Fawn's Devotion. Dir. James Young Deer. Pathé, 1910.

White Feather. Dir. Robert D. Webb. Perf. Robert Wagner, John Lund, Debra Paget, Jeffrey Hunter, Eduard Franz, Noah Beery Jr., Virginia Leith, Emile Meyer, Hugh O'Brian, Milburn Stone, Iron Eyes Cody. 20th Century-Fox, 1955.

The Yaqui Girl. Dir. James Young Deer. Perf. Virginia Chester. Pathé, 1911.

Notes

ABBREVIATIONS

AMPAS   Margaret Herrick Library, Academy of Motion Picture Arts
             and Sciences, Beverly Hills, Calif.
DMA, BYU   Cecil B. DeMille Archives, L. Tom Perry Special Collections
             Library, Harold B. Lee Library, Brigham Young University,
             Provo, Utah
MOMA   Celeste Bartos International Film Study Center, Museum of
             Modern Art, New York

INTRODUCTION

1. Exceptions to this include the works of S. Elizabeth Bird, Maryann Oshana, and Angela Aleiss, which are foundational to the history of Native American women's representation in cinema.

2. As Robert Berkhofer reveals, this construction of Native Americans as Other to white Europeans and Americans illuminates the general themes that form mainstream understandings of Indians. These themes are based on the dichotomous noble/ignoble savage structure but are complicated by differing degrees of rationalism, reason, passion, and use value. Throughout American history, they have been used together or separately as American social needs demanded. For instance, individually, they were used by the Puritans to envision the Indian as a bloodthirsty savage, a minion of the devil whose purpose was to test their religious strength. By the citizens of the early Republic, they were developed into the romantic noble savage, who, as an extension of the Golden Age, was a representational critic of European society and culture. As such, this figure is a signifier of freedom from social convention and from the artificial civilization that chained Western man. According to Berkhofer, together these images of "the good and bad Indian came to demonstrate what the life of man was like in the original state of nature." Berkhofer, *White Man's Indian*, 76, 47. Also see Berkhofer for a thorough tracing of the image of the Indian from Columbus through American federal Indian policy.

3. See Leslie Fiedler's *The Return of the Vanishing American*, which

probes the psychological ramifications of American literature's construction of the Indian as the white man's alter ego/companion/lover. Fiedler argues that white America, through its texts and its myth of the West, has positioned the Indian at the "heart of the Western" and, thus, with the westerner. Fiedler goes so far as to surmise that if the Indian is extinguished from the West, then so too is the white westerner—the American. Fiedler, *Return of the Vanishing American*, 21.

   4. Bernardi, *Birth of Whiteness*, 5.

   5. Omi and Winant, *Racial Formation*, 56.

   6. Anderson, *Imagined Communities*; Bhabha, "Other Question," 18.

   7. Lewis, *American Adam*, 5.

   8. Ibid.; Slotkin, *Gunfighter Nation*, 10–12. Slotkin defines "savage war" as a "mythic figure and an operative category of military doctrine" that is based on the premise that Western culture cannot coexist with "primitive natives" in any other way than through the subjugation of the latter group. Underlying this is the idea that "ineluctable political and social differences" are inherent in "blood and culture" that prevent cohabitation without violence. Slotkin, *Gunfighter Nation*, 12.

   9. Fiedler, *Return of the Vanishing American*, 24.

   10. Freud, "Fetishism," 152–57.

   11. Kolodny, *Lay of the Land*, 4, 10; Raleigh quoted in Kolodny, *Lay of the Land*, 11.

   12. E. McLung Fleming quoted in Fiedler, *Return of the Vanishing American*, 66.

   13. Green, "Pocahontas Perplex," 702. Green's work, which focuses on the American Queen and Princess figures, has been instrumental in opening a dialogue on Native American women in film.

   14. The male noble and ignoble savage figures exist at this time as well, but it is the female presence that entices the European male in a sexually aggressive and dominating way.

   15. Faery, *Cartographies of Desire*, 96.

   16. Green, "Pocahontas Perplex," 702.

   17. Fiedler, *Return of the Vanishing American*, 66.

   18. Bird, "Tales of Difference," 94.

   19. Fiedler, *Return of the Vanishing American*, 65.

   20. Throughout this work, the term "Whiteness" is used as a symbolic construct, an ideal image of purity, ultimate civilization, and culture that is held as a utopian model of excellence and desire. Within the colonial structure that continually produces the Celluloid Princess stereotype, Whiteness, which is presented in a dominant, white, Anglo-Saxon or western European male, is positioned against her racial background. In addition, Native Americans are continually juxtaposed to a white cultural norm, one based on particular cultural, social, political, and sometimes religious ideologies supporting a hegemoni-

cally racialized national identity. My use of this term and my reading of how it is manifested in film grow out of the foundational scholarship on Whiteness and critical race theory by Daniel Bernardi and Richard Dyer.

21. There is a disturbing parallel in the construction of the Princess as a child and as a part of the land that "desires" taming. Throughout American history, American politicians, missionaries, and intellectuals have equated Native Americans mentally and socially with children in need of paternal guidance in the form of intervention by the dominant culture. All too often, this understanding of Native Americans has arisen out of the belief that, because Native Americans do not know how to use the land properly (tame it and cultivate it, as Europeans and Americans do), they should lose it. That the Princess, as a representative of the American land, desires the white colonizers' taming influence suggests that she, too, subscribes to the paternalistic idea that her people are incapable of cultivating the land and should be removed from it at all costs.

22. Tilton, *Pocahontas*, 7–8.

23. Ibid., 1; Faery, *Cartographies of Desire*, 100.

24. Tilton, *Pocahontas*, 55, 7, 55. At least two films adapt the Pocahontas-Rolfe narrative during the silent period: *Pocahontas, Child of the Forest* (1908) and *Pocahontas* (1910). One in 1953, although titled *Captain John Smith and Pocahontas*, focuses on her marriage to Rolfe. More recently, the Pocahontas-Smith theme seems to be the motivating force behind Disney's 1995 *Pocahontas* and its video spin-offs, *Pocahontas: The Musical Tradition Continues* (1995) and *Pocahontas II: Journey to a New World* (1998). Significantly, and unlike the Celluloid Princess, Pocahontas does not die in these narratives, suggesting that her particular iconic status exempts her from filmic death. For this reason, and because other incarnations of the Celluloid Maiden have been ignored, I have chosen not to write about Pocahontas.

25. Kasdan and Tavernetti, "Native Americans in a Revisionist Western," 121.

26. Tompkins, *West of Everything*, 4, 39, 6–7.

27. Slotkin, *Gunfighter Nation*, 10.

28. Schatz, *Boom and Bust*, appendixes 5 and 7.

29. The film industry also uses stereotypical images of Asian, African American, and Hispanic women. How these images are read often depends on the historical power relations between each group and the American government.

ONE. DEATH, GRATITUDE, AND THE SQUAW MAN'S WIFE

The epigraph to this chapter comes from Mayer, "Broken Doll," 192.

1. Pearson, "Revenge of Rain-in-the-Face," 275. I use the term "Celluloid Princess" to differentiate cinematic representations of Native American women from other material culture and popular culture depictions of the Native princess figure.

2. During the early film period, Indian films constituted a genre, separate from the western, that focused primarily on Indian characters and plots. Hundreds of films depicted various images and themes related to Indian subjects. Some were romantic portrayals of Native American life, love, and noble spirit; others were decidedly unromantic in their negative portrayals of Native Americans as violent savages and distinct Others to whites. Native American women were more prominently featured in these early films than at any other time in history—and the Princess figure emerges at this time. Indian films later merged to become a subgenre of the western. See Bowser, *Transformation of Cinema*, 173.

3. U.S. federal Indian policy has been affected by geography, motive of the government in relation to particular tribes, and political swings. Pre- and early-twentieth-century policy can be broken down into three periods: the Indian removal period, which tends to be dated 1828–1840 and discussed in terms of the Indian Removal Act of 1830, but which can be pushed back to the post–French and Indian War period, with the removal of northeastern tribes from their homelands; the reservation period, 1834–1887; and the allotment period, 1887–1934, under the General Allotment Act of 1887, also known as the Dawes Act. The philosophy of assimilation underscored all periods but was emphasized more forcefully when tribes did not assimilate on their own or through the mechanism deemed appropriate at the time.

4. The term "imperial nostalgia" was coined by anthropologist Renato Rosaldo to explain the nostalgia often felt by agents of colonialism (for example, officials and missionaries) for the "colonized culture as it was 'traditionally' (that is, when they first encountered it). The peculiarity of their yearning, of course, is that agents of colonialism long for the very forms of life they intentionally altered or destroyed." Rosaldo, *Culture and Truth*, 69.

5. Smith, "Shooting Cowboys and Indians," 68. Also see Abel, *Red Rooster Scare.*

6. Langman, *Guide to Silent Westerns*, ix; Schatz, "Western," 45–46. At least six hundred Indian films and westerns were released between 1909 and 1913 alone. Langman, *Guide to Silent Westerns*, ix. Also see Friar and Friar, *Only Good Indian*, 85–104, and Hilger, *From Savage to Nobleman*, 24.

7. Hilger, *From Savage to Nobleman*, 1–16; Jowett, *Democratic Art*, 62.

8. There are only a few catalogues and annotated filmographies available on the images of Native Americans or Native American themes in film. Bataille and Silet's two works, *Images of American Indians on Film* and *The Pretend Indians*, offer bibliographies and edited writings on the subject. Friar and Friar's *The Only Good Indian* includes a thorough filmography categorized by terms and themes. Hilger's *The American Indian in Film* and *From Savage to Nobleman* are seminal catalogues of films from the early silent period through the 1980s. Annotations reference westerns and Indian films as early as 1894 (Friar and Friar) and 1903 (Hilger); however, it is not until 1908 that what I am terming the Celluloid Princess emerges in these film lists. Thus I have based my

analysis of the figure on the years it clearly surfaces. I extend the film analysis into 1931 to encompass two talkies, *The Squaw Man* and *Oklahoma Jim*, that clearly fit with the early silent films more readily than they do with the westerns of the 1930s.

9. Later Celluloid Princess figures that emerge from this early blueprint include Sonseeahray (*Broken Arrow*, 1950), Kamiah (*Across the Wide Missouri*, 1951), Running Deer (*A Man Called Horse*, 1970), Swan (*Jeremiah Johnson*, 1972), and Isabel Two (*Legends of the Fall*, 1994).

10. Wiebe, *Search for Order*.

11. Morgan quoted in Dippie, *Vanishing American*, 103.

12. Slotkin, *Gunfighter Nation*, 10–12. Also see Slotkin, *Regeneration through Violence*.

13. Hilger, *From Savage to Nobleman*, 9–11.

14. D. W. Griffith's *Iola's Promise* (1912) opens with two miners attacking Iola. They appear only in the first seconds of the film; the rest of the narrative portrays only good white settlers and miners, who contrast with Iola's angry and volatile people. Though white villains do emerge in Indian films depicting the tragic demise of Native America, according to Langman's studies of silent films, Native American, half-breed, and Mexican characters were predominant among the villains of the early period. Often they appeared in westerns as the antithesis of the white hero, but the "studios occasionally made attempts to deal sympathetically" with these groups. Langman, *Guide to Silent Westerns*, xiii–xiv. Also see Langman, *American Film Cycles*.

15. Unsigned review of *Red Wing's Gratitude*, *Moving Picture World*, 567.

16. Bowser, *Biograph Bulletins*, 239.

17. *Iola's Promise* differs from *Red Wing's Gratitude*, *The Broken Doll*, and other helper films slightly in that Iola's safety is threatened by a group of white men, who seem to be intent on raping her. This sexual violence emerges in films Griffith made after leaving Biograph but does not seem to play into the general helper films of the time. Iola is not threatened just by white men; members of her own tribe also treat her poorly. After Jack, a white miner, rescues her, she promises to help him find gold and returns to her village. Her attempts to tell a number of Indian men about what has happened result in their roughly pushing her aside. However, just as in the other helper films, the maiden risks her life to repay the white man's kindness.

18. Griffith seemed quite concerned with the topic of child abuse, which also surfaces briefly in *Iola's Promise* (1912) and prominently in his famous film *Broken Blossoms* (1919). All three films present a female child who suffers some form of abuse from a parental figure—usually male, with the exception of *The Broken Doll*. And all three films underscore the young woman's crossing of racial lines, which results in her death. As Christine Gledhill's work on melodrama, *Home Is Where the Heart Is*, points out, the threats to family unity are main threads in many of Griffith's films.

19. Henderson, *D. W. Griffith*, 37.

20. James Young Deer is well known today as one of the few early-period Native American film directors. He worked for such leading film companies as Biograph, Vitagraph, Kalem, Luben, New York Motion Picture Co. (producer of the Bison label), Selig, and Pathé. Brownlow, *War*, 331. He is particularly well remembered for his creation of "strong, willful, and individual Indian characters" who, whether defending themselves against abusive whites or attempting to assimilate into western European culture, always stood as "equals . . . on their own terms." Many of his early films dealt with themes of prejudice, racism, and assimilation with the underlying message that it was "fear and prejudice, rather than the savagery of Indians[, that] created hostility between two peoples." Smith, "Shooting Cowboys and Indians," 88. James Young Deer's films worked within the system to provide realism and depth rather than the stereotypical renditions of Indians common at the time.

Griffith made around thirty short Indian films during his tenure at Biograph. They cover the gamut in their representations of Native Americans from the romantic and peaceful to the extremely violent and savage. Griffith did not write the scripts and was under obligation to Biograph to produce what was popular at the time, suggesting that he was no different from other directors in producing contradictory depictions. With that said, what does arise in his films, in part because of his extraordinary directing skills and his authority over the majority of the film process, is the accentuating of particular racial biases through editing, framing, and the latitude allowed to actors. See Daniel Bernardi's analysis of *That Chink at Golden Gulch* in "Voice of Whiteness." Perhaps Griffith is remembered most critically for the aesthetic and racist qualities of his films *Birth of a Nation* (1915) and *Broken Blossoms* (1919).

21. Langman, *Guide to Silent Westerns*.

22. Unsigned review of *Red Wing's Gratitude*, *Moving Picture World*, 567; Bowser, *Transformation of Cinema*, 175; *Views and Films Index*, 16 October 1909, quoted in Smith, "Shooting Cowboys and Indians," 95; *Moving Picture World*, "Accuracy in Indian Subjects," 48; Bush, "Moving Picture Absurdities," 733; unsigned review of *Lo, the Poor Indian*, *Moving Picture World*, 10–11.

23. Mayer, "*Broken Doll*," 192; Bowser, *Transformation of Cinema*, 55. Roberta Pearson's *Eloquent Gestures* offers a detailed historical and textual analysis of the changing styles of acting that appear in D. W. Griffith's Biograph pictures. Also see Bernardi, "Voice of Whiteness," which analyzes Griffith's use of a mixture of acting techniques with narrative approach to reinforce certain stereotypes.

24. Mayer, "*Broken Doll*," 193.

25. Slotkin, *Gunfighter Nation*, 10.

26. Bowser, *Biograph Bulletins*, 386.

27. *The Vanishing American* is a fascinating film for a number of reasons, including the changes made from Zane Grey's 1925 novel. The film capital-

izes on the romantic nostalgic sentiments of the late 1920s and the concern over Indian policy on the reservations to create a narrative mixture of stereotypes and social commentary. Riley, "Trapped in the History of Film," 58. Grey worked in conjunction with Paramount to create the screenplay, so his primary objectives remain clearly ingrained in the film. A number of things, however, are different. Nophaie's East Coast education is eliminated, and missionaries, who are heavily critiqued by Grey, are erased, displaced onto the white Indian agents. The interracial romance between Nophaie and Marion is truncated so that it never comes to fruition in the film as it does in the novel. The Nophas (Nophaie's people) are killed by poverty and influenza. In addition, a lengthy social Darwinist evolution sequence is added to the film that overemphasizes the "doomed and vanishing" race motif but continues Grey's theme of evolutionary Darwinism; the result is two distinctly separate sections of the film. And, finally, Nophaie is accidentally shot by his own people while trying to defend the whites, rather than dying from influenza as he does in the novel. Also see Aleiss, "'Vanishing American.'"

28. Zinn, *People's History of the United States*, 339; Dinnerstein, Nichols, and Reimers, *Natives and Strangers*, 123; Wiebe, *Search for Order*, 226.

29. Smith, "Shooting Cowboys and Indians," 116.

30. The plot also resembles hero stories of other cultures and past eras, such as the Greek Jason-Medea and the Mexican La Lloran–Cortes narratives; however, they differ in two significant respects. In the Greek and Mexican stories, the wife kills her own children as revenge for her abandonment. The squaw man stories, or lover films, eliminate this element, displacing the violence onto the woman herself and freeing the hero to raise his children in his own culture. The squaw man story also has deep historical roots in the North American fur trade and early colonial period, when Native American women offered companionship and economic security to white frontiersmen. See Hodes, *Sex, Love, Race*, and Smits, "'Squaw Men.'"

31. Smith, "Shooting Cowboys and Indians," 112; Gunning, "Cinema of Attraction," 68; Higashi, *DeMille and American Culture*, 1, 8, 17.

32. Bergsten, *Biograph Bulletins*, 365.

33. Champagne, *Chronology*, 228, 236, 237. The allotment policy, passed into law in 1887 as the Dawes Act, divided reservation lands into 160-acre parcels for the male heads of families. The land was held in trust for twenty-five years, or until the owner was deemed ready to manage the land appropriately, at which time he was granted citizenship. By 1906, sixty-five thousand Native Americans had become citizens through the allotment process, but millions of acres of reservation land were also lost to white homesteaders, ranchers, and mineral companies. Dippie, *Vanishing American*, 193. The system aided in the attempt to assimilate Native Americans into European American and patriarchal standards of citizenship through farming and single-family landholding as opposed to communal ownership. The policy was not successful

in fully acculturating Native Americans or in "weaning" them of their tribal worldview.

34. Bowser, *Transformation of Cinema*, 38.

35. Loughney, *"Kentuckian,"* 56.

36. Unsigned review of *White Fawn's Devotion*, *Moving Picture World*, 1061.

37. Generally, lover films do not show Native women aside from the primary Princess figure, but *White Fawn's Devotion* (1910) presents Native American women more accurately than do the other films. In this film, a number of tribal women come to the child's aid when she returns to her mother's people for help. Depicted in tribal dress, they work as a unit to care for the "dead" mother and child, offering a hint at the women's network behind the braves. For these reasons, and in light of its profeminist and pro-Native tone, *White Fawn's Devotion* is unique among the lover films. Both Angela Aleiss and Jacquelyn Kilpatrick attribute this film to James Young Deer. Aleiss, "Surprising Silents," 35; Kilpatrick, *Celluloid Indians*, 19. Certainly, the film's differences from the norm reflect his influence. A number of inconsistencies in the chronology of Young Deer's work and in the work itself, however, suggest he did not have full control of the material. According to Smith, Young Deer worked for New York Motion Picture Co. until the end of 1910, when Pathé hired him. *White Fawn's Devotion* was released in June 1910, suggesting that the film's release preceded his time at Pathé. Smith, "Shooting Cowboys and Indians," 101. There are also elements in the film that work against Young Deer's stamp of realism—for example, the Native characters in the film are dressed in long johns, and the child is bullied and slapped by the chief when she attempts to refuse to kill her father. Smith's chapter 3, "A Genuine Indian and His Wife: James Young Deer, Lillian Red Wing, and the Bison-Brand Western," offers a thorough history of Young Deer's career and influence on early westerns and Indian films.

38. The configuration of Nat-U-ritch's name changes slightly over the course of the three films and seventeen years: Nat-U-ritch in 1914, Naturitch in 1918, and finally Naturich in 1931. The 1931 version arrives at a spelling that leaves no doubt that Naturich is a child of nature who embodies the qualities of the wild. Script files, DMA, BYU.

39. The *Squaw Man* films offer a unique opportunity for film historians because they reflect the changes in film style from the early silent period to the early sound era, the maturation of a prominent filmmaker, and the power of the filmic image to convey ideology. DeMille's skill as a filmmaker lay in his ability to continually adapt to the rapidly changing film industry and to audience demands. He rose to fame in the late 1910s and early 1920s for knowing what his fans wanted to see. At the time, he was most famous for his stylish sex comedies and melodramas—his early Jazz Age films—that addressed the "genteel middle-class" but also showcased "ostentatious consumption that appealed to lower-middle-class and working-class female spectators." Higashi, *DeMille*

and American Culture, 142. In addition, the racial dichotomies and stereotypes presented in these films foreshadow DeMille's later westerns and nation-building epics, like *The Plainsman* (1937), *Union Pacific* (1939), *Northwest Mounted Police* (1940), and *Unconquered* (1947), which were not atypical of 1930s and 1940s portrayals of Native Americans. In short, DeMille's lover films, more so than *The Kentuckian* and *White Fawn's Devotion*, echo the sentiments of mainstream America during the late 1910s and early 1930s.

40. Blaisdell, review of *The Squaw Man*, 1243. Winnebago actress Lillian St. Cyr, also known in Hollywood as Princess Red Wing or Lillian Red Wing, was born in Nebraska in 1883 and died in 1974. According to Andrew Smith, she grew up on the Omaha-Winnebago reservation and, with her husband, James Young Deer, worked for many of the East Coast film companies (Biograph, Kalem, Selig, and New York Motion Picture Co.). Smith, "Shooting Cowboys and Indians," 94.

41. Smith, "Shooting Cowboys and Indians," 115.

42. Unsigned review of *The Squaw Man*, *Variety*, 41.

43. This phenomenon is not unique to Hollywood's casting for Native American roles; it is one that occurs in the representation of other ethnic minority groups as well—white actors in blackface, for example.

44. Burgess and Valaskakis, *Indian Princesses and Cow-girls*, 30; Hershfield, "Dolores Del Río," 145. The Mexican Spitfire films Vélez made for RKO in the pre–World War II era were part of their top series productions. Schatz, *Boom and Bust*, 57.

45. Jowett, *Democratic Art*, 190; Knight quoted in Jowett, *Democratic Art*, 188–89.

46. The film industry had practiced self-censorship since the 1910s; however, by the 1930s, the industry was under extreme pressure from religious organizations, women's groups, social service groups, and other concerned public organizations and individuals to severely curtail the latitude directors had in content. In particular, gambling, prostitution, drug use, criminal activity, interracial sexual relations—indeed, overt sexual relations of any kind—were considered taboo. When films depicted such activities, they most often included some type of punishment for those transgressing in order to get the films past the censorship boards. The process could be arduous, with scripts repeatedly being rewritten for such items as passionate kissing and suggestive clothing. The leading film companies supported the self-censorship process, and in 1930, the Motion Picture Association of America published a set of very clear guidelines titled *A Code to Govern the Making of Motion Pictures: The Reasons Supporting It and the Resolution for Uniform Interpretation*.

47. The Meriam report detailed the conditions on reservations where land had been allotted into individual family plots under the General Allotment Act of 1887, and it resulted in an "influential set of recommendations for modifying government policy." Economic changes and many reforms to Indian health

services, education, and welfare resulted; however, as Edward Spicer points out, these reforms were built on the same "foundations as the existing policy, namely, the assumption that the Indians were in a kind of wardship relationship to the United States government." Spicer, *Short History*, 99, 100. As commissioner of Indian Affairs under Franklin D. Roosevelt, John Collier initiated federal policies that reinstated some level of sovereignty to Native American tribes, recognized their cultural integrity, promoted cultural pluralism, and began the long task of reversing the effects of the allotment system. Following the recommendations of the Meriam report, his Indian Reorganization Act helped to restore millions of acres of land to reservations, improved health-care and education systems, and allowed tribal governance on a greater level than that seen during the previous fifty years. Tribes' criticism of his project generally revolved around the structuring of tribal governments on the federal government system rather than on traditional tribal models.

48. Dyer, *White*, esp. chap. 3, "The Light of the World."

49. Zinn, *People's History of the United States*, 378–83.

50. Douglas, *Purity and Danger*, 115.

51. *Oklahoma Jim* is the only example that I uncovered in my research of the Princess's committing suicide out of shame. It is also an anomaly among the other silent film examples in that the Princess figure is a small character part that simply provides a plot device for the rest of the narrative. See the discussion of the film later in this chapter.

52. Smith, "Shooting Cowboys and Indians," 115.

53. Unsigned review of *Oklahoma Jim*, *Film Daily*, 10.

TWO. WHITE-PAINTED LADY

1. *Broken Arrow* is based on the book by Elliott Arnold and on the true story of Tom Jeffords, an ex-Indian scout, superintendent for the Arizona mail during the 1860s and 1870s, and peace negotiator between General O. O. Howard and the Chiricahua Apaches. The film narrates, through Jeffords's voice, his interaction on behalf of the Arizona mail to parley with Cochise, the growth of his friendship with Cochise, and the resulting period of peace. The fictional love affair between Jeffords and Sonseeahray is heightened in the film and plays a central role in presenting the cultural aspects of Apache life. The film continues to hold a place of honor as a western that presents a truly sympathetic view of the Apaches. O'Conner, *Hollywood Indian*, 50, 49. Also see Arnold, *Blood Brother*.

2. Bhabha, "Other Question," 18.

3. Zinn, *People's History of the United States*, 416–17.

4. In 1940, the House Un-American Activities Committee, led by Martin Dies, had attempted to "uncover evidence of Communist influence in Hollywood which could be behind the intense anti-Nazi activity then emerging

in the film capital." Jowett, *Democratic Art*, 393–94. Unable to substantiate his claims and thwarted by the Roosevelt administration's promotion of the film industry as a morale-boosting tool for the war effort, Dies dropped the allegations.

5. Zinn, *People's History of the United States*, 417–23; Sklar, *Movie-Made America*, 397.

6. President's Committee on Civil Rights quoted in Zinn, *People's History of the United States*, 440; Zinn, *People's History of the United States*, 440–42.

7. Fixico, *Termination and Relocation*, 134; Debo, *Short History*, 371–72. Francis Paul Prucha's *Documents of United States Indian Policy* provides actual text from the annual report of the commissioner of Indian Affairs on the relocation program and substantial documentation of the termination policy. Prucha, *Documents*, 237–38. Also see Prucha, *Great Father*; Deloria and Lytle, *Nations Within*; Cornell, *Return of the Native*; and Philp, *Indian Self-Rule*. For more information on Native Americans and World War II and for Native Americans' reactions to termination and relocation, see Bernstein, *Toward a New Era*; Franco, *Crossing the Pond*; and Townsend, *World War II*. Also see Nabakov, *Native American Testimony*, 332–54.

8. In 1950, thirty-eight westerns were made, an increase from twenty-five in 1949. The numbers fluctuated but continued an upward trend that peaked at forty-six in 1956. There was a decline from 1957 to 1962 because of television competition and "the collapse of the legal and economic structures that had sustained the studio system." While movie westerns may have declined, television westerns increased during these years, suggesting that the genre's appeal was stronger than ever during the cold war crises. Slotkin, *Gunfighter Nation*, 347–48.

9. Coyne, *Crowded Prairie*, 69.

10. Ibid., 71, 69.

11. Aleiss, "From Adversaries to Allies," 180, 183, 180.

12. *Devil's Doorway* (Anthony Mann) was produced earlier than *Broken Arrow*, but, according to Richard Slotkin, "its story was so uncompromising in its presentation of White greed and bigotry that the studio delayed its release until the success of Fox's *Broken Arrow* indicated that the public was ready to accept it." Slotkin, *Gunfighter Nation*, 367. *Broken Arrow* proved successful, grossing $3.5 million, and was influential in "reshaping Hollywood's representation of the Indian." Coyne, *Crowded Prairie*, 70. In fact, "*Broken Arrow* was one of the first movie Westerns to be adapted into a television series." Manchel, "Cultural Confusion," 92. Also see Tuska, *American West in Film*, 243.

13. According to Tom Holm, professor of American Indian studies at the University of Arizona, Sonseeahray's headdress is constructed like those worn by male Apache mountain spirit dancers. Its appearance here represents an incorrect cinematic attempt at authenticity.

14. Lewis, *American Adam*, 1, 5, 128.

15. Baird, "'Going Indian,'" 155.

16. Hatch, review of *Broken Arrow*, 23. Five years after *Broken Arrow*, Delmer Daves would coscript *White Feather* (1955), which reworks the earlier narrative. In this film, which was directed by Robert Webb after Daves left 20th Century-Fox, Appearing Day (also played by Debra Paget) does not die but lives to have a son who goes to West Point. As Michael Walker points out, it was still unusual in 1955, even after the success of *Broken Arrow*, for an interracial marriage to be allowed to succeed. One bold exception to this is the 1952 film *The Big Sky*, in which the racist young hero falls in love with a Native woman and stays to live with her people. Walker, "Westerns of Delmer Daves," 133–36.

17. Slotkin, *Gunfighter Nation*, 349, 367. Slotkin's observation is particularly true of *Broken Lance* and *Broken Arrow*. *Broken Lance*'s director, Edward Dmytryk, was a casualty of the blacklists; *Broken Arrow*, which condemned racism and intolerance, was scripted by blacklisted writer Albert Maltz, also one of the Hollywood Ten. Walker, "Westerns of Delmer Daves," 127. Michael Blankfort fronted the script for Maltz and won a Screen Writers Guild award for it while Maltz was in prison for refusing to "cooperate with the House Committee on Un-American Activities investigation of Communist influence in Hollywood." Although a contract between the two writers stated a fee of 10 percent for Blankfort, he did not accept any money. After the McCarthy era, Blankfort succeeded in getting the Screen Writers Guild to correct the records to reflect Maltz's authorship, but he was unable to persuade 20th Century-Fox to change the credits on the film. *Los Angeles Times*, "Mending 'Broken Arrow.'"

18. *Across the Wide Missouri*, film synopsis submitted to Production Code office, file 1508, AMPAS.

19. Nash, "Hidden History," 13; O'Meara, *Daughters of the Country*.

20. Talbot Jennings, *Across the Wide Missouri*, plot synopsis, 1950, production files, Turner MGM Collection, AMPAS.

21. Talbot Jennings to Mr. Lewis at MGM, 1950, file 69, Turner MGM Collection, AMPAS.

22. Zinn, *People's History of the United States*, 417, 419, 421.

23. Unsigned review of *Across the Wide Missouri*, *Time*, 110; Dippie, *Vanishing American*, 338–39.

24. "Going native" refers to the act of marrying into the tribe or rejecting Western civilization for the ideologies, lifestyles, and cultures of Native peoples. For a thorough discussion of "going native," see chapter 5. In this case, Devereaux remains an icon of the historical western cattle barons and does not give up Western culture for Comanche culture. But the film depicts him as the old vanguard being replaced by the new West represented by cattle companies, stock trading, and eastern legal systems. His marriage to the Princess and his isolation from the white community reinforce this idea.

25. Manchester, *Glory and the Dream*, 374; Moses, *American Movie Classics*, 61. Dmytryk's own dealings with intolerance—he was blacklisted by the

House Un-American Activities Committee in 1947—may have influenced the liberal stance in these films, but without more information, it is impossible to determine exactly what his intent was with this material. According to Lary May, Dmytryk served part of his jail sentence, during which "he changed his mind. Seeking to secure the opportunity to work again, he named his communist allies to HUAC," confessed publicly, and began directing films that appeared to be atonements for his Communist sympathies. May cites *The Caine Mutiny* (1954) as one of these. May, *Big Tomorrow*, 198, 203. Released the same year as *The Caine Mutiny*, *Broken Lance* does not appear to be an anti-Communist film; its sympathetic rendering of the victims of prejudice and its request for tolerance seem to point toward a more liberal agenda.

    26. Coyne, *Crowded Prairie*, 70.

    27. Ibid., 85, 69. The race riots that erupted in Little Rock, Arkansas, in 1957 over desegregation of the public schools resulted in President Eisenhower's sending in the 101st Airborne to restore order and escort African American school children into the previously white schools. Manchester, *Glory and the Dream*, 799–810, offers a detailed summary of the Little Rock incident.

    28. Powe, review of *Last Train from Gun Hill*.

    29. Bernardi, *Classic Hollywood*, xv.

    30. Higson, "Concept of National Cinema," 54.

    31. Bhabha, "Other Question," 66.

    32. Douglas, *Purity and Danger*, 114.

    33. Slotkin, *Gunfighter Nation*, 383, 353.

THREE. WHAT LIES BENEATH THE SURFACE

The epigraph to this chapter comes from Cecil B. DeMille, *Northwest Mounted Police*, story notes, 31 July 1939, box 554, DMA, BYU.

    1. Baron Valentin Mandelstamm to DeMille, 24 January 1940, *Northwest Mounted Police*, boxes 554 and 559, folder 8, DMA, BYU. The letter informs DeMille of the slang meaning of Lupette and suggests that the director find a better name for the character. The film opened on March 7, 1940, with the character's name changed to Louvette.

    2. Bhabha, "Other Question," 19.

    3. Ibid., 27.

    4. Green, "Pocahontas Perplex," 702.

    5. Ibid., 711; Smits, "'Squaw Men'"; Smits, "'Squaw Drudge.'"

    6. Musser, "Ethnicity," 65.

    7. Jones quoted in Smits, "'Squaw Men,'" 37.

    8. Doane, *Femmes Fatales*, 2–3.

    9. Schatz, *Boom and Bust*, appendixes 5 and 7.

    10. Bowser, *Biograph Bulletins*, 365.

    11. Hilger, *From Savage to Nobleman*, 51.

12. See chapter 1 for discussion of the *Squaw Man* films.

13. Elsie Janis, *The Squaw Man*, dialogue script, scene 196, box 1260, file 7, DMA, BYU; Lenore Coffee to Cecil B. Demille, 27 December 1930, *The Squaw Man*, box 295, DMA, BYU.

14. The Production Code of 1930 (created by the Motion Picture Producers and Distributors of America) was designed as a self-regulatory code of ethics for the film industry, which underwent repeated attacks from the public regarding the sexual, violent, and inappropriate subject matter of its products from the early silent period onward. Beginning as a voluntary program, but switching to a mandatory regulation by 1934, the code presented guiding principals of morality and virtue based on mainstream American ideals. Also known as the Hays Code after William H. Hays, president of the Motion Picture Producers and Distributors of America, or the Breen Code after Joseph Breen, director of the Production Code Administration, the code governed film imagery from 1934 to 1968. It was revised in 1956 and again in 1966 in an attempt to "keep up with liberalization," but miscegenation was one of the unchanging taboos of a code that was finally replaced with the current rating system in 1968. Konigsberg, *Complete Film Dictionary*, 151, 220. In the early 1930s, prior to the mandatory enforcement of the code, Hollywood films notoriously challenged the main tenets of the code's ethical intent by suggesting what the "spectator *doesn't* see." Mae West's sexual innuendoes, the "promiscuous embrace of sex" in "sex films," and gangster films' celebration of vices, for example, resulted in public and church groups' demands for tighter regulation. The crackdown on film products by the code in 1934 led to a period of extremely tight regulation that would loosen in the 1940s, after Joseph Breen left the position for a "short interregnum at RKO in 1940–41," and would never return to the same level of strict control. Doherty, *Pre-Code Hollywood*, 11, 102, 342.

15. According to Lea Jacobs's study of precode Hollywood, the use of ellipsis, fade-to-black, and other techniques to suggest sex became one of the industry's innovative ways to sidestep the Production Code regulations. Thus "ideas which were occluded at the level of dialogue or action could be emphasized by visual means." Jacobs, *Wages of Sin*, 112.

16. *The Squaw Man*, casting files, box 303, DMA, BYU; Itershfield, "Delores Del Rio," 145.

17. López, "Are All Latins from Manhattan," 404–24, 412.

18. Gevinson, *Within Our Gates*, 1158.

19. Foster, "Art of Fetishism," 254; Mulvey, "Visual Pleasure," 22, 25.

20. Slim Girl's statement reflects the fractured sense of self many Native Americans felt at the time, straddling two different cultural systems and worldviews. Overall, the film underscores the then-popular liberal sentiment that mainstream American intrusion into Native culture contaminated the purity and innocence of those cultures. Such perspectives supported a pluralistic approach to Native-federal relationships, and cultural separation rather than as-

similation. The Indian Reorganization Act, which was signed into law in the same year as the film's release, promoted this liberal approach to Indian policy. The result was an overturning of assimilationist policies, such as the Dawes Act, in favor of cultural pluralism and tribal identity. Tribal governments were reinstated, albeit redesigned to fit an American federal model, to offer a certain amount of autonomy. Simultaneously, Native cultural difference was celebrated rather than condemned. See Prucha, *Great Father*; Deloria and Lytle, *Nations Within*; Cornell, *Return of the Native*; and Philp, *Indian Self-Rule*.

21. Bhabha, "Other Question," 27.

22. *Frozen Justice*, film synopsis, 1926–1927, William Fox Dramatic Productions, Chamberlin Collection no. 123, vol. 39, pp. 2–3, AMPAS.

23. Unsigned review of *Frozen Justice*, n.d., Chamberlin Collection no. 123, vol. 39, p. 2, AMPAS; unsigned review of *Frozen Justice*, *Film Daily*; unsigned review of *Frozen Justice*, *New York Times Film Reviews*, 565; Bige, review of *Frozen Justice*, 25.

24. Katz, *Film Encyclopedia*, 1385.

25. Memorandum from Mr. Breen to Dr. Wingate, 4 December 1933, and report by Mr. Breen to William Hayes, 22 March 1934, *Laughing Boy*, 1934, Production Code files, AMPAS.

26. Jacobs, *Wages of Sin*, 33, 34, 41.

27. Aleiss, "From Adversaries to Allies," 45.

28. In 1930, A westerns "made up 2.6 percent of all films produced by the seven major studios, and 21.4 percent of all Westerns," but by 1934 there were no A westerns produced. Slotkin suggests that the Depression-era recovery and the failure of American industrial and capitalist society to prevent the Depression may have caused dissatisfaction with themes that promoted American expansionism. Slotkin, *Gunfighter Nation*, 255, 256.

29. Aleiss, "Prelude to World War II," 51; John C. Flinn quoted in Balio, *Grand Design*, 194. In addition, the Hollywood studios started their economic comeback from the Depression years. The money allocated to, and the increase in, A westerns may reflect the studios' increased production.

30. Schatz, *Hollywood Genres*, 50; Slotkin, *Gunfighter Nation*, 257–58. By 1939, the A western constituted 2.3 percent of all films, a doubling of its status a year earlier, and between 1939 and 1941, the genre averaged "18.6 percent of all Westerns and 2.7 percent of all productions." Slotkin, *Gunfighter Nation*, 278.

31. Richard Slotkin defines the historic epic, the cult of the outlaw, and the classic as three categories adapted by the Hollywood film industry in the late 1930s and early 1940s to resolve "the problem of making movies out of American mythology" and alternative ideologies about the idealized frontier at the time. Slotkin, *Gunfighter Nation*, 286.

32. Schatz, *Hollywood Genres*, 48.

33. Slotkin, *Gunfighter Nation*, 286–88, 292.

34. *Northwest Mounted Police*, story notes, 6 June 1939, box 552, DMA, BYU.

35. Cecil B. DeMille, "In Chicago Tonight" (Chicago premiere of *North-west Mounted Police*, 27 October 1940), box 387, folder 6, DMA, BYU.

36. DeMille, *Northwest Mounted Police*, story notes, 31 July 1939.

37. Commander Weade, *Northwest Mounted Police*, story notes, 31 July 1939; *Northwest Mounted Police*, story notes, 13 October 1939, box 554, DMA, BYU.

38. Slotkin, *Gunfighter Nation*, 290–91; Cawelti, *Six-Gun Mystique Sequel*, 151.

39. Pye, "Criticism and the Western," 13; Cawelti, *Six-Gun Mystique Sequel*, 30–31, 31, 34.

40. Aleiss, "Prelude to World War II," 27, 25. Three years prior to America's entrance into the war in 1941, "the Office of War Information—a federal agency that advised the film industry on its promotion of war-related themes . . . advis[ed] producers to treat 'dark-skinned peoples' as allies to American heroes. 'Our sincerity,' the agency explained, 'is judged by the attitude and treatment we accord those dark-skinned peoples within our own borders.'" Aleiss, "Prelude to World War II," 31.

41. Joseph Breen to Luigi Luraschi at Paramount Studios, 18 July 1940, *Northwest Mounted Police*, Production Code files, AMPAS; Schatz, *Boom and Bust*, 466, 472; López, "Are All Latins from Manhattan," 409.

42. Aleiss, "From Adversaries to Allies," 100; Jowett, *Democratic Art*, 326; Schatz, *Boom and Bust*, 279; Zinn, *People's History of the United States*, 407; Schatz, *Boom and Bust*, 137; Dinnerstein, Nichols, and Reimers, *Natives and Strangers*, 247. On African American troop segregation, see Zinn, *People's History of the United States*, 406, and Franco, *Crossing the Pond*, 132. Two recent works on Native American servicemen of World War II make clear that Native Americans were successfully integrated with whites into mixed units. Native Americans' efforts for the war overseas and at home were praised by individuals, the federal government, and the armed services. Even so, stereotypes about the scouting and war skills of Native Americans, which survived from popular culture folklore and the not-so-distant Indian wars, perpetuated the image of them as more naturally conditioned for battle—"natural Ranger[s]." Townsend, *World War II*, 134. Also see Bernstein, *Toward a New Era*.

43. The studio's net profits for the year were about $120 million, up from $66 million in 1945. Schatz, *Boom and Bust*, 289–90.

44. Ibid., 371; Fenin and Everson, *Western*, 265–66.

45. Schatz, *Boom and Bust*, 481; Slotkin, *Gunfighter Nation*, 286; Schatz, *Hollywood Genres*, 48, 50–51; Lyons, "My Darling Clementine," 5.

46. Simmon, "Concerning the Weary Legs," 149–66.

47. Bignell, "Method Westerns," 113.

48. Schatz, *Hollywood Genres*, 113; Jackson, *Language of Cinema*, 96.

49. Lyons, "My Darling Clementine," 8; Gallafent, "Four Tombstones," 305; Brand quoted in John Ford to Joseph Breen, 5 March 1946, *My Darling*

Clementine, Production Code files, AMPAS. Harry Brand's qualification of Chihuahua as an entertainer came after negotiations with the Production Code office about her label as a prostitute. As a result of the Production Code officials' reaction, Ford modified her occupation from prostitute to saloon entertainer, but not without firing off a scathing letter to Joseph Breen. In the letter, Ford suggests that Breen reread the script, keeping in mind that certain elements depict the reality of the West. In particular, "It would be very easy for us to cheat . . . and call our girls hostesses in the saloon, but just between the two of us nobody is fooled, and I think that if for once we treat the matter with honesty and avoid anything that is in bad taste, there cannot possibly be any complaint from anyone." John Ford to Joseph Breen, 5 March 1946.

50. Coyne, *Crowded Prairie*, 38.

51. See, for example, Maltby, "Better Sense of History," 34–49, and Aleiss, "Race Divided."

52. Gallafent, "Four Tombstones," 305.

53. Schatz, *Hollywood Genres*, 114; Schatz, *Boom and Bust*, 342; O'Hara, review of *Duel in the Sun*, 33; unsigned review of *Duel in the Sun*, *Variety*, 14. A "raw, sex-laden, western pulp fiction," *Duel in the Sun* met with extreme resistance and censorship from the Production Code Administration and condemnation from a number of organizations, including the Daughters of the American Revolution, the California Federation of Business and Professional Women's Clubs, the American Association of University Women, the Catholic League of Decency, and the public in general. Unsigned review of *Duel in the Sun*, *Variety*, 14. The Production Code files on the film reveal an enormous amount of correspondence with the Production Code office from citizens, religious organizations, and women's groups. Many of the letters from women follow a specific format, suggesting that they were part of a campaign of some type. Selznick also received numerous letters of concern about the sexual content from the Protestant Film Commission, the Church Federation of Los Angeles, and the national Legion of Decency. *Duel in the Sun*, Production Code files, AMPAS.

54. Lang, *American Film Melodrama*, 6; Doane, *Femmes Fatales*, 227; Wood, "*Duel in the Sun*," 190.

55. Doane, *Femmes Fatales*, 2.

56. Jerome Pryor's analysis of the film focuses on its connection to Greek tragedy and on its dance and storytelling patterns. As he explains, the Orizaba is named after the "highest mountain in Mexico . . . a volcano, where rain dances have been performed," which links it to fertility rituals. Pryor, "*Duel in the Sun*," 8–19.

57. Much of the overt racism voiced in the film comes from Senator McCanles, who taunts Pearl by calling her Pocahontas, remarks on her dark skin, and orders "that squaw" out of his house. Lewt mimics his father in this, remarking, on seeing her father's picture, "This must be the white side."

58. Until this point in the film, Pearl has always slept in the nude. The white nightgown seems to indicate her attempt at being a chaste "good girl" after Sam's murder. The contrast of her dark skin next to the white cloth also metonymically connects her to Laura Belle and moral goodness. The nightgown's design corresponds to Laura Belle's high-collared dresses, and the contrasting color tones recall an early scene in the film in which Pearl's dark skin is juxtaposed to Laura Belle's light skin. Sitting in Laura Belle's parlor, Pearl kisses her hand and cries that she wants to be like her. Laura Belle leans over and places her face next to Pearl's. The juxtaposition of Lillian Gish's pallor to Jennifer Jones's darkly tinted skin illustrates the vast difference between the women's coloring and metaphorically contrasts their inner beings. Pearl's passionate darkness overwhelms Laura Belle's frail and suppressed character.

59. The ending rewrites that of the novel by Niven Busch, in which Pearl kills Lewt and then returns to marry Jesse. Busch's 1944 story "flouted racial boundaries by unleashing the carnal instincts that traditionally had been restrained by social taboos" and by promoting an interracial marital union as a happy ending—a twist the Production Code Administration could not condone in light of Pearl's actions. Aleiss, "From Adversaries to Allies," 159. Selznick's alteration reinforces the film's underlying theme of transgression and violent passion but also ensures the melodramatic and western ideological adherence to paternalism and moral law.

60. Doane, *Femmes Fatales*, 2.

61. Aleiss, "From Adversaries to Allies," 159; Zinn, *People's History of the United States*, 440.

62. Dinnerstein, Nichols, and Reimers, *Natives and Strangers*, 257–58.

63. Slotkin, *Gunfighter Nation*, 333.

64. Cawelti, *Six-Gun Mystique Sequel*, 92; Aleiss, "From Adversaries to Allies," 166; Coyne, *Crowded Prairie*, 48.

65. Slotkin describes outlaw westerns as films that celebrate the careers of famous outlaws, such as Jesse James, within the historical and iconographic devices of the genre, but with a tendency for social criticism. His classification of outlaw westerns looks primarily at the late-1930s and early-1940s films, such as *The Oklahoma Kid* (1939) and *Jesse James* (1939). Slotkin, *Gunfighter Nation*, 293. Although later in date, *Colorado Territory* contains elements of the outlaw western, such as the outlaw hero himself and the questioning of particular social assumptions, values, and methods of achieving progress and civilization.

66. Lucas, "Saloon Girls," 305.

67. Unsigned review of *Colorado Territory*, *Newsweek*, 88–89.

68. Fenin and Everson, *Western*, 276–77.

69. Lucas, "Saloon Girls," 305.

70. Unsigned review of *Colorado Territory*, n.d., clipping files, MOMA.

71. Schatz, *Boom and Bust*, 197; Haralovich, "Film Advertising," 127, 129, 152, 128.

72. Bhabha, "Other Question," 26.

73. Doane, *Femmes Fatales*, 209–48, 212.

74. JanMohamed quoted in Apter and Pietz, *Fetishism as Cultural Discourse*, 7.

75. Doane, *Femmes Fatales*, 235.

76. Dinnerstein, Nichols, and Reimers, *Natives and Strangers*, 249; Schatz, *Boom and Bust*, 135; Manchester, *Glory and the Dream*, 248–49.

FOUR. THE ONLY GOOD INDIAN IS A DEAD INDIAN

1. Stember, *Sexual Racism*, ix.

2. Unsigned review of *Arrowhead*, *Variety*, 6.

3. *Arrowhead*, film files, MOMA. The United States' reservation policy is often broken down into two primary periods—before the Civil War (1834–1860) and during and after the war (1861–1887). These dates suppose the policy ended with the 1887 passage of the Dawes Act, which began a policy of breaking up tribally held reservation lands into privately held family plots.

4. Toriano's recent return from this school is an important detail because it hints at the history of military, mission, and Bureau of Indian Affairs boarding schools that were part of the United States' and religious groups' efforts to "civilize" Native Americans through education. The earliest schools date to 1842, when the Bureau of Indian Affairs was created as part of the War Department. Sharpes, "Federal Education," 1. The United States' education policy for Native Americans was one of forced assimilation, designed to uproot the child and drastically refocus his view of the world from that of a tribal person to that of a western European American. *Arrowhead*'s story date, 1878, is particularly important because this was the founding year of the first federally administered military-style boarding school, the Carlisle Indian Industrial School in Carlisle, Pennsylvania. The school was the brainchild of Captain Richard H. Pratt, whose experiences reforming Apache prisoners at Fort Marion, Florida, informed the structure and ideology of Carlisle. Many children returned from Carlisle and other boarding schools angry, distanced from their kin because they no longer spoke their languages, and culturally caught between two worlds. For more information on boarding schools and their legacy for Native Americans, see Adams, *Education for Extinction*; Archuleta, Child, and Lomawaima, *Away from Home*; and Child, *Boarding School Seasons*.

5. Tuska, *American West in Film*, 249; unsigned review of *Arrowhead*, *Daily Variety*, 3.

6. Zinn, *People's History of the United States*, 416–21, 412.

7. Slotkin, *Gunfighter Nation*, 405.

8. The film industry was investigated by the House Un-American Activities Committee from 1946 to 1960 to discover and purge any "Communist influence." Between 1947 and 1952, "the motion picture community bore the brunt of the committee's all-out campaign to increase public awareness of the

'insidious danger' communism posed for the American way of life." Jowett, *Democratic Art*, 393, 394. The campaign devastated the Hollywood community, which suffered losses of actors, writers, producers, technicians, and others to allegations of Communist activity. In the face of the accusations, the industry retreated, turned its back on many, and in some cases participated in condemning the accused. Sklar, *Movie-Made America*, 397.

9. According to Richard Slotkin, thirty-one westerns were produced in 1948, twenty-five in 1949, thirty-eight in 1950, forty in 1952, thirty-six in 1954, and forty-six in 1956. Slotkin, *Gunfighter Nation*, 347. Jowett translates this into percentages of feature-length pictures approved by the Motion Picture Association of America. He records 25.2 percent in 1947, 23.7 percent in 1948, 26.3 percent in 1949, 27.1 percent in 1950, 18 percent in 1951, 20.3 percent in 1952, 17.7 percent in 1953, and 22.1 percent in 1954. Jowett, *Democratic Art*, 369.

10. Coyne, *Crowded Prairie*, 70.

11. Nita's occupation as Bannon's laundress adds a historical note of accuracy to the film. A number of historical works have documented the role of Native women at the American and French forts as laundresses, cooks, and companions. See Smits, "'Squaw Men,'" 29–61; Nash, "Hidden History," 10–34; and O'Meara, *Daughters of the Country*.

12. May, *Big Tomorrow*, 208.

13. Scheuer, review of *Arrowhead*; unsigned review of *Arrowhead*, *Hollywood Reporter*.

14. *Arrowhead*, screenplays and script treatments, fall 1951, Production Code files—scripts, AMPAS; *Arrowhead*, shooting script, Paramount Pictures Production Code files, AMPAS; Kovel, *White Racism*, 57.

15. Suicide is a characteristic death linked to the Princess figure rather than the Sexualized Maiden. As mentioned in chapter 1, the silent-period filmmakers utilized suicide as a favorite method for eliminating the Princess figure from the narrative. The only other instances of self-sacrifice in the 1940s and 1950s Celluloid Maiden films are Señora Devereaux's in *Broken Lance* (1954) and Hannah's in *Unconquered* (1947). Hannah is an interesting case because she is an atypical Princess whose violence places her in the subcategory of Celluloid Maiden closer to these 1950s Sexualized Maidens.

16. *Mackenna's Gold*, Columbia Pictures publicity files, Production Code files, AMPAS.

17. *Mackenna's Gold*, scripted by Carl Foreman and based on the novel by Will Henry, was produced in 1967 and "intended as a 1968 reserved-seat attraction in Cinerama," but the film was "held up for nearly a year until Columbia Pictures decided to release it on a continuous release." *Filmfacts*, 330.

18. Omi and Winant, *Racial Formation*, 2, 138; Brody, Dumenil, and Henretta, *America*, 834–37; Zinn, *People's History of the United States*, 451.

19. Brody, Dumenil, and Henretta, *America*, 848; Coyne, *Crowded Prairie*, 122.

20. Coyne, *Crowded Prairie*, 122, 124. Coyne notes that, between 1963 and 1968, the number of cinemas declined, as did weekly attendance. Television westerns remained common, ranging from thirteen to twenty per year, but lost popularity to cops-and-robbers dramas after 1968. Hollywood's production of westerns fluctuated, but the genre remained a staple for the industry: a "paltry six in 1963, but seventeen in 1964, eighteen in both 1965 and 1966, and nineteen in 1967." Coyne, *Crowded Prairie*, 122.

21. Unsigned review of *Mackenna's Gold*, *Variety*, 6.

22. As Mackenna and Inga flee the canyon, they discard the gold in their pockets, as if to rid themselves of its evil influence. However, unbeknownst to them, Sergeant Tibbs filled their saddlebags with gold prior to his death in the canyon; therefore, the couple ride off rewarded for their morality.

23. *Mackenna's Gold*, script files, Gregory Peck Collection, AMPAS.

24. Cecil B. DeMilles's Celluloid Maiden, Hannah, in *Unconquered* (1947) must be mentioned as a figure that foreshadows Hesh-ke. Hannah is a unique case because she, like Look (*The Searchers*) and Flo (*In Cold Blood*), is a hybridized fallen Princess type—a combination of the femme fatale Sexualized Maiden and a Princess of high social standing. Like Hesh-ke, she is depicted as having a terrible temper and raging jealousy, and she also attacks the white heroine frequently.

25. Brody, Dumenil, and Henretta, *America*, 850–54; Zinn, *People's History of the United States*, 515–17; Brody, Dumenil, and Henretta, *America*, 858, 846.

26. The nudity in the scene deserves special mention. It is the first of such nude scenes in any of the Celluloid Maiden films I analyzed, and it signals relaxing standards of morality and acceptability in the Production Code and American society. In an attempt to keep up with the changing morals and realities of the time, Hollywood, following the lead of British and American productions such as *Bonnie and Clyde* and *The Graduate* in 1967, and *Midnight Cowboy* and *Easy Rider* in 1969, incorporated progressively riskier and more violent images into films. In the early 1960s, the Motion Picture Association of America had streamlined the Production Code regulations in an attempt to make the rating system more reflective of the time, but it finally replaced the old system in 1968 with the ratings X, R, M, and GP. See Jowett, *Democratic Art*, 434–35.

27. Green, "Pocahontas Perplex," 703, 711.

28. Slotkin, *Gunfighter Nation*, 468.

29. Thompson, "*The Searchers*," 1502–5; Coyne, *Crowded Prairie*, 76. Coyne reports that the film made $4.9 million at the box office, making it the sixteenth-most-successful western by 1981 standards. Coyne considers the application of the praise "best-ever Western" far from helpful and suggests that the film may have been "over-analysed and certainly over-praised." He does agree that the film is "nevertheless impressive," with stunning photography and a

complex narrative that is "alternately poignant and gripping." Coyne, *Crowded Prairie*, 76. A sampling of 1956 reviews reveals the critics' disappointment with Ford's epic western. *America's* film critic found it "curiously deficient"; *Film in Review* felt it left "much to be desired"; *Sight and Sound* concluded that "the parts did not coalesce and the essential theme never came alive"; *Commonweal* condemned the plot and subplot as unsatisfactory; and the *Nation* suggested that the film carried the theme of "prejudice to an extreme, even by movie frontier standards. . . . *The Searchers* is a picnic for sadists in very beautiful country." In 1961, however, the *Motion Picture Herald* gave the film an "excellent" rating and praised its "well-written screenplay." Unsigned review of *The Searchers*, *America*, 272; unsigned review of *The Searchers*, *Film in Review*, 284–85; Anderson, review of *The Searchers*, 94–95; unsigned review of *The Searchers*, *Commonweal*, 274; Hatch, review of *The Searchers*, 536; unsigned review of *The Searchers*, *Motion Picture Herald Product Digest*, 140.

30. Thompson, "*The Searchers*," 1502; Roth, "'Yes, My Darling Daughter,'" 67; Slotkin, *Gunfighter Nation*, 461–62; Pye, "Double Vision," 229.

31. Pye, "Double Vision," 230.

32. Tompkins, *West of Everything*, 41.

33. Pye, "Double Vision," 231; Lehman, "Looking," 261. Pye's and Lehman's articles offer the most thorough analyses of Look. Although they do not discuss her as a fallen Princess figure, their work informs my understanding of the ways in which racializing practices within filmic traditions create the character.

34. Both Pye and Lehman discuss this scene. Lehman's shot-by-shot analysis of the sequence reveals that Martin runs over the area where Look's body should have landed, and that this missing shot is replaced by that of her dead body in the Comanche village. Lehman suggests that the uncomfortable treatment of Look and Ford's inability to follow this sequence through with the continuity editing style typical of Hollywood reveal a psychological response of repression on Ford's part. Lehman, "Looking," 259–92.

35. In Le May's novel, Look leaves Martin after eleven days, riding off with an unknown Indian. Through hearsay years later, Martin learns that a Comanche woman who called herself Look had died a captive. Le May, *Searchers*, 114–15.

36. Peter Lehman proposes that the film's western conventions allowed Ford to displace black-white racial tensions "into the past and onto another race," a race that was no longer "actively contemplated, let alone feared by the average white American in 1956." He continues that interracial sexuality, particularly between black men and white women, was a controversial topic at the time. Lehman, "Looking," 263–64. Marty Roth makes a similar conclusion, noting that, "in a Ford film, an African-American man would never do it to a white daughter—although an Indian would." Roth, "'Yes, My Darling Daughter,'" 69. I do not disagree with either scholar about the displacement of black-white

tensions onto Native American subjects. The ability of a filmmaker to make such a translation and to construct the film in such a way as to underscore the particulars of historical white–Native American racial tensions, however, suggests that racism toward Native Americans also continues to control the American imagination. In short, the power of Ford's racializing imagery deserves to be analyzed within Native American–white tensions also.

37. Pye, "Double Vision," 231.

38. Again, see Pye, "Double Vision," and Lehman, "Looking."

39. The phrase "nonfiction novel" appears in a number of film reviews and is credited to Capote, who used it to describe his crafting of the documentary-novel *In Cold Blood*. See unsigned review of *In Cold Blood*, *Time*, 78; unsigned review of *In Cold Blood*, *Variety*, 6; Schickel, review of *In Cold Blood*, 10; and Conroy, review of *In Cold Blood*, 28–29.

40. Capote, *In Cold Blood*, acknowledgments; Crowther, review of *In Cold Blood*, 60.

41. Capote, *In Cold Blood*, 123–33.

42. Fiedler, *Return of the Vanishing American*, 14. In keeping with Fiedler's comparison of the novel to a western, many of the film reviewers at the time compared the film to *Bonnie and Clyde* (1967), a gangster film built on a western generic framework. There are connections between gangster films and the western, as Richard Slotkin has shown, and the urban gangster films of the late 1960s build on this history. Slotkin, *Gunfighter Nation*, 260–65. For reviews that mention *Bonnie and Clyde*, see Hatch, review of *In Cold Blood*, 28; Crowther, review of *In Cold Blood*, 60; and Conroy, review of *In Cold Blood*, 28–29.

43. The casting of Thurman may signal the film industry's attempt to utilize Native American actors and to achieve a greater degree of authenticity after a fifty-year hiatus. Readers will recall that Lillian Red Wing was the last Native actress cast in a Celluloid Maiden role (*The Squaw Man*, 1914).

44. Capote's focus on the American social welfare system may have referenced the expansion of such programs by the Johnson administration, which increased federal aid to elementary and secondary education, urban renewal, and social welfare programs. See Brody, Dumenil, and Henretta, *America*, 833–39.

45. Crowther, review of *In Cold Blood*, 60–61; Kozloff, review of *In Cold Blood*, 148.

46. A similar example surfaces in the popular television series *Star Trek* in 1968; however, the Native American woman in the *Star Trek* episode is a Princess figure, not a Sexualized Maiden. In "The Paradise Syndrome," Captain Kirk, "suffering from amnesia," becomes the "medicine chief for a tribe of Native-Americans on a planet far from Earth." He falls in love with and marries Miramanee, a "submissive and often scantily clad native girl." He eventually leaves Miramanee after regaining his memory, because he realizes that she will

never fit into his world and he cannot remain in hers. Bernardi, *"Star Trek" and History*, 44–46.

47. Omi and Winant, *Racial Formation*, 19.

FIVE. FREE LOVE AND VIOLENCE

1. In general, when the white hero has a close male Indian friend, that Indian falls into the noble savage category. He, like the princess, represents the best of his people and is open to assimilation or integration with whites.

2. McCarthy, "Westers, Not Westerns," 123. McCarthy refers specifically to the mountain man character, which he differentiates from the cowboy hero; however, I see a similarity in how the Celluloid Maiden works in these films to encourage the revisionist western hero to reject civilization.

3. Kasdan and Tavernetti, "Native Americans in a Revisionist Western," 121.

4. Huhndorf, *Going Native*, 18; Fiedler, *Return of the Vanishing American*, 24.

5. Slotkin, *Gunfighter Nation*, 631.

6. The term "savage reactionary," coined by Michael Marsden and Jack Nachbar, refers to the Indian who "is a killer because he detests the proper and manifest advancement of a White culture clearly superior to his own and often because of his own primal impulses." This character is contrasted to the "Noble Anachronism," or the noble Indian. Marsden and Nachbar, "Indian in the Movies," 609.

7. Zinn, *People's History of the United States*, 460.

8. Bataille and Silet, *Pretend Indians*, 72; Cook, *Lost Illusions*, 174, 297; Zinn, *Twentieth Century*, 255–300.

9. Blue Cloud quoted in Hertzberg, "Indian Rights Movement," 318. In addition to Hertzberg's article, see Champagne, *Chronology*, 367–82.

10. Cook, *Lost Illusions*, 174; French, "Indian in the Western Movie," 104; Baird, "'Going Indian,'" 278. Elliot Silverstein, the director of *A Man Called Horse*, intended an authentic rendering of Sioux culture, and his introduction to the film indicates that he relied on government documents and on information gathered from the American Museum of Natural History, the Library of Congress, and the Smithsonian Institution. In addition, "the rituals dramatized have been documented from the letters and painting of George Catlin, Carl Bodmer, and other eye witnesses of the period." The film incorporated the Sioux language into "80% of the dialogue" and hired hundreds of Native Americans as extras. Georgakas, "They Have Not Spoken," 26. Ideally, Silverstein would also have incorporated "authentic Sioux chants accompanied by equally authentic Indian pipes, drums, and rattles," but this idea was replaced with a contemporary musical score during postproduction editing. Knight, review of *A Man Called Horse*, 52. As Churchill observes, in addition to the musical

score, the hallucination montages—also added to Silverstein's dismay—and a liberal mixing of Indian elements result in a "myriad of . . . errors [that] made the widely publicized 'authenticity' of this film deleterious to an understanding of Native peoples, past and present." The film "depicts a people whose language is Sioux, whose hairstyles range from Assiniboin through Nez Perce to Comanche, whose tipi design is Crow, and whose Sun Dance ceremony and the lodge in which it is held are both typically Mandan." Churchill, *Fantasies of the Master Race*, 238.

11. Promotional materials, A *Man Called Horse*, Cinema Center Films, in the author's possession; unsigned review of A *Man Called Horse*, *America*, 538.

12. Fiedler, *Return of the Vanishing American*, 167; Georgakas, "They Have Not Spoken," 26; Fiedler, *Return of the Vanishing American*, 167.

13. Unsigned review of A *Man Called Horse*, *Time*, 103.

14. Prats, *Invisible Natives*, 178.

15. The film accentuates a common misunderstanding about "buying" a bride in Native cultures. For many tribes, the gift of horses and other items to the woman's father was not a purchase of a woman as a commodity; rather, it was proof of the man's ability to take care of the woman in a manner agreeable to the family. In many cases, as the film does illustrate, women had the right to turn down a would-be husband.

16. Farber, review of A *Man Called Horse*, 61; Prats, *Invisible Natives*, 178.

17. Unsigned review of A *Man Called Horse*, *Time*, 103. Native American groups protested the film's depiction of the Sioux as savages and, as Stephen Farber points out, "rightly objected to the intimation that the white Anglo-Saxon is the natural leader of the tribe." Farber, review of A *Man Called Horse*, 61. The American Indian Movement protested the film's distorted view of Native Americans and later withdrew its support of *Jeremiah Johnson* out of fear of similar negative stereotyping. Champagne, *Chronology*, 374.

18. Kilpatrick, *Celluloid Indians*, 84; French, "Indian in the Western Movie," 105; Hartung, review of *Little Big Man*, 447.

19. The most in-depth critiques of these aspects of the film from the period are Kael, review of *Little Big Man*, 50–52; Braudy, "Difficulties of *Little Big Man*," 30–33; Burgess, review of *Little Big Man*, 30–32; Kaufmann, review of *Little Big Man*, 18, 25; and Turner, "*Little Big Man*, the Novel and the Film," 154.

20. O'Conner, *Hollywood Indian*, 68; Cook, *Lost Illusions*, 174.

21. Cowen, "Social-Cognitive Approach," 368; Kasdan and Tavernetti, "Native Americans in a Revisionist Western," 125. During the brief Hollywood renaissance (1969–1970), which initiated a "remarkable aesthetic revival that produced the *auteur* directors," such as Stanley Kubrick, Francis Ford Coppola, and Robert Altman, Arthur Penn entered a short period of "bankability." The

decline of the studio system and the resulting reliance on independent directors opened the door to a number of directors, like Penn, whose "iconoclasm and independence had thus far prevented them from entering the Hollywood mainstream." Cook, *Lost Illusions*, 69–73. This moment offered Penn the ability to express his liberal and antiestablishment views in films such as *Bonnie and Clyde*, *Alice's Restaurant*, and *Little Big Man*.

22. The massacre scenes reference two episodes in American history: the Washita River massacre of November 1868 and the similar slaughter of women and children in Vietnam. In 1868, Lieutenant Colonel George Armstrong Custer led the Seventh Cavalry in an unprovoked attack on Chief Black Kettle's Cheyennes, who were camped in Indian territory along the Washita River. The elimination of the Motion Picture Association of America's Production Code in 1968 allowed filmmakers to present more graphic sexual and violent images. This is quite evident in the harshly realistic massacre scenes that frame the cavalry's vicious attack on the peaceful village. Quite a few shots follow the riding down of a woman or child and the shooting, spearing, and dying that follow. Sunshine is shot three times before she dies; after each shot, she rises and attempts to run farther away from the soldiers. Both her one-year-old strapped to her back and the newborn in her arms are shot. The parting image of her is a high-angle shot of her lying face down in the snow, a blossoming red stain on her back where her son would be.

23. As Walter Zinn explains, during the 1960s and 1970s, norms of sexual behavior changed drastically: open marriages, premarital sexual relations, co-ed living arrangements, same-sex partnerships, and communal living broke traditional barriers of normative societal behavior. In addition, the feminist movement opened doors for more freedom of expression in dress, careers, and sexual behavior for the nation's women. Zinn, *People's History of the United States*, 297–99.

24. Kupferer, *Ancient Drums*, 162. Also see Grinnell, *Cheyenne Indians*.

25. Pye, "*Ulzana's Raid*," 263. Among the many who have pointed out the allegorical connections between *Little Big Man*'s massacre scenes and the images presented in the press coverage of My Lai are Cook, *Lost Illusions*, 163; Kilpatrick, *Celluloid Indians*, 93; Slotkin, *Gunfighter Nation*, 631; and Kasdan and Tavernetti, "Revisionist Western," 130. Slotkin offers a thorough analysis of the article in *Life* that presented the information about the My Lai massacre to the public and the manner in which this particular episode significantly altered American support of the war. Slotkin, *Gunfighter Nation*, 578–91.

26. Writers of promotional materials for *A Man Called Horse* and film reviewers took great care to mention that the role of Running Deer marked the cinematic debut of Corinna Tsopei, a former Miss Greece and Miss Universe. Promotional materials, *A Man Called Horse*, Cinema Center Films, in the author's possession; Keneas, review of *A Man Called Horse*, 103; Bell, review of *A Man Called Horse*, 318; Logsdon, "Princess and the Squaw," 14.

27. Slotkin, *Gunfighter Nation*, 631.

28. Brody, Dumenil, and Henretta, *America*, 871–72, 880, 883; Zinn, *Twentieth Century*, 302–6.

29. Champagne, *Chronology*, 386.

30. The twenty points included demands that treaty relations be reestablished between the federal government and tribes; that the termination policies, Public Law 280 in particular, be repealed; that the Native American land base be increased; and that cultural and economic conditions for Native peoples be improved. See Deloria, *Behind the Trail of Broken Treaties*, 48–53.

31. Champagne, *Chronology*, 386.

32. Zinn, *Twentieth Century*, 523, 524; Champagne, *Chronology*, 394. Also see Michael Apted's documentary film *Incident at Oglala* (1992); Matthiessen, *In the Spirit of Crazy Horse*; and Deloria, *Behind the Trail of Broken Treaties*.

33. Wallmann, *Western*, 163.

34. The American Adam incorporates the qualities of a truly all-American man whose connection to nature and individualism is a rejection of European corruption. This mythic garden scenario sets the stage for American nationalism and expansionism. For a thorough discussion of the myth of the American Adam, see chapter 2. Also see Lewis, *American Adam*; Kolodny, *Land before Her*; Kolodny, *Lay of the Land*; and Fiedler, *Return of the Vanishing American*.

35. Eugene D. Genovese, "A Massive Breakdown," *Newsweek*, 6 July 1970, 21–22, quoted in Wallmann, *Western*, 163.

36. Kael, review of *Jeremiah Johnson*, 50–51. Johnson's alienation and need for solitude must have resonated with the viewing public; although *Jeremiah Johnson* received mixed reviews from the critics, it earned $21.9 million, making it the fifth-most-popular film of 1972. These numbers also indicate that it surpassed in profits both *A Man Called Horse*, which earned only $6 million in 1970, and *Little Big Man*, which took in $17 million in 1971. Cook, *Lost Illusions*, 498.

37. McAllister, "You Can't Go Home," 35–36.

38. The collaborative screenplay by Edward Anhalt and John Milius merges aspects of Fisher's novel and Thorp and Bunker's biography. Johnson's gentle spirit favors Fisher's hero Sam Minard, while the film's other characters are extracted from Thorp and Bunker's work, whose hero John Johnson is a violent and aggressive character more akin to that of Del Gue in the film. According to Mick McAllister, it was a "controversial film, panned by the New York critics, hailed in the *Journal of Popular Film* as a movie of tragic dimensions, the first ecological western." McAllister, "You Can't Go Home," 35.

39. Boyum, review of *Jeremiah Johnson*; McAllister, "You Can't Go Home," 39. *Wall Street Journal* reviewer Joy Gould Boyum points out that the tale is one of the American landscape while discussing the poetry and beauty of the "legend's locale" and the motion picture medium's ability to "quite literally bring this landscape to us." Boyum, review of *Jeremiah Johnson*.

40. McCarthy, "Westers, Not Westerns," 118; McAllister, "You Can't Go Home," 39; McCarthy, "Westers, Not Westerns," 123.

41. Mick McAllister presents this aspect of the film slightly differently, but no less accurately: "This is Swan's land, and it demands Swan's language and ways. It is Johnson, not Swan, who must change and adapt, and his changes must be organic and whole, consistent with the moral and practical necessities of his adopted world. Until Swan's death, his chances for transformation seem good." McAllister, "You Can't Go Home," 41–42.

42. Ibid., 47.

43. Ibid., 39.

44. *Jeremiah Johnson*, press book, AMPAS; Winsten, review of *Jeremiah Johnson*.

45. The film gets its name and plot from the novel by Marilyn Durham.

46. Nash and Ross, *Motion Picture Guide*, 1856.

47. Ibid. (italics mine).

48. Huhndorf, *Going Native*, 2, 3–5.

49. Cook, *Lost Illusions*, 69, 73.

SIX. GHOSTS AND VANISHING INDIAN WOMEN

The epigraphs to this chapter come from Kilpatrick, *Celluloid Indians*, 124, and Burgoyne, *Film Nation*, 39.

1. I refer the reader to the words of David Mayer that introduced chapter 1: "Historians of American culture have long and effectively argued that the identity of the Native American and Native American's encounters with European invaders constitute a palimpsest upon which our current preoccupations and understandings and world-views are constantly reinscribed." Mayer, "*Broken Doll*," 192.

2. Burgoyne, *Film Nation*, 10.

3. Kilpatrick, *Celluloid Indians*, 124.

4. Slotkin, *Gunfighter Nation*. See especially the introduction, which offers a substantial description of patterns of reciprocal influence.

5. Zinn, *People's History of the United States*, 580, 583.

6. Ibid., 552; Omi and Winant, *Racial Formation*; Lipsitz, *Time Passages*, 25; Zinn, *People's History of the United States*, 582–613. Also see Frankenburg, *Displacing Whiteness*, and Berlant, *Queen of America*.

7. Wesley Ruggles's *Cimarron* (1931) was the first western to receive the Academy Award for Best Picture.

8. See Grist, "*Unforgiven*," 294–301.

9. Slotkin, *Gunfighter Nation*, 655.

10. *Incident at Oglala*, also released in 1992, is narrated by Robert Redford. The film concentrates on the 1975 incident at Pine Ridge, South Dakota, in which two FBI agents and one Native American were killed. Apted negotiates

this material by interviewing members of the community invaded by the FBI and their reaction, twenty years later, to the "reign of terror" during that period (1972–1975). In 1972, the American Indian Movement was called in by tribal traditionalists to protest and actively respond to the violent actions of the corrupt tribal government led by Dick Wilson, his Guardians of the Oglala Nation (the "GOON Squad"), and the federal government. A seventy-one-day siege ended in the surrender of American Indian Movement members and continued military reign by Wilson and his group. Leonard Peltier was one of those arrested; he continues to be held in prison even after ample evidence has been found to suggest his innocence. For a detailed history of the events behind Apted's documentary, see Matthiessen, *In the Spirit of Crazy Horse.*

11. Burgoyne, *Film Nation,* 35–56.

12. Arnold, "Reframing the Hollywood Indian," 356. According to Arnold, Aquash was found shot in the head with her hands cut off at the wrists.

13. Green, "Pocahontas Perplex," 702.

14. Winona LaDuke and Wilma Mankiller come to mind as two high-profile political figures. In addition, a close look at the fishing protests in the Northwest, the Navajo demonstration against the Black Mountain Coal Company, and the O'odham U.S.-Mexico border disputes reveals women as primary participants.

15. The Ghost Dance initially came in a vision to the Northern Paiute spiritual leader Wovoka while he was ill. During his vision, he saw former generations of Native Americans, and God told him to spread peace, honesty, and love among the people. God also gave him the Ghost Dance to take back to the people. The dance became the basis for the Ghost Dance religion among the Plains and Great Basin tribes. "Among the Teton Lakota, devastated by war, reservations, poverty, and disease, Wavoka's admonitions of peace are forgotten." Champagne, *Chronology,* 184, 239. Wavoka's teachings were used by militant leaders of the Lakota to motivate a few to commit violence against whites. Fear of Sioux attacks spurred the government to outlaw the dance in 1880.

16. Walton, "Hollywood and the Indian Question," 12.

17. Macnab, review of *Silent Tongue,* 54.

18. Paul Streufert makes a convincing case that Shepard relies on both Greek drama and Native oral tradition in composing the film's narrative structure. Streufert, "Revolving Western," 27–41.

19. Thomas, review of *Silent Tongue.*

20. The following works indicate the range of responses: Axtell, *Beyond 1492;* Summerhill and Williams, *Sinking Columbus;* Gray, "Trouble with Columbus"; *Time,* "Beyond the Year 2000"; *Newsweek,* "1492–1992"; and Barreiro, "View from the Shore."

21. Summerhill and Williams, *Sinking Columbus,* 114; Dark with Harris, *New World,* 58; Zinn, *People's History of the United States,* 600; Omi and Wi-

nant, *Racial Formation*; Berlant, *Queen of America*; Summerhill and Williams, *Sinking Columbus*, 119.

22. Miller-Monzon, *Motion Picture Guide*, 208.

23. Smith, "Mythmaking," 370.

24. Burgoyne, *Film Nation*, 39.

25. Omi and Winant, *Racial Formation*, 147; Kilpatrick, *Celluloid Indians*, 124.

26. Omi and Winant, *Racial Formation*, 56.

27. Thomas, "Colonialism," 1–7.

CONCLUSION

1. Turner, *Significance of the Frontier*.

2. Phillip Deloria's *Playing Indian* provides an interesting look at the ways in which Americans have used the image of the Indian to suit particular identity needs. Deloria suggests, "The self-defining pairing of American truth with American freedom rests on the ability to wield power against Indians—social, military, economic, and political—while simultaneously drawing power from them. Indianness may have existed primarily as a cultural artifact in American society, but it has helped *create* these other forms of power, which have then been turned back on native people." Deloria, *Playing Indian*, 191.

3. See Jaimes and Halsey, "American Indian Women," and Lawrence, "Indian Health Service."

4. *Sexual Assault in Indian Country*, 4; Greenfield and Smith, *American Indians and Crime*, 6, 4.

Works Cited

FILM REVIEWS

Anderson, Lindsay. Review of *The Searchers*. *Sight and Sound* 26 (1956): 94–95.

Bell, Arthur. Review of *A Man Called Horse*. *Commonweal*, 26 June 1970, 318.

Bige. Review of *Frozen Justice*. *Variety*, 29 October 1929, 25.

Blaisdell, George. "A Man with the Bark On." Review of *The Squaw Man*. *Moving Picture World*, 28 February 1914, 1243.

Boyum, Joy Gould. "Two Wild Folklore Heroes." Review of *Jeremiah Johnson*. *Wall Street Journal*, 1972, 6.

Conroy, Frank. "Violent Movies." Review of *In Cold Blood*. *New York Review of Books*, 11 July 1968, 28–29.

Crowther, Bosley. Review of *In Cold Blood*. In *The New York Times Film Reviews* (New York: Times Books, 1967), 60.

Farber, Stephen. "*A Man Called Horse* and *Flap*." Review of *A Man Called Horse*. *Film Quarterly* 24 (1970): 61.

Hartung, Philip T. "Six Easy Pieces." Review of *Little Big Man*. *Commonweal*, 5 February 1971, 447.

Hatch, Robert. Review of *Broken Arrow*. *New Republic*, 31 July 1950, 23.

———. Review of *In Cold Blood*. *Nation*, 1 January 1968, 28.

———. Review of *The Searchers*. *Nation*, 23 June 1956, 536.

Kael, Pauline. Review of *Jeremiah Johnson*. *New Yorker*, 30 December 1972, 50–51.

———. Review of *Little Big Man*. *New Yorker*, 26 December 1970, 50–52.

Kaufman, Stanley. Review of *Little Big Man*. *New Republic*, 26 December 1970, 18, 25.

Keneas, Alex. "Indian Pudding." Review of *A Man Called Horse*. *Newsweek*, 25 May 1970, 102–4.

Knight, Arthur. "A Man Called Camel." Review of *A Man Called Horse*. *Saturday Review of Literature*, 2 May 1970, 52.

Kozloff, Max. Review of *In Cold Blood*. *Sight and Sound* 37 (1968): 148–50.

Macnab, Geoffrey. Review of *Silent Tongue*. *Sight and Sound* 3 (1993): 54.

O'Hara, Shirley. "The Bigger They Are." Review of *Duel in the Sun*. *New Republic*, 19 May 1947, 33–34.

Powe. Review of *Last Train from Gun Hill*. *New York Times*, 15 April 1959.

Review of *Across the Wide Missouri*. *Time*, 19 November 1951, 110–11.

Review of *Arrowhead*. *Daily Variety*, 15 June 1953, 3.

Review of *Arrowhead*. *Hollywood Reporter*, 15 June 1953.

Review of *Arrowhead*. *Variety*, 17 June 1953, 6.

Review of *Colorado Territory*. "Reluctant Bandit." *Newsweek*, 27 June 1948, 88–89.

Review of *Duel in the Sun*. *Variety*, 1 January 1947, 14.

Review of *Frozen Justice*. *Film Daily*, 25 August 1929.

Review of *Frozen Justice*. "Lenore Ulric's First Talker." In *The New York Times Film Reviews* (New York: Times Books, 1929), 565.

Review of *In Cold Blood*. *Variety*, 13 December 1967, 6.

Review of *In Cold Blood*. "Anatomy of a Murder." *Time*, 22 December 1967, 78.

Review of *Lo, the Poor Indian*. "Poor Lo on the Warpath." *Moving Picture World*, 4 March 1911, 10–11.

Review of *Mackenna's Gold*. *Variety*, 26 March 1969, 6.

Review of *A Man Called Horse*. *America*, 16 May 1970, 538.

Review of *A Man Called Horse*. "Home of the Braves." *Time*, 11 May 1970, 103.

Review of *Oklahoma Jim*. *Film Daily*, 27 December 1931, 10.

Review of *Red Wing's Gratitude*. *Moving Picture World*, 23 October 1909, 567.

Review of *The Searchers*. *America*, 9 June 1952, 272.

Review of *The Searchers*. *Film in Review*, June–July 1956, 284–85.

Review of *The Searchers*. *Motion Picture Herald Product Digest*, 27 May 1956, 140.

Review of *The Searchers*. "Looking, Looking Everywhere." *Commonweal*, 15 June 1956, 274.

Review of *The Squaw Man*. *Variety*, 8 November 1918, 41.

Review of *White Fawn's Devotion*. *Moving Picture World*, 18 June 1910, 1061.

Scheuer, Philip K. "'Arrowhead' Achieves Authentic Indian Drama." Review of *Arrowhead*. *Los Angeles Times*, 10 September 1953, 13.

Schickel, Richard. "Cold Blood Shouldn't Be That Simple." Review of *In Cold Blood*. *Life*, 12 January 1968, 10.

Thomas, Kevin. "Shepard's 'Tongue' a Supernatural Western Tale." Review of *Silent Tongue*. *Los Angeles Times*, 25 February 1994.

Winsten, Archer. "Redford 'Mountain Man' in 'Jeremiah Johnson.'" Review of *Jeremiah Johnson*. *New York Post*, 2 December 1972.

ARTICLES AND BOOKS

Abel, Richard. *The Red Rooster Scare—Making Cinema American, 1900–1910.* Berkeley: University of California Press, 1999.

Adams, David Wallace. *Education for Extinction: American Indians and the Boarding School Experience, 1875–1928.* Lawrence: University Press of Kansas, 1995.

Aleiss, Angela. "From Adversaries to Allies: The American Indian in Hollywood Films, 1930–1950." PhD diss., Columbia University, 1991.

———. "Native Americans: The Surprising Silents." *Cineaste* 21, no. 3 (1995): 34–35.

———. "Prelude to World War II: Racial Unity and the Hollywood Indian." *Journal of American Culture* 18, no. 2 (1995): 25–34.

———. "A Race Divided: The Indian Westerns of John Ford." *American Indian Culture and Research Journal* 18, no. 3 (1994): 167–86.

———. "'The Vanishing American': Hollywood's Compromise to Indian Reform." *Journal of American Studies* 25, no. 3 (1991): 467–72.

Anderson, Benedict. *Imagined Communities: Reflections on the Origin and Spread of Nationalism.* London: Verso, 1983.

Apter, Emily, and William Pietz, eds. *Fetishism as Cultural Discourse.* Ithaca, N.Y.: Cornell University Press, 1993.

Archuleta, Margaret L., Brenda J. Child, and K. Tsianina Lomawaima, eds. *Away from Home: American Indian Boarding School Experiences, 1989–2000.* Phoenix, Ariz.: Heard Museum, 2000.

Arnold, Ellen L. "Reframing the Hollywood Indian: A Feminist Re-Reading of *Powwow Highway* and *Thunderheart.*" In *American Indian Studies: An Interdisciplinary Approach to Contemporary Issues,* edited by Dane Morrison, 347–62. New York: Lang, 1997.

Arnold, Elliott. *Blood Brother.* Lincoln: University of Nebraska Press, 1947.

Axtell, James. *Beyond 1492: Encounters in Colonial North America.* Oxford: Oxford University Press, 1992.

Baird, Robert. "'Going Indian:' *Dances with Wolves* (1990)." In Rollins and O'Conner, *Hollywood's Indian,* 153–69.

Balio, Tino. *Grand Design: Hollywood as a Modern Business Enterprise, 1930–1939.* Vol. 5 of *History of the American Cinema.* Berkeley: University of California Press, 1993.

Barreiro, Jose, ed. "View from the Shore: American Indian Perspectives on the Quincentenary." Special issue, *Northeast Indian Quarterly,* Fall 1990.

Bataille, Gretchen M., and Charles L. P. Silet, eds. *Images of American Indians on Film: An Annotated Bibliography.* New York: Garland, 1985.

———, eds. *The Pretend Indians: Images of Native Americans in the Movies.* Ames: Iowa State University Press, 1980.

Berger, Thomas. *Little Big Man.* New York: Dell Publishing, 1964.

Bergsten, Bebe, ed. *Biograph Bulletins, 1896–1908.* Los Angeles: Locare Research Group, 1971.

Berkhofer, Robert, Jr. *The White Man's Indian: Images of the American Indian from Columbus to the Present.* New York: Random House, 1979.

Berlant, Lauren. *The Queen of America Goes to Washington City: Essays on Sex and Citizenship.* Durham, N.C.: Duke University Press, 1997.

Bernardi, Daniel, ed. *The Birth of Whiteness: Race and the Emergence of U.S. Cinema.* New Brunswick, N.J.: Rutgers University Press, 1996.

————, ed. *Classic Hollywood, Classic Whiteness.* Minneapolis: University of Minnesota Press, 2001.

————. *"Star Trek" and History: Race-ing toward a White Future.* New Brunswick, N.J.: Rutgers University Press, 1998.

————. "The Voice of Whiteness: D. W. Griffith's Biograph Films (1908–1913)." In Bernardi, *Birth of Whiteness,* 103–28.

Bernstein, Alison R. *Toward a New Era in Indian Affairs: American Indians and World War II.* Norman: University of Oklahoma Press, 1991.

Bhabha, Homi. "The Other Question . . . Homi K. Bhabha Reconsiders the Stereotype and Colonial Discourse." *Screen: Incorporating Screen Education* 24, no. 6 (1983): 18–36.

Bignell, Jonathan. "Method Westerns: The Left-Handed Gun and One-Eyed Jacks." In Cameron and Pye, *Book of Westerns,* 99–122.

Bird, S. Elizabeth. "Tales of Difference: Representations of American Indian Women in Popular Film and Television." In *Mediated Women: Representations in Popular Culture,* edited by Marian Meyers, 91–109. Cresskill, N.J.: Hampton Press, 1999.

Bowser, Eileen, ed. *Biograph Bulletins, 1908–1912.* New York: Farrar, Straus and Giroux, 1973.

————. *The Transformation of Cinema: 1907–1915.* Vol. 2 of *History of the American Cinema.* Berkeley: University of California Press, 1994.

Braudy, Leo. "The Difficulties of *Little Big Man.*" *Film Quarterly* 25 (1971): 30–33.

Brody, David, Lynn Dumenil, and James A. Henretta. *America: A Concise History.* 2nd ed. Vol. 2, *Since 1865.* Boston: Bedford/St. Martin's, 2002.

Brownlow, Kevin. *The War, the West, the Wilderness.* New York: Knopf, 1979.

Burgess, Marilyn, and Gail Guthrie Valaskakis. *Indian Princesses and Cow-girls: Stereotypes from the Frontier.* Montreal, Quebec: Oboro, 1995.

Burgoyne, Robert. *Film Nation: Hollywood Looks at U.S. History.* Minneapolis: University of Minnesota Press, 1997.

Bush, Stephen. "Moving Picture Absurdities." *Moving Picture World,* 16 September 1911, 733.

Cameron, Ian, and Douglas Pye, eds. *The Book of Westerns.* New York: Continuum, 1996.

Capote, Truman. *In Cold Blood.* 1965. New York: Random House, 1993.

Cawelti, John G. *The Six-Gun Mystique Sequel.* Bowling Green, Ohio: Bowling Green State University Popular Press, 1999.

Champagne, Duane, ed. *Chronology of Native North American History from Pre-Columbian Times to the Present.* Detroit, Mich.: Gale Research, 1994.

Child, Brenda J. *Boarding School Seasons: American Indian Families, 1900–1940.* Lincoln: University of Nebraska Press, 1993.

Churchill, Ward. *Fantasies of the Master Race: Literature, Cinema and the Colonization of the American Indians.* Edited by M. Annette Jaimes. Monroe, Maine: Common Courage Press, 1992.

Cook, David A. *Lost Illusions: American Cinema in the Shadow of Watergate and Vietnam, 1970–1979.* Vol. 9 of *History of the American Cinema.* Berkeley: University of California Press, 2000.

Cooper, James Fenimore. *The Last of the Mohicans.* Ware, Hertfordshire, U.K.: Wordsworth Editions, 1993.

Cornell, Stephen. *The Return of the Native: American Indian Political Resurgence.* New York: Oxford University Press, 1988.

Cowen, Paul S. "A Social-Cognitive Approach to Ethnicity in Films." In Friedman, *Unspeakable Images,* 353–78.

Coyne, Michael. *The Crowded Prairie: American National Identity in the Hollywood Western.* London: Tauris, 1997.

Dark, K. R., with A. L. Harris. *The New World and the New World Order: U.S. Relative Decline, Domestic Instability in the Americas, and the End of the Cold War.* New York: St. Martin's Press, 1996.

Debo, Angie. *A Short History of the Indians of the United States.* Norman: University of Oklahoma Press, 1989.

Deloria, Philip J. *Playing Indian.* New Haven, Conn.: Yale University Press, 1998.

Deloria, Vine, Jr. *Behind the Trail of Broken Treaties: An Indian Declaration of Independence.* Austin: University of Texas Press, 1974.

Deloria, Vine, Jr., and Clifford Lytle. *The Nations Within: The Past and Future of American Indian Sovereignty.* New York: Pantheon, 1984.

Dinnerstein, Leonard, Roger L. Nichols, and David M. Reimers. *Natives and Strangers: A Multicultural History of Americans.* New York: Oxford University Press, 1996.

Dippie, Brian W. *The Vanishing American: White Attitudes and U.S. Indian Policy.* Lawrence: University Press of Kansas, 1982.

Doane, Mary Ann. *Femmes Fatales: Feminism, Film Theory, Psychoanalysis.* New York: Routledge, 1991.

Doherty, Thomas. *Pre-Code Hollywood: Sex, Immorality, and Insurrection in American Cinema, 1930–1934*. New York: Columbia University Press, 1999.

Douglas, Mary. *Purity and Danger: An Analysis of Concepts of Pollution and Taboo*. New York: Random House, 1970.

Durham, Marilyn. *The Man Who Loved Cat Dancing*. New York: Harcourt Brace Jovanovich, 1972.

Dyer, Richard. *White*. London: Routledge, 1997.

Faery, Rebecca Blevins. *Cartographies of Desire: Captivity, Race, and Sex in the Shaping of an American Nation*. Norman: University of Oklahoma Press, 1999.

Fenin, George N., and William K. Everson. *The Western from Silents to Cinerama*. New York: Orion Press, 1962.

Fiedler, Leslie A. *The Return of the Vanishing American*. New York: Stein and Day, 1968.

Filmfacts. Vol. 12. Los Angeles: Division of Cinema, University of Southern California, 1969.

Fisher, Vardis. *Mountain Man: A Novel of Male and Female in the Early American West*. New York: Morrow, 1965.

Fixico, Donald. *Termination and Relocation: Federal Indian Policy, 1945–1960*. Albuquerque: University of New Mexico Press, 1986.

Foster, Hal. "The Art of Fetishism: Notes on Dutch Still Life." In Apter and Pietz, *Fetishism as Cultural Discourse*, 251–65.

Franco, Jere Bishop. *Crossing the Pond: The Native American Effort in World War II*. Vol. 7 of *War and the Southwest*. Denton: University of North Texas Press, 1999.

Frankenberg, Ruth, ed. *Displacing Whiteness: Essays in Social and Cultural Criticism*. Durham, N.C.: Duke University Press, 1997.

French, Philip. "The Indian in the Western Movie." In Bataille and Silet, *Pretend Indians*, 98–105.

Freud, Sigmund. "Fetishism." 1927. In *The Future of an Illusion, Civilization and Its Discontents and Other Works (1927–1931)*, 152–57. Vol. 21 of *Standard Edition of the Complete Psychological Works of Sigmund Freud*. London: Hogarth Press.

Friar, Ralph E., and Natasha A. Friar. *The Only Good Indian . . . The Hollywood Gospel*. New York: Drama Book Specialists, 1972.

Friedman, Lester, ed. *Unspeakable Images: Ethnicity and the American Cinema*. Urbana: University of Illinois Press, 1991.

Gallafent, Edward. "Four Tombstones, 1946–1994." In Cameron and Pye, *Book of Westerns*, 302–11.

Georgakas, Dan. "They Have Not Spoken: American Indians in Film." *Film Quarterly* 25 (1972): 26–32.

Gevinson, Alan, ed. *Within Our Gates: Ethnicity in American Feature Films, 1911–1960*. Berkeley: University of California Press, 1997.

Gledhill, Christine, ed. *Home Is Where the Heart Is: Studies in Melodrama and the Woman's Film*. London: British Film Institute, 1987.

Gray, Paul. "The Trouble with Columbus." *Time*, 7 October 1991, 52–56.

Green, Rayna. "The Pocahontas Perplex: The Image of Indian Women in American Culture." *Massachusetts Review* 16, no. 4 (1995): 698–714.

Greenfield, Lawrence A., and Steven K. Smith. *American Indians and Crime*. Washington, D.C.: Office of Justice Programs, Bureau of Justice Statistics, U.S. Department of Justice, 2000.

Grey, Zane. *The Vanishing American*. New York: Grosset and Dunlap, 1925.

Grinnell, George Bird. *The Cheyenne Indians: Their History and Ways of Life*. 2 vols. New York: Cooper Square Publishers, 1962.

Grist, Leighton. "*Unforgiven*." In Cameron and Pye, *Book of Westerns*, 294–301.

Gunning, Tom. "The Cinema of Attraction: Early Film, Its Spectator and the Avant-Garde." *Wide Angle* 8, nos. 3–4 (1986): 63–70.

Haralovich, Mary Beth. "Film Advertising, the Film Industry, and the Pin-up: The Industry's Accommodations to Social Forces in the 1940s." In *Current Research in Film: Audiences, Economics, and Law*, vol. 1, edited by Bruce A. Austin, 127–64. Norwood, N.J.: Ablex, 1985.

Harrison, Jim. *Legends of the Fall*. New York: Dell, 1978.

Henderson, Robert M. *D. W. Griffith: The Years at Biograph*. New York: Farrar, Straus and Giroux, 1970.

Hershfield, Joanne. "Dolores Del Río, Uncomfortably Real: The Economics of Race in Hollywood's Latin American Musicals." In Bernardi, *Classic Hollywood*, 139–56.

Hertzberg, Hazel Whitman. "Indian Rights Movement, 1887–1973." In Washburn, *History of Indian-White Relations*, 305–23.

Higashi, Sumiko. *Cecil B. DeMille and American Culture: The Silent Era*. Berkeley: University of California Press, 1994.

Higson, Andrew. "The Concept of National Cinema." In *Film and Nationalism*, edited by Alan Williams, 52–67. New Brunswick, N.J.: Rutgers University Press, 2002.

Hilger, Michael. *The American Indian in Film*. Metuchen, N.J.: Scarecrow Press, 1986.

———. *From Savage to Nobleman: Images of Native Americans in Film*. Lanham, Md.: Scarecrow Press, 1995.

Hodes, Martha, ed. *Sex, Love, Race: Crossing Boundaries in North America*. New York: New York University Press, 1999.

Huhndorf, Shari M. *Going Native: Indians in the American Cultural Imagination*. Ithaca, N.Y.: Cornell University Press, 2001.

Jackson, Kevin. *The Language of Cinema*. New York: Routledge, 1998.

Jacobs, Lea. *The Wages of Sin: Censorship and the Fallen Woman Film, 1928–1942*. Berkeley: University of California Press, 1995.

Jaimes, M. Annette, and Theresa Halsey. "American Indian Women: At the Center of Indigenous Resistance in Contemporary North America." In *The State of Native America: Genocide, Colonization, and Resistance*, edited by M. Annette Jaimes, 311–44. Boston: South End Press, 1992.

Jowett, Garth. *Film: The Democratic Art*. Boston: Little, Brown, 1976.

Kasdan, Margo, and Susan Tavernetti. "Native Americans in a Revisionist Western: *Little Big Man* (1970)." In Rollins and O'Conner, *Hollywood's Indian*, 121–36.

Katz, Ephraim, ed. *The Film Encyclopedia*. Edited by Fred Klein and Ronald Dean Nolen. 3rd ed. New York: HarperCollins, 1998.

Kilpatrick, Jacquelyn. *Celluloid Indians: Native Americans in Film*. Lincoln: University of Nebraska Press, 1999.

Kitses, Jim, and Gregg Rickman, eds. *The Western Reader*. New York: Limelight Editions, 1998.

Kolodny, Annette. *The Land before Her: Fantasy and Experience of the American Frontiers, 1630–1860*. Chapel Hill: University of North Carolina Press, 1984.

———. *Lay of the Land: Metaphor as Experience and History in American Life and Letters*. Chapel Hill: University of North Carolina Press, 1975.

Konigsberg, Ira. *The Complete Film Dictionary*. New York: Meridian, 1987.

Kovel, Joel. *White Racism: A Psychohistory*. New York: Pantheon Books, 1970.

Kupferer, Harriet J. *Ancient Drums, Other Moccasins: Native North American Cultural Adaptation*. Englewood Cliffs, N.J.: Prentice Hall, 1988.

La Farge, Oliver. *Laughing Boy*. New York: Signet, 1929.

Lang, Robert. *American Film Melodrama: Griffith, Vidor, Minelli*. Princeton, N.J.: Princeton University Press, 1989.

Langman, Larry. *American Film Cycles: The Silent Era*. Vol. 22 of *Bibliographies and Indexes in the Performing Arts*. Westport, Conn.: Greenwood Press, 1998.

———. *A Guide to Silent Westerns*. Vol. 13 of *Bibliographies and Indexes in the Performing Arts*. New York: Greenwood Press, 1992.

Lawrence, Jane. "The Indian Health Service and the Sterilization of Native American Women." *American Indian Quarterly* 24, no. 3 (2000): 400–419.

Le May, Alan. *The Searchers*. New York: Harper and Brothers, 1954.

Lehman, Peter. "Looking at Look's Missing Reverse Shot: Psychoanalysis and Style in John Ford's *The Searchers*." In Kitses and Rickman, *Western Reader*, 259–92.

Lewis, R. W. B. *The American Adam: Innocence, Tragedy and Tradition in the Nineteenth Century*. Chicago: University of Chicago Press, 1955.

Lipsitz, George. *Time Passages: Collective Memory and American Popular Culture*. Minneapolis: University of Minnesota Press, 1990.

Logsdon, Judith. "The Princess and the Squaw: Images of American Indian Women in Cinema Rouge." *Feminist Collections* 13, no. 4 (1992): 13–17.

López, Ana M. "Are All Latins from Manhattan? Hollywood, Ethnography, and Cultural Colonialism." In Friedman, *Unspeakable Images*, 404–24.

Los Angeles Times, "Mending 'Broken Arrow,'" 29 June 1991.

Loughney, Patrick. "*The Kentuckian*." In *The Griffith Project*, edited by Paolo Cherchi Usai. Vol. 1, *Films Produced in 1907–1908*, 55–56. London: British Film Institute, 1999.

Lucas, Blake. "Saloon Girls and Ranchers' Daughters: The Woman in the Western." In Kitses and Rickman, *Western Reader*, 301–20.

Lyons, Robert, ed. "*My Darling Clementine*": *John Ford, Director*. New Brunswick, N.J.: Rutgers University Press, 1984.

Maltby, Richard. "A Better Sense of History: John Ford and the Indians." In Cameron and Pye, *Book of Westerns*, 34–49.

Manchel, Frank. "Cultural Confusion: *Broken Arrow* (1950)." In Rollins and O'Conner, *Hollywood's Indian*, 91–106.

Manchester, William. *The Glory and the Dream: A Narrative History of America, 1932–1972*. Boston: Little, Brown, 1974.

Marsden, Michael, and Jack Nachbar. "The Indian in the Movies." In Washburn, *History of Indian-White Relations*, 607–16.

Matthiessen, Peter. *In the Spirit of Crazy Horse*. New York: Penguin, 1991.

May, Lary. *The Big Tomorrow: Hollywood and the Politics of the American Way*. Chicago: University of Chicago Press, 2000.

Mayer, David. "*The Broken Doll*." In *The Griffith Project*, edited by Paolo Cherchi Usai. Vol. 4, *Films Produced in 1910*, 191–94. London: British Film Institute, 2000.

McAllister, Mick. "You Can't Go Home: Jeremiah Johnson and the Wilderness." *Western American Literature* 13, no. 1 (1978): 35–50.

McCarthy, Cormac. *Blood Meridian, or, The Evening Redness in the West*. New York: Random House, 1985.

McCarthy, Patrick. "Westers, Not Westerns: Exteriorizing the 'Wild Man Within.'" *Journal of Popular Film and Television* 23, no. 3 (1995): 117–29.

Miller-Monzon, John, ed. *The Motion Picture Guide: 1995 Annual (Films of 1994)*. New York: Baseline, 1994.

Moses, Robert, ed. *American Movie Classics: Movie Companion*. New York: Hyperion, 1999.

Moving Picture World, "Accuracy in Indian Subjects," 10 July 1909, 48.

Mulvey, Laura. "Visual Pleasure and Narrative Cinema." In *Visual and Other Pleasures*, 14–28. Bloomington: Indiana University Press, 1989.

Musser, Charles. "Ethnicity, Role-Playing, and American Film Comedy: From *Chinese Laundry Scene* to *Whoopee* (1849–1930)." In Friedman, *Unspeakable Images*, 39–81.

Nabakov, Peter. *Native American Testimony: A Chronicle of Indian-White Relations from Prophecy to the Present, 1492–2000*. New York: Penguin, 1991.

Nash, Gary B. "The Hidden History of Mestizo America." In Hodes, *Sex, Love, Race*, 10–34.

Nash, Jay Robert, and Stanley Ralph Ross, eds. *The Motion Picture Guide: 1927–1983*. Vol. L–M. Chicago: Cinebooks, 1986.

Newsweek, "1492–1992: When Worlds Collide; How Columbus's Voyages Transformed Both East and West," special issue, Fall/Winter 1991.

O'Conner, John E. *The Hollywood Indian: Stereotypes of Native Americans in Films*. Trenton: New Jersey State Museum, 1980.

O'Meara, Walter. *Daughters of the Country: The Women of the Fur Traders and Mountain Men*. New York: Harcourt, Brace and World, 1968.

Omi, Michael, and Howard Winant. *Racial Formation in the United States from the 1960s to the 1990s*. 2nd ed. New York: Routledge, 1994.

Pearson, Roberta A. *Eloquent Gestures: The Transformation of Performance Style in the Griffith Biograph Films*. Berkeley: University of California Press, 1992.

———. "The Revenge of Rain-in-the-Face? Or, Custers and Indians on the Silent Screen." In Bernardi, *Birth of Whiteness*, 274–99.

Philp, Kenneth R., ed. *Indian Self-Rule: First-Hand Accounts of Indian-White Relations from Roosevelt to Reagan*. Salt Lake City, Utah: Howe Bros., 1986.

Prats, Armando José. *Invisible Natives: Myth and Identity in the American Western*. Ithaca, N.Y.: Cornell University Press, 2002.

Prucha, Francis Paul, ed. *Documents of United States Indian Policy*. 2nd ed. Lincoln: University of Nebraska Press, 1990.

———. *The Great Father: The United States Government and the American Indians*. 2 vols. Lincoln: University of Nebraska Press, 1984.

Pryor, Jerome. "*Duel in the Sun*, a Classical Symphony." *New Orleans Review* 17, no. 4 (1990): 8–19.

Pye, Douglas. "Criticism and the Western." Introduction to Cameron and Pye, *Book of Westerns*, 9–21.

———. "Double Vision: Miscegenation and Point of View in *The Searchers*." In Cameron and Pye, *Book of Westerns*, 229–35.

———. "*Ulzana's Raid*." In Cameron and Pye, *Book of Westerns*, 262–68.

Riley, Michael J. "Trapped in the History of Film: *The Vanishing American*." In Rollins and O'Conner, *Hollywood's Indian*, 58–72.

Rollins, Peter C., and John E. O'Conner, eds. *Hollywood's Indian: The Portrayal of the Native American in Film*. Lexington: University Press of Kentucky, 1998.

Rosaldo, Renato. *Culture and Truth: The Remaking of Social Analysis*. Boston: Beacon Press, 1989.

Roth, Marty. "'Yes, My Darling Daughter': Gender, Miscegenation, and Generation in John Ford's *The Searchers*." *New Orleans Review* 18, no. 4 (1991): 65–73.

Schatz, Thomas. *Boom and Bust: American Cinema in the 1940s*. Vol. 6 of *History of the American Cinema*. Berkeley: University of California Press, 1997.

———. *D. W. Griffith: An American Life*. New York: Simon and Schuster, 1984.

———. *Hollywood Genres: Formulas, Filmmaking, and the Studio System*. New York: Random House, 1981.

Sexual Assault in Indian Country: Confronting Sexual Violence. National Sexual Violence Resource Center. 2000.

Sharpes, Donald K. "Federal Education for the American Indian." *Journal of American Indian Education* 19, no. 1 (1979): 19–22.

Simmon, Scott. "Concerning the Weary Legs of Wyatt Earp: The Classic Western According to Shakespeare." In Kitses and Rickman, *Western Reader*, 149–66.

Sklar, Robert. *Movie-Made America: A Cultural History of American Movies*. Rev. ed. New York: Vintage Books, 1994.

Slotkin, Richard. *Gunfighter Nation: The Myth of the Frontier in Twentieth-Century America*. Norman: University of Oklahoma Press, 1992.

———. *Regeneration through Violence: The Mythology of the American Frontier, 1600–1860*. New York: HarperCollins, 1973.

Smith, Andrew Brodie. "Shooting Cowboys and Indians: Silent Western Films, American Culture, and the Birth of Hollywood." PhD diss., University of California, Los Angeles, 2000.

Smith, Patrick A. "Mythmaking and the Consequence of 'Soul History' in Jim Harrison's *Legends of the Fall*." *Studies in Short Fiction* 36, no. 4 (1999): 369–80.

Smits, David D. "The 'Squaw Drudge': A Prime Index of Savagism." *Ethnohistory* 29, no. 4 (1982): 281–306.

———. "'Squaw Men,' 'Half Breeds,' and Amalgamators: Late Nineteenth-Century Anglo-American Attitudes toward Indian-White Race-Mixing." *American Indian Culture and Research Journal* 15, no. 3 (1991): 29–61.

Spicer, Edward H. *A Short History of the Indians of the United States*. New York: Van Nostrand Reinhold, 1969.

Stember, Charles Herbert. *Sexual Racism: The Emotional Barrier to an Integrated Society*. New York: Elsevier, 1976.

Streufert, Paul D. "The Revolving Western: American Guilt and the Tragically Greek in Sam Shepard's *Silent Tongue*." *American Drama* 8, no. 2 (1999): 27–41.

Summerhill, Stephen J., and John Alexander Williams. *Sinking Columbus: Contested History, Cultural Politics, and Mythmaking during the Quincentenary*. Gainesville: University Press of Florida, 2000.

Thomas, Robert K. "Colonialism: Domestic and Foreign." *New University Thought* 4, no. 4 (1967): 1–7.

Thompson, Don K. "*The Searchers*." *Magill's Survey of Cinema* 4 (1980): 1502–5.

Thorp, Raymond W., and Robert Bunker. *Crow Killer: The Saga of Liver-Eating Johnson*. Bloomington: Indiana University Press, 1959.

Tilton, Robert S. *Pocahontas: The Evolution of an American Narrative*. Cambridge: Cambridge University Press, 1994.

Time, "Beyond the Year 2000," special issue, Fall 1992.

Tompkins, Jane. *West of Everything: The Inner Life of Westerns*. New York: Oxford University Press, 1992.

Townsend, Kenneth William. *World War II and the American Indian*. Albuquerque: University of New Mexico Press, 2000.

Turner, Frederick Jackson. *The Significance of the Frontier in American History*. Edited by Harold P. Simonson. New York: Ungar, 1963.

Turner, John. "*Little Big Man*, the Novel and the Film: A Study in Narrative Structure." *Literature/Film Quarterly* 5 (1977): 154–63.

Tuska, Jon. *The American West in Film: Critical Approaches to the Western*. Vol. 11 of *Contributions to the Study of Popular Culture*. Westport, Conn.: Greenwood Press, 1985.

Walker, Michael. "The Westerns of Delmer Daves." In Cameron and Pye, *Book of Westerns*, 123–60.

Wallmann, Jeffrey. *The Western: Parables of the American Dream*. Lubbock: Texas Tech University Press, 1999.

Walton, John. "Hollywood and the Indian Question: Political, Radical or Ecological Symbol." *Multicultural Education* 1, no. 2 (1993): 12–13.

Washburn, Wilcomb E. *History of Indian-White Relations*. Vol. 4 of *Handbook of North American Indians*. Washington, D.C.: Smithsonian Institution, 1988.

Wiebe, Robert H. *The Search for Order, 1877–1920*. New York: Hill and Wang, 1967.

Wood, Robin. "*Duel in the Sun*: The Destruction of an Ideological System." In Cameron and Pye, *Book of Westerns*, 189–95.

Zinn, Howard. *A People's History of the United States: 1492–Present*. New York: HarperCollins, 1995.

———. *The Twentieth Century: A People's History*. New York: Perennial, 2003.

RESEARCH ARCHIVES

Cecil B. DeMille Archives, L. Tom Perry Special Collections Library, Harold B. Lee Library, Brigham Young University, Provo, Utah.
D. W. Griffith Collection, Celeste Bartos International Film Study Center, Museum of Modern Art, New York.
Film and Television Archive, University of California, Los Angeles.
Film and Video Center, George Gustav Heye Center, National Museum of the American Indian, New York.
Margaret Herrick Library, Academy of Motion Picture Arts and Sciences, Beverly Hills, Calif.
Motion Picture, Broadcasting, and Recorded Sound Division, Library of Congress, Washington, D.C.

Index

CPSIA information can be obtained at www.ICGtesting.com
Printed in the USA
BVOW010957300712

296544BV00001B/1/P